Leading Becomes You

"Dr. Natalie Pickering is the kind of person who, if you met her in line in the grocery store, would strike up an animated, humorous conversation with you, all the while offering curative advice that you would later, sitting in your car realize, significantly impacted your life and wellbeing. I know. I've had that conversation with her. The next best thing to calling her for an actual appointment is to read her animated, skillfully written practical guide to becoming the kind of leader who knows how to lead from their own skin. Five stars!"

– Jamie Winship, Author, Speaker, Founder, *Identity Exchange*

"Drawing on her extensive experience as a coach and consultant, Dr. Natalie Pickering offers a fresh, actionable perspective on how to reinvigorate your leadership presence and impact. At a time when leadership must show up everywhere, every day, this book arrives as an essential guide. Through data-driven insights, real-world examples, and thoughtful encouragement, Dr. Pickering leads readers toward a powerful blend of reflection and action".

– Mary Cianni PhD, Clinical Associate Professor of Organizational Consulting, New York University, Author of *The Consultant's Compass: Navigating Success with Courage, Curiosity, and Compassion*

"Whether we arrived by grit or by simple evolution, those of us in the lead car—pole position—don't need another book on how to go faster, tighten our turns, avoid the wall, or find the perfect groove on the track. What we do need is a guide—someone who can gently help us trace that persistent rattle that's followed us from car to car. Someone who can explain why an orange car in the rearview mirror triggers more anxiety than any other. Someone who can help us step back and ask: why am I so driven to be the best at driving in circles? Good news: Natalie has written that book. Get it. Read it. Then—thoroughly, confidently, and purposefully—enjoy the ride."

– Barney M. Davis, Jr. M.D. Psychiatrist, *Barnabas International*

"Dr. Natalie Pickering and her training have had the biggest impact on my personal and professional development—incredibly more impactful than anyone else in the leadership and professional growth industry. This book provides the "what do I do" for awareness-building and the framework for inner work. It is extremely practical for anyone just getting started in their personal-meets-professional-growth journey and equally impactful for more seasoned leaders and professionals. Don't miss this life-changing field guide."

– M. Valentina Escobar-Gonzalez, MBA, Co-author of
The Most Amazing Marketing Book Ever

"This book is amazing! I'm recommending it to all my leadership coaching clients. It's not just a book. It's a game plan. Dr. Natalie not only addresses the root causes of so many leadership issues, she shows how to use them to fertilize your leadership renewal. Do yourself a favor and get this book right now."

– Marc A. Pitman, Author of *The Surprising Gift of Doubt*

"Wow! Instead of the usual book detailing symptoms of leader discontent, Leading Becomes You offers a tested and true blueprint from an experienced psychologist and coach's clinical expertise. It is a deep work but an easy and enjoyable read. I have personally seen the dramatic impact Dr. Pickering's work has on the wide variety of managers, supervisors, and leaders with whom she works. I compiled a list of gift recipients as I read this book!"

– Cynthia Mealer, PhD, Clinical Psychologist

"Leading Becomes You both challenged and encouraged me. Engagingly written, with stories from the author's own life as well as her years of practice helping clients discover their authentic self-as-leader. Having recently completed a career chapter in non-profit executive service, I'm looking ahead to my next chapter. Leading Becomes You gave me the language and tools to navigate this next phase of leadership successfully. I wish I could have read it thirty years ago. You won't regret this read."

– Tim Rickel, Former Vice-President, *WGM*

LEADING BECOMES YOU

A Real-World
Framework for Leading
from the Inside Out

Natalie K. Cupples Pickering, PhD

**Leading Becomes You: A Real-World Framework for
Leading from the Inside Out**
©2025 Natalie K. Pickering

For more information: www.drnataliepickering.com

Cover art and graphical illustrations by Lorraine Coolidge.
Formatting by Laura Murray.

Library of Congress Cataloging-in-Publication Data
Name: Pickering, Natalie K., author.
Title: Leading becomes you: a real-world framework for leading from the inside out/ Natalie Pickering.
Includes bibliographical references.
Identifier: LCCN 2025913601
ISBN 979-8-9990556-1-3 (hardcover) | ISBN 979-8-9990556-0-6 (e-book)
ISBN 979-8-9990556-2-0 (paperback)

In memory of Mom and to Dad, Mark, Seilah, Carsten, and Nicole. Thank you for your gracious presence in my re-becoming.

TABLE OF CONTENTS

—————

PART 1

PART 2

INTRODUCTION

Every year, right around the end of summer, I find myself standing in front of the sad, scraggly leftovers in the grocery store's garden section. The ones shoved together on one wooden pallet with old dirt dried into thin plastic squares. Half-priced. Half-forgotten. Their cheap containers are heat-warped and cracked, roots coiled tight like clenched fists. They haven't been watered in days. The blooms are brittle. The stems slouch under their own weight.

Most people pass by without a second glance.

But I can't. I always stop. I always choose one.

Not because it's pretty and vibrant—it's not. It looks haggard, rough around the edges, like it's been fighting to survive in silence. But I pick it up because I can see it's still alive. And because I know what it's like to feel worn down, overlooked, and spent…but still not done.

Back home, the dry mass is easily removed from its flimsy plastic pot. The roots are packed tight into the shape of their confinement, spiraling in on themselves with nowhere to go, shaped by too many seasons in too small a space. The soil is dry, depleted. And yet—there's still something in it, trying.

Hoping for more. Knowing the potential just hasn't been realized.

It's not past saving—it's past pretending. It's in the wrong container.

That's how I recognize root-bound leaders.

Some look obviously worn—tired, frayed, stretched too thin.

Others have managed to keep a couple of bright clinging blooms in place to sell the story of vitality while the roots beneath choke for freedom. The attempt to manage the image of "all is well" barely covers the quiet unraveling beneath.

They've outgrown this version of success.

The roles, rhythms, and expectations that once carried them now stifle them.

They've mastered the outer business with success and accolades, but the inner business has gone untended.

They've spent years tending to everything but their inner life.

Flourishing feels far away.

This book is for them. And if any of that feels familiar, it's for you!

It's about what happens when you stop pushing through, performing, climbing, winning, agreeing, comparing—and start tending inward. When you loosen the gripped roots, rework the soil, and finally give yourself room to grow again.

Left too long like that, the trapped, exhausted plant would eventually lose growth potential and won't make it. Like a leader unaware that the person they're becoming isn't really them. The leader who has never done the deeper inner business of clarifying their personalized and authentic approach.

Can you relate? Do you know you have more to offer but the constricting demands of imposter chatter, diluted impact, second-guessing, and disconnection tighten around you like plastic walls? You're doing all the leader things—communicating, deciding, rallying—but it's not fun, let alone fulfilling. Something feels off. Missing. Confused. You've realized that ignoring your root tangles is not sustainable. The disconnection from yourself and others widens. You're surviving but not thriving, even if it all looks good from the outside.

This book is your repotting!

I'm sharing the complete how-to guide to loosening the root tangles and flimsy ill-fitting leadership container that constricts you. I've built the map to rediscover your own leader pot, your own soil, and your own self-as-leader flourishing landscape—the space, story, and strength to lead from your own skin and recover the story and soul of your leadership. I've time-tested the system for "how to" look more closely at the flimsy pot, how you got there, and the plan to make sure it doesn't happen again.

Because flourishing doesn't happen when you lead like someone else. It happens when you lead like *you*.

This book is your blueprint for answering two big questions:

1. Who is my self-as-leader and what does my unique leadership approach and strategy look like, sound like, feel like?

2. How do I transform my dry, unrealized inner leader terrain to flourishing for the long-term fulfillment of myself, my team, the people I love?

—————————— WHY THIS APPROACH? ——————————

I have worked alongside C-suite executives, directors, managers, and front-line supervisors nearly every day for years. As an executive coach, corporate trainer and consultant, I have been trusted to journey with hundreds of leaders navigating their most defining moments—transitions, crises, turnarounds, reinventions. I have a front-row seat to what leaders wrestle with behind the curtain—and what helps them rise. I also have enough distance to maintain candor and objectivity. I wrote this book not from the direct perspective of a corner office but from something bigger: years of listening, asking, reflecting, and helping leaders find their way back to the kind of leadership that's not just effective but deeply human, sustainable, and true.

The method I've designed draws from synthesizing hundreds of leadership discoveries and recoveries based on patterns I've witnessed across leader stories—about what unlocks trust, clarity, resilience, and influence in today's fast-shifting world and marketplace.

My approach is not a fit for leaders who believe they've arrived, that growth is for the less experienced, or who believe that deeper work is a waste of time. This approach is designed for the humble leader who wants to lead beyond competencies and performance metrics, from foundational integrity—the leader who wants to lead from alignment with their values, empower their team, and drop anchor in their authentic one-of-a-kind self-as-leader.

Woven throughout the book are practical steps, exercises, questions, and suggestions, all with research and real-world time-testing behind them. My clinical specialization in PTSD and experience walking with many through stressful stories of awful to new places of resilience, post-trauma growth and hard-earned identity rediscovery is here too.

As an entrepreneur, I'm well-versed in the leadership required to run a successful business. I'm proud that most of my work is from word-of-mouth testimonials. I've built a practice that leaders trust. But more than that, I've built a body of work rooted in the belief that leadership, at its best, begins with the courage to return home to your self—and lead from there.

My own leadership journey was forged via living and working international-ally, weathering personal crises and wastelands, sitting across from struggling people and tragic stories, and navigating my own seasons of loss, faceplant and too-tight pots. I've done every step in the book.

A core premise of the Leading Becomes You model is that the most pow-erful and effective leaders are those who are deeply rooted in self. I call this leader identity clarity. They are also connected to purpose, to mission, and to those they lead. This connection to others and to the hard work and soul of leadership intersects with identity clarity to foster flourishing. Without strong identity clarity or connection, the leader's "inner terrain" is fragmented, bogged down, desolate, and fragmented—like a swamp, wasteland, or petrified forest. I see this in overfunctioning, burnout, and self-erasure. It can also show up as too much ego with too little humility. Balance is essential. If a leader is hyper-focused on their pre-determined identity and not connected to purpose or people, they lead from a trapped, rigid, and isolated place. We will look more closely at each terrain in Chapter 8. On the following graphic you can see the dimension of identity clarity on the horizontal axis and the dimension of connection on the vertical axis. We will explore these dimensions in Part One of the book. In Part Two, I will guide you step-by-step through the four As: awareness, acceptance, assimilation and authentic activation—the process for moving from the three languishing terrains of swamp, wasteland, or petrified forest to the flourishing meadow. The four A's are how you break out of the too-tight pot, detangle your rootboundness, and replant your self-as-leader for flourishing.

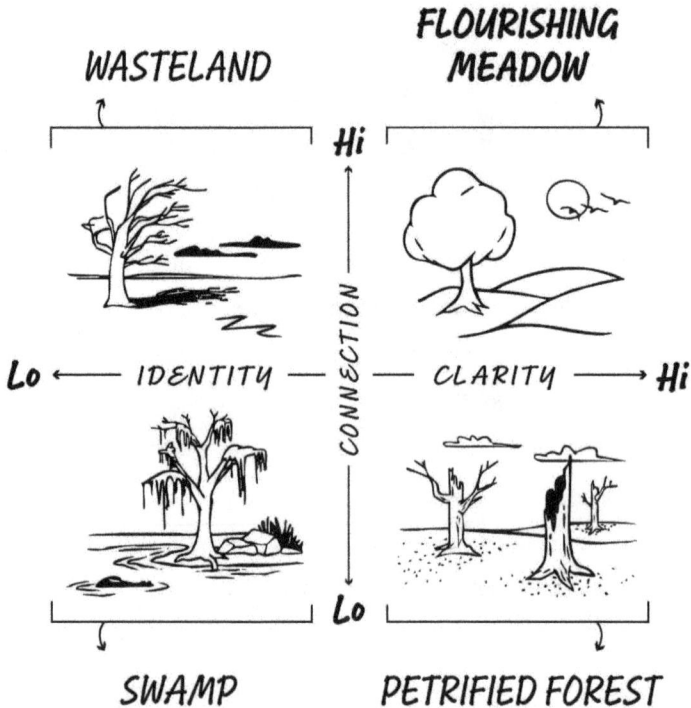

LEADING BECOMES YOU MODEL
©Dr. Natalie Pickering

WASTELAND

FLOURISHING MEADOW

Hi

Lo ← IDENTITY — CONNECTION — CLARITY → Hi

Lo

SWAMP

PETRIFIED FOREST

I have helped many leaders transform their flimsy plastic container to their one-of-a-kind pot and flourishing landscape. The work ahead will illuminate your own path to identity clarity and connection, so that your leadership approach is grounded in who you are and attuned to what and whom and why you lead. Your leader transformation produces an unstoppable force for flourishing impact via stability, trust, and commitment to your self-as-leader becoming and rebecoming

This connection-meets-identity-clarity formula fuels sustainable performance, fosters psychological safety, and cultivates cultures where both people and purpose can thrive. Prioritizing leader identity development is one of the most powerful—and most overlooked—performance strategies in modern leadership. While organizations invest heavily in skills training, strategic planning, and performance metrics, few address the core question shaping every decision a leader makes: *Who is this leader becoming while performing, managing, and influencing?*

> " Who is this leader becoming while performing, managing, and influencing?

Identity clarity and connection via the Leading Becomes You process becomes a force multiplier! It strengthens decision-making, builds trust, improves delegation, and fosters authentic presence. The model frees you up to enjoy this leadership trek you've undertaken. It's not a soft skill—it's the invisible infrastructure behind your choice to lead for as long as you want to!

THE LEADING BECOMES YOU CADRE

Throughout our journey, I'll share stories from the cadre of other leaders who have navigated the Leading Becomes You journey. Names and details have been changed or combined to protect confidentiality.

Sophia, a regional director at a national healthcare network, was known across her system for her reliability, responsiveness, and drive. When the COVID-19 pandemic hit, she stepped in with remarkable steadiness—absorbing crises and holding operations together.

For the first year, she was recognized by her team and senior leadership as indispensable. But behind the apparent steadiness, Sophia was slowly unraveling.

She rarely slept through the night. Her inbox overflowed by sunrise. Her staff and multiple teams leaned on her for decisions. Her husband noticed that she no longer laughed. When colleagues asked how she was, her response was an automatic: "I'm fine—just a lot going on."

Sophia was trapped in a leadership terrain I call the wasteland, a combination of low identity clarity and overconnectedness to others' agendas. She was still showing up effectively—but as a version of herself that ran on obligation rather than presence. Her leadership identity had quietly fused with overfunctioning. She'd long stopped asking, "Who am I as a leader?" and instead lived in a cycle of reactive service perpetuated by the global crisis facing her industry. Everyone else's needs came first. Her voice had gone silent, and she lost sight of the sweet spot of her impact capability.

Her team initially thrived under her consistency—but then began to show wear and tear too. They adopted her pace, stopped initiating, and waited for her signal before acting. Innovation slowed. Morale dipped. But Sophia was too depleted to notice, let alone intervene.

"I felt like I was watching myself lead," she said in a coaching session. "And I didn't feel anything."

When she stepped back, Sophia was met with the inner business of a new ache: the deeper grief of disconnection and the reality of how long she had been leading in a fog, drifting farther from her original purpose in this role: to be a human-centered transformative leader. Something in her—the smallest root—wanted to find her way back, not just out.

Our coaching focused on rebuilding a rhythm of returning to her self-as-leader. The big picture goal of striking the balance between healthy identity clarity and connection follows the four As process you will learn in Part Two: awareness, acceptance, assimilation, and authentic activation. I designed the four As to support leaders with one customizable process that simultaneously supports inner leader transformation while sustaining outer connection.

Sophia's progression through the four As you will learn looked like this:

1. *Awareness*: Of your self-as-leader. Of your current state. How you got here. What's working. What's not. Sophia began noticing her emotional landscape instead of numbing it. Anger, fatigue, grief—though uncomfortable, all were welcomed. She tracked the systems and moments that made her go quiet inside. Your awareness phase includes gathering the primary influences of your self-as-leader story—the seasons, situations, people, and places that have significantly impacted your leadership, for good, for challenging, for growth. This may be positive, uncomfortable, or likely both. Giving voice to the good stuff *and* the hard stuff not only illuminates debris that may be holding you back but recovers forgotten strengths for your self-as-leader superpowers.

2. *Acceptance*: Of your self-as-leader impact. Of your story's impact on you. Of strengths. Weaknesses. Failures. Wins and Losses. Acknowledging where you are versus where you wish you were. Sophia acknowledged that her old leadership model had unconsciously rewarded her pain and that staying silent had once been protective. But no longer. Intentional acceptance recognizes the impact of the significant events and experiences you discover in the awareness phase. Acceptance shines a light on how your roots got tangled and focuses on making peace with the hard realities of true leadership growth and moving forward unhindered.

3. *Assimilation*: Of insights. Truths. Lessons. Connecting your leader self with your full story. Of your leader soul. Integrating your discoveries from the awareness phase and acknowledgements in the acceptance phase. Sophia revisited her values, not as an exercise,

but as a reorientation. She created her own three "non-negotiables" for future leadership, namely *emotional truth, strategic patience, and shared ownership*. The assimilation phase brings together your new awareness and acceptance. It answers, "What will your re-rooted and just-like-you leader identity and approach yield from new insights?" You will repurpose the yuck (aka composting) for your best self-as-leader now.

4. *Authentic activation*: Of your re-potted self-as-leader. Your intentional vision for how you move forward in your leadership. Slowly, Sophia began experimenting. She delegated a key project without micro-managing. She spoke honestly at a directors' meeting about burn-out and boundaries. She asked her team what they needed from her, rather than assuming and taking it all on herself. Once you move through the four As process once, I encourage you to do it again… and again. You will realize the necessity of revisiting and translating ongoing a-ha's into a rhythm for yourself and your team. Growth requires consistent pruning and weeding of the flourishing meadow.

Sophia started sleeping again.

Her team, sensing the shift, began to reengage. A senior staff member said to Sophia, *"I don't know what you're doing, but I would follow your leadership anywhere."*

Even admired leaders can live in terrains of depletion and disconnection. Recovery isn't about speed—it's about returning to self, re-rooting in clarity and connection, and leading from that soil. This is the becoming journey you have undertaken!

LEADERSHIP IS EVERYWHERE

Leadership goes well beyond a formal title. Leadership happens the moment someone looks to <u>you</u> for how to be. It means shaping wherever you are by how <u>you</u> show up.

Leadership happens when:
- The cashier in the cafeteria remembers your name.
- A co-worker generously shares credit with colleagues.
- The commuter gives up their seat.
- A new hire asks brave questions.
- An older sibling invites her little brother to the movies.
- The group text initiator encourages the team.
- A parent models apologizing and follow-through.
- The volunteer shows up every time

But the very best leadership happens when leaders break free from flimsy plastic container constraints of what a leader *should* be and grows into an authentic leader of their very own!

> " Leadership happens the moment someone looks to <u>you</u> for how to be.

YOUR PERSONAL LEADERSHIP FIELD GUIDE

The leaders I work with often act *out* leadership—and even demonstrate incredible competency—but are not necessarily truly embodying it. Depending on the stage of their career, this limitation may stem from a lack of experience, diminished confidence, or the disbelief that there's any growth needed. Sometimes they've lost awareness that their leader persona is performative. Younger leaders second-guess their decisions and wonder, "Am I doing leadership right?" But even experienced leaders, like Sophia, may not realize they're following someone else's playbook or outdated leadership norms. And no matter their level of experience, leaders (aka people) are inevitably carrying some debris or residue from a tough season or a difficult environment—and it's interfering with their maximal effectiveness.

In any of these situations, internal leadership convictions get stunted by pressure to stick with the familiar or play it safe in the flimsy plastic mold dependent on external validation and other people's definitions. This is a fast track to stagnancy, lack of influence, and frustration. *Leading Becomes You* is the template for writing the only field guide your leadership should follow: *your own*!

_____ FLOURISHING LEADER TERRAIN _____

Flourishing, represented by the flourishing meadow, is the goal for your personal leadership terrain—a land of wholeness, presence, identity, and connection. It's the leadership landscape that nourishes you and those around you.

Here is the map and model for the journey ahead:

LEADING BECOMES YOU MODEL

©Dr. Natalie Pickering

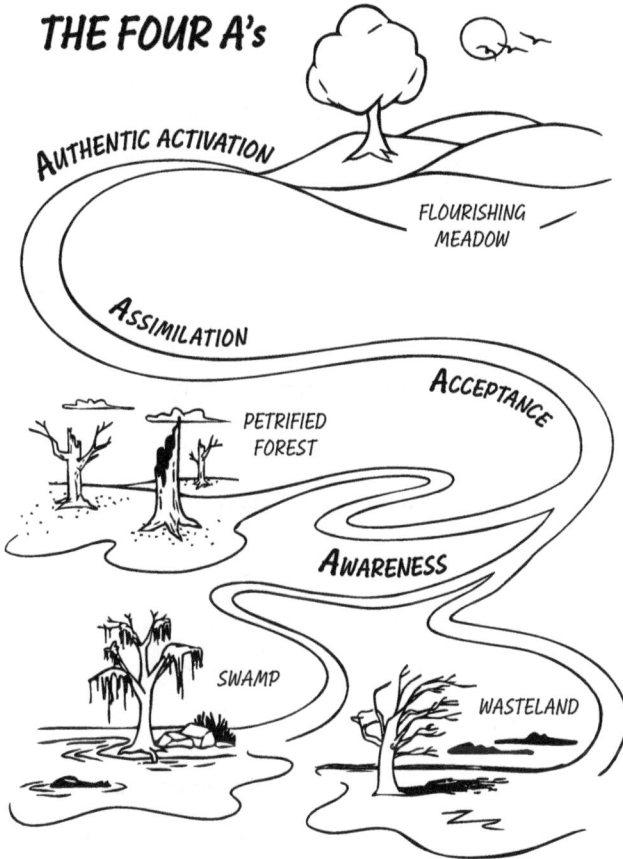

THE FOUR A's

AUTHENTIC ACTIVATION

FLOURISHING MEADOW

ASSIMILATION

ACCEPTANCE

PETRIFIED FOREST

AWARENESS

SWAMP

WASTELAND

Once you break your rootbound self-as-leader free from the plastic and untangle the old scripts and ill-fitting habits that may be creating swamp, wasteland, or petrified forest terrain (I'll show you how), you will rebuild the flourishing meadow where your self-as-leader can thrive. Your Leading Becomes You process includes pruning and cultivating your flourishing self-as-leader. (Oh, and don't forget composting!)

True leadership isn't about pushing past your limits, compromising your well-being, working harder, or proving yourself. The Leading Becomes You process is a recommitment to a personalized leadership approach rooted in fulfillment and authenticity.

While I wrote this book, a monumental joint international research effort assessed human flourishing via 200,000 participants from more than 20 geographically and culturally diverse countries and territories. Among the key findings of the *Global Flourishing Study,*[1] are some that are particularly relevant for the leaders I support and a central motivation for this book:

a.   Meaning and purpose are central predictors of sustained human (and leader) flourishing. They are often more influential than income or education: "In wealthy, resource-rich contexts, people are languishing in meaning, connection, and fulfillment."

b.   Character strengths, including forgiveness, gratitude, and ethical integrity, are strongly related to long-term well-being and leadership trust.

c.   Flourishing is positively associated with resilience, engagement, and healthier relationships, both personally and professionally. (Who doesn't want more of that?)

d.   Workplace environments that foster alignment between personal identity and job role contribute to higher levels of meaning, job satisfaction, and overall flourishing.

e.   Spirituality and religious beliefs are protective factors that enhance coherence and emotional well-being in high-stress contexts.

Taken together, these findings match my observation that leaders are especially at risk of languishing when they lose sight of inner terrain traps like:

- High visibility with low social and psychological support
- High responsibility with low relational safety or trust

- High achievement with low identity clarity and sense of self

Despite leaders' credentials, responsibilities, and accolades, they quietly find themselves trapped in an inner leader terrain that does not look or feel like flourishing. More specifically, they talk about feeling:

- Lost in every direction, lacking meaningful connection, driven by survival or approval, at the mercy of image and success-in-the-moment, a terrain of buried potential—like a *swamp*.
- Externally engaged and even motivated; realizing that while they appear competent they are internally untethered, dry, and scattered; chasing perfection; tying worth to others' agendas; their imposter and inner critic chatter limit solid ground—like a *wasteland*.
- Guarded; realizing they've become overly confident in their ways; locked in on self-protection and resistant to the risk of vulnerable growth, honesty, and acknowledging limits; unapproachable; a well-defined identity but walled off—like a *petrified forest*.

If you don't actively design your inner leadership terrain, you will default, like all humans, to safety or survival.

Your inner terrain will be clogged or depleted by the extremes of diluted self-insight or flooded misplaced connection. And your leadership will look and feel more like languishing than flourishing.

WELCOME TO THE CADRE

You join an incredible community of leaders who have undertaken this journey. I have personally walked the journey too. I know what confinement feels like—trying to lead from other people's field guides, squeezing myself into expectations versus following my intuition, leading from "shoulds" for survival. I'll share those stories and some personal experiences—seasons of loss and learning, examples of staying trapped and investing years of pursuit for goals that were not mine. I've stifled my real self-as-leader because someone deemed her unrealistic. Personal and professional faceplants resulted in quitting my job to start a business and quitting my business to start a job.

The executives, managers, first-time supervisors, team leaders, intrapreneurs, and entrepreneurs I support have faced the very same nagging tension between ambition and alignment. When they recognized they were rootbound, they courageously asked: "Is it possible to stay true to myself while leading others? "

And the answer is Yes!

Your commitment to the Leading Becomes You journey positions you among the ranks of many others who have detangled, re-rooted, and expanded their leadership approaches. It's a leader re-becoming—and the work is sacred.

WHAT IT ISN'T

Before you proceed, I feel compelled to share that this approach is not a quick fix. There are plenty of books with three-easy-step, "Believe it to achieve it" tactics and strong-sounding mantras that, frankly, don't work. Not without the deep work. "Dream big" and "Do it scared" and "Do what I do" formulas promise leadership outcomes with minimal work and a believe to achieve devoid of how-to. If you're looking for fast and easy, this isn't the book for you. If you're looking for what works, has been time-tested with hundreds of leaders like you, and you recognize that worthwhile pursuits—like a leadership rebecoming—take deep, intentional time and work, you are absolutely in the right place.

The self-as-leader transformation is exciting, hopeful, and transformational. It can also be uncomfortable, foggy, and fragile. Holding all of this in tension is part of the process. Because the path to effective leadership is filled with the same tension. Your deepest and most long-lasting impact requires intentionality and the courage to redefine leadership on your terms. That's why you chose this book!

" The self-as-leader transformation is uncomfortable, foggy, and fragile.

New tools await you in each chapter. The timeline is yours. The process is a premise for leadership becoming.

Welcome to your reclaimed, real-life, re-rooted Leading Becomes You—the one-size-fits-*you* leadership approach written for you, by you.

Let's get you out of that flimsy container and find the flourishing pot for you!

For additional leader tools, visit: www.drnataliepickering.com

PART 1

"Honesty is often very hard. The truth is often painful. But the freedom it can bring is worth the trying."

– Fred Rogers

"Life is not easy for any of us. But what of that? We must have perseverance and, above all, confidence in ourselves. We must believe we are gifted for something and that this thing must be attained."

– Marie Curie

CHAPTER 1

THE
HONEST LEADER

Courage to Look Deep
So You Can Lead Deep

You are your leadership and your leadership is you. Behind the title, role, decision-making, and visioning lives your personal agency. Behind the strategy, operations, and results lies your humanity—managing uncertainty, team dynamics, and the human aspects of effectiveness. Others look to you for direction. They know your commitment to them. The responsibility is great. But when leadership feels like you're planted in the wrong pot, no amount of wins and outcomes lead to fulfillment.

If you're honest with your self-as-leader, do any of these resonate?

- ☐ I'm leading from a place that doesn't feel like my own.

- ☐ I've been skidded to a stop by an unexpected challenge—upheaval, exhaustion, others' choices.

- ☐ My current path or role does not align with my self-as-leader or the leader I want to be.

- ☐ I'm plagued by "shoulds" and "dos" and "don'ts" and "can'ts" in my head that are not mine.

- ☐ Flourishing seems like an impossible reality from my current state.

- ☐ I'm busy all the time, but it feels more hamster wheel than purposeful.

- ☐ I feel like a fraud.

- ☐ I juggle everything but feel like I'm failing at all of it.

- ☐ I don't know how to make a real impact in a way that is my own.

These realities of the human experience can be especially heightened for leaders. One reality is that life and leadership ebb and flow from seasons of hostile terrain to seasons of smooth, open flourishing—with some wilderness stretches in between. But the ebb of hostile terrain is perpetuated when leaders don't commit to the inner business of self-awareness and consistent recalibration. External terrain factors of work pace and responsibility, not all within your control, will certainly deplete your leadership of nutritive energy and attention. Our work in *Leading Becomes You* is to intentionally do business with what you can control—your inner terrain factors.

> "Short-term distractions of high-octane leadership hustle and cultural demands for warp speed don't disguise troubled terrains for long.

Like most leaders, you adapt, perform, and push forward. But over time, debris from unexamined patterns and expectations, inherited ill-fitting leadership styles, external factors like leader betrayal trauma and moral injury, and unchecked stress leads to swamp, wasteland, or petrified forest terrain. These terrains become significantly more troublesome when old, inherited, or unconsidered ways of leading stop working and the soul of leadership feels clogged. Short-term distractions of high-octane leadership hustle and cultural demands for warp speed don't disguise troubled terrains for long. Top it off with the unspoken leadership rule pollutant—"Keep up appearances, no matter the cost"—and the tangling rootbound cycle will deplete anyone's self-as-leader landscape.

_____ REALIZING UNSUSTAINABILITY _____

High-achieving leaders and entrepreneurs are often the least likely to admit they feel off course. Whether you lead in a not-for-profit, a business, or a committee, there are clear rewards for decisiveness, productivity, and confidence. High performers can operate at full capacity while internally grappling with many inner business terrain factors like the erosion and acid rain examples of:

- *Limiting mindset*, ranging from overconfidence to imposter phenomenon.
- *Emotional exhaustion*, a key factor of work-related burnout. You are leading effectively but experience a growing personal depletion.
- *Performance-based identity*, a wide-open trap for high-capacity people whose tangled tentacles run deep from deriving self-worth from success.
- *Disconnection from purpose*, wondering what the point is, if work holds meaning, and whether it reflects your deepest values.

There are other examples, and we will explore them. For now, getting honest about the now is where your transformation revival begins. Whether you are experiencing a big change like a new role or an opportunity, you've left a role (by choice or not), or you are coming through a tough season of leadership life, I'm confident this process will equip you to navigate your story with hard-earned clarity and intention.

FROM THE CADRE

There is courage and motivation to be tapped in naming the tension and assessing the reality of your inner leader terrain. The following insights are from people like you—high insight leaders who have walked this process with me. Here are their initial pre-process thoughts:

"I feel unqualified for this position, which leads me to being too easily influenced by others' opinions. I often choose and act based on what I think others value without considering my own perspective."

— Male Physician Leader

"I am a strong and capable leader and have not felt insecure about my work very often. My challenges now are these personal insecurities. I have worked on them for years, but this upheaval in my life showed me I have a ways to go."

— Female Top 30 Under 30 Lawyer

"I'm good at keeping up appearances on the outside so that others do not know I second-guess myself constantly. It's exhausting."

— Female Human Resources Leader

"Generally, I am a confident person. I like myself, I know who I am, and I am decisive. But this work situation has led to rejection I didn't know existed. The imposter is loud, even though I know that I am good at leading this organization. This crazy insecurity is not me."

— Female Executive International Not-for-Profit

Here are their responses after working through the Leading Becomes You process:
- "I cannot believe how freeing this is. It's like a weight off my chest."
- "I will never forget this before and after. I know I have more to sort, but now I know how. I see the importance of slowing down, making the next decision, how to recognize the old rules, and leading from my own lens. What a game-changer."

- "The life and leadership rules I've followed for so long are much clearer. They don't define my approach anymore. That awful failure season I've kept replaying is now just a chapter. It doesn't define me. I can trust my team and myself."
- "I wasn't letting myself live or lead like myself. My obligation to hours and performance and people's view of me had trapped me. I did not know I could drive to work feeling this freed up."

That's where you're going. Just ahead is freedom to vision, dream, and create. It can be very challenging for many leaders trapped by a tight perspective of productivity. But research shows that leaders who set aside time for personal growth and reflection are more effective, resilient, and influential than those who do not.[2]

NEXT STEPS: SCHEDULE IT

Transformation cannot happen in the margins of an overloaded schedule. You are not here to gather more ideas but to take action in shaping your self-as-leader.

Right now, I encourage you to block time in your calendar for deeper reflection—time to roll around the questions, and yes, roll around the emotions in your heart, mind, and soul for a bit. Make the appointment recurring. Whether it's 30 minutes before work, a Sunday morning, or a midday walk, set aside consistent time for your leader re-becoming process.

_____ PREMISES _____

As an Enneagram 1 straight-shooter, I feel compelled to share my other key premises for the Leading Becomes You journey:

1. No final destination.

I like the terms "re-flourishing," "re-becoming," and "re-rooting"—or I guess I just like the prefix "re"—to remind me that the journey *is* the destination! Like a multiday hike on the Appalachian Trail, there are hard trail sections with wet tent washouts and blisters mixed in with sunny days and beautiful vistas. The leader growth process is never complete. Research shows that managers do not become more effective just because they gain experience over time.[3] Intentionality is required. You're learning a process that I encourage you to revisit at least annually. Put next year's self-as-leader personal strategic planning retreat on the calendar now.

Life and leadership flourishing is not linear and direct. You will experience peaks and valleys. I know you know this, but it helps to be reminded sometimes.

The journey is not a nice, straight, always-up-and-to-the-right kind of line. It's more like a scribble with loops and ups and downs that, over time, generally point up—but with lots of downs in between.

NOT LIKE THIS

LIKE THIS

The reality of this work is a reflection of the gritty fiber of a leader like you...

rolling up your sleeves (even if part of you is a little unsure) to expand your horizon of flourishing influence on yourself and others.

Re-becoming is not arrival. Leader identity is an iterative process over the course of your life and leadership. I'm so thrilled that you are committed to it!

2. No three-easy-steps.

You will be fighting the allure of our hyper-hustle, busy-only culture. But deep work does not happen with a diet of sound bites, podcasts, and social media infographics. Some slowdown is required to pull yourself out of the swirling. The good news is you can stop trying everything to see if something sticks because you'll have the process for deep, real change and lead-like-you discovery.

3. No one but you.

Only you can write your leadership approach. If you search for books about "how to lead well" or "leadership 101," you will find hundreds of "what worked for me" stories. I have certainly benefited from the ideas in many of these. However, someone else's blueprint does not perfectly translate to my situation. That's why I'm giving you the framework to build your *own* personalized "how to lead well" framework. And of course, effective leadership also requires adaptability. There is a lot of "it depends" when it comes to industry, organization size, culture, experience, team dynamics. The focus here is on you-as-leader and how you step into the inevitable and necessary situational agility.

4. **No solo treks.**

We need another set of eyes on our leadership life. Personally, my support has varied depending on my season of life and career—I've worked with a coach, a mentor, a peer coach, or a therapist. Their higher ground perspectives have been invaluable.

You'll be spending deep reflection on your inner leadership landscape. If you've been in leadership for any length of time, you know about blind spots. True to their words, we don't recognize them. That's why Leading Becomes You cannot be done solo.

This next statement may be surprising coming from a psychologist but here it is. My corollary premise is that self-help does not truly exist and is, in fact, contradictory. When my life and leader terrain has gotten out of hand, it was not helpful to look for solutions within myself. Self was part of the problem. My honesty has limitations. So does yours. The personal part of personal growth only gets you so far. Yes, this method I'm showing you certainly incorporates deeper introspection. *And* I'm advocating that you invite a trek-mate to your process. Don't worry—I'll remind you again!

> "Self-help does not truly exist and is, in fact, contradictory.

If you need further convincing that re-becoming and defining your leader identity cannot be done in isolation, here's some science:

- *Neurobiology*: Blind spots happen because the brain likes stability. The brain's Default Mode Network (DMN)[4] builds and locks in your sense of self—even if your perception is not completely true or accurate. Plus, your emotion system prioritizes safety, which is why you get defensive or prickly when someone points out that blind spot or growth edge. Looking at your human leader suit only from the inside is like choosing navy or black socks in a dark closet.

- *Social Psychology:* Your identity is one part how you see yourself and one part how you think others perceive you. At a social gathering, we might say something like:

"Hi, my name is ___. I live near ___ and work with ____ (another guest) at _____."

When we meet someone new, we share identity-related information without even thinking about it. But what we share shifts with the setting and often includes what we think this person might most want to know about us, which is deeply intertwined with how we want to see ourselves.

· Leadership retreat: "I'm Natalie, and my work focuses on helping leaders reconnect with who they are so they can lead with clarity."
· Networking breakfast: "I'm Natalie Pickering. I'm an organizational psychologist who partners with organizations to develop leaders who are both high-performing and deeply human."
· Neighborhood cookout: "I'm Natalie. We live in the blue house on the corner with the struggling garden."
· Wedding reception: "I work in leadership development. I help people and teams work and lead from who they are."

The details might stay the same, but the story you choose to tell about yourself changes and that choice reveals a lot about how identity works in everyday life. As leaders, this is even more true: our identity is socially informed, shaped by how we read the perceptions of others and tailor our introductions to align with (or challenge) those expectations. Leadership and social psychology research shows we all do this. We spotlight the parts of ourselves most relevant to the moment, blending what we think others want to know with how we most want to see ourselves

5. Your leader becoming is bigger than you

The process I'm teaching you for re-potting, re-rooting, and re-flourishing has benefits far beyond your personal leadership fulfillment, though you get that too! The beautiful bonus of your work is the widespread flourishing meadow impact on others in your circle of influence. Your growth pursuit of self-as-leader exemplifies that you're committed to wholehearted influence.

6. No more toxic terrains.

If you're putting in the work to prune and root your leader self, your flourishing landscape needs to be set up for your long-term thriving and nurture. We will do that in the last phase of the journey, which I call authentic activation. Most leadership books outline a process of transformation but overlook the essential foundation of identity clarity and long-term sustainability. You will design your personal leader flourishing landscape. Two-for-one, I've got you covered!

CHAPTER RECAP

Here's where your gritty self-as-leader is headed. Let's summarize:

☐ *Unchecked terrain factors deplete leaders:* You will gain clarity on the size and contributors to your version of adverse self-as-leader inner terrain.

☐ *Leadership is personal:* You will discover what real alignment in leadership looks like to you.

☐ *Honest reflection sparks transformation:* You will untangle from expectations and outdated leadership scripts that no longer serve you.

☐ *Support is essential:* You will recognize that leadership does not have to be lonely.

☐ *Long-range effectiveness:* You will develop a sustainable, long-term framework for your leadership resilience and purposeful impact.

You've already exhibited the most important quality of a flourishing leader: the willingness to be honest.

Now, let's go.

LEADING BECOMES YOU BREAKTHROUGHS

In the following space, take a few moments to write notes for what resonated with you from this chapter.

Which of the premises feels particularly important?

Are there aspects of your personal or professional re-becoming already coming to mind that you would like to focus on?

"It takes courage to grow up and become who you really are."

– E. E. Cummings

"Knowing ourselves is something so important that I wouldn't want any relaxation ever in this regard, however high you may have climbed into the heavens."

– St. Teresa of Avila

CHAPTER 2

WHAT'S A LEADER IDENTITY?

Fine-Tuning the Target

The essence of leadership is influence. I like the definition of leadership that says leadership is *how your influence makes people feel*. If so, then knowing and choosing what kind of influence you want your leadership to have is only as effective as your intentional exploration of your own inner leadership landscape. As I described in Chapter 1, a leader's terrain is impacted by both internal and external factors. Once we get clear in this chapter on what a leader identity is, I will show you how to explore and realize the internal factors and external experiences that inform your present leader identity and impact.

—————— AM I A LEADER EVERYWHERE? ——————

A leader's identity refers to their self-concept as a leader. It's how you would answer the question: "How much have you internalized the role of leading as part of your identity?"[5]

A common question in my leadership identity workshops is: "Does my leadership identity change? I feel like a different person when I'm at home versus at work. I'm decisive at work and quieter and more expressive in my personal life. Is that a problem?"

Without fail, everyone in the room nods in agreement.

It's a good question. And the answer is... It depends!

It depends on *how much* compartmentalization is happening between how you show up at your job and your home life. It's normal to have some differences in how we present ourselves in our professional and personal spaces. One reason is our unique core internal motivation and drivers—our responses to questions like, what do I need the most from this situation? It might be respect, connection, control, or security. We are strongly wired to recognize whether these deep, sometimes unconscious, motivations get rewarded in a particular context—personal or professional. Our first of the four As in Part Two, awareness, will help you make these connections for yourself.*

For example, I am personally very motivated by giving people the right solution. At work, I am highly aware of opportunities where I can provide well-researched answers to the question (often overly researched). I consistently show up with that lens and over time my expected social role matches my drive to solve problems. At home, my relationships carry a different and deeper level of warmth, softness, and vulnerability. My means of solving problems in that context is highly relational and personalized. I love to solve problems for my family, but our relationships reinforce other aspects of my presence such as protection, empathy and deep connection. This makes it easier for me to say, "I'm not sure about that, but let's figure it out together."

Sometimes leaders describe feeling like two different people entirely. Or they receive feedback that "no one knows the real me," which can lead to distrust. Sometimes there are multiple and *very* different versions of self that morph completely based on the situation. When the differences between several versions of "work me" or "home me" or "friend me" are so significantly incongruent, it's possible to lose track of your authentic self in the extremes. Balance is the goal, and some integration may be part of the work. The awareness phase we will work on in Chapters 6 and 7 will equip you with enhanced realization and tools for a more intentional reflection of the why and how of your different "versions of me," and the assimilation phase will help you integrate them.

---

* Psychologists call this identity fragmentation—when the different "selves" we show in work, home, and social roles feel so disconnected it creates strain and inauthenticity.

Some indicators that your leadership identity may be fragmented on the unhealthier side of the spectrum include:

- Consistent feelings of being fake and inauthentic
- A sense of disconnected relationships, both personally and professionally
- Difficulty "switching gears" when roles or circumstances change
- A steady sense of performing rather than showing up as yourself
- Feeling powerless to control the different roles you are living and leading
- Drastically different behaviors in different contexts and settings
- Avoiding any overlap between personal and professional (e.g., never sharing personal information at work)
- Others noticing how differently you show up depending on the circumstances or who is in the room

These feelings and behaviors may be reflective of the inner leader terrain I refer to as the swamp with a hyperfocus on a polished but empty version of identity. One reason this compartmentalization happens is when a leader struggles to see themselves as a leader. When a leader has not stepped into believing in their own self-as-leader identity, research confirms the potential fallout. The leader with low identity clarity often struggles with decreased morale, performance, and even burnout due to behavior inconsistency and related uncertainty of followers. Not to mention lack of fulfillment and satisfaction for the leader.[6]

Leadership skills and sustainability both develop through a deeply internalized self-as-leader foundation. Authentic leadership rooted in clear self-as-leader identity is also connected to stronger ethical leadership. Your revived leadership identity should remain mostly consistent and authentic across contexts, while still allowing space for intentional shifts between your various roles and situations that require an agile response.

Now that we have a sense for why leaders need identity clarity, I'll note that this leader identity does not live alone. The terms identity, self, and personality are often used interchangeably, but mean different things. Besides this distinction mattering greatly to us psychologists, a brief look at the differences will be helpful as you dig deep into your Leading Becomes You process. Once we distinguish the general difference between identity, self, and personality, we will zoom back in on some nuances related specifically to leadership identity.

To better understand *leader* identity, let's break down the three critical elements of every leader as human—who you are before you step into leading and influence.

- *Self.* The relationship between I (subject) and Me (object)—your deeply personal core beliefs, values, and motivations.
- *Identity.* The construction of your life story of self, including the roles you occupy in leadership and life—how you define yourself within your family, community, and organization and how others perceive you.
- *Personality.* The outward expression of your self-as-leader identity—your behaviors, decision-making patterns, habits, and relational style. How you express your story of self in life and leadership.

To distinguish between these, imagine a sculpture:

The *raw marble block*, still buried in the dirt, represents your *self*—the unrefined essence of your potential.

When the raw stone is placed *in the hands of the sculptor*—shaped by life experiences, upbringing, and choices—it takes on a unique *identity*.

Once sculpted, it is polished and *exhibited with personality*. The features of your leadership self emerge under different lightings, sometimes harsh and dramatic, other times soft and subdued.

Michelangelo's philosophy for his work is also beautifully appropriate for your Leading Becomes You journey, "I saw the angel in the marble and carved until I set him free."[7] Your focus is the discovery and recovery of your very own authentic leadership *identity*, which is packed between your essence of leader *self* and the display of your *personality* visible to the world.

THE ICEBERG OF PERSONALITY

A leader's personality, for example their introversion or extroversion, significantly influences their interaction with the team, communication style, and how they inspire others. You've likely taken personality-based assessments in your professional journey. Some common ones are the Myers-Briggs Type Indicator (the four letters, like INTJ), the Hogan, the NEO-PI (Big Five), or the Enneagram (nine numbers around a circle)*. Other assessments like the DISC look at workplace behavior styles.[8] These are helpful frameworks that offer leaders, teams and organizations a way to communicate about work styles, communication and conflict styles, preferences, and how we can organize and respect the beautiful diversity of the workplace! The science of personality debates the relative impact of nature—how much personality is impacted by genetic hardwiring—and

---

* I'm a huge fan of this tool. It has a fascinating history and frankly, a less fascinating research backing. My hunch for the limited research is that the tool is publicly available. No one owns the Enneagram, per se, so anyone can use it, make their own assessment, etc. So the investment in research and the lucrative business associated hasn't been prioritized. Having used the tool with hundreds of people via psychotherapy, coaching, team and leader development training, my experience is that people resonate with it deeply. It also offers many practical applications for coaches, leaders, and teams.

nurture—external influences like your family and life experience. Nature and nurture, mushed together, comprise your unique personality, including your traits, interests, and values. It's how someone might portray you in charades!

My favorite way to think about personality is the metaphor of an iceberg.

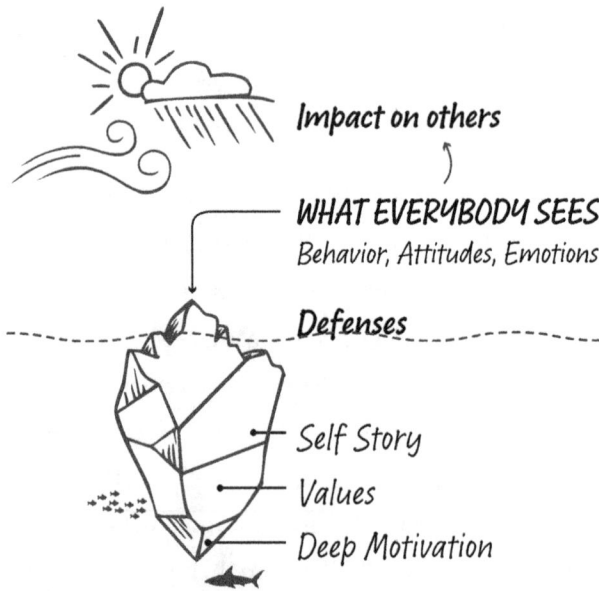

Impact on others

WHAT EVERYBODY SEES
Behavior, Attitudes, Emotions

Defenses

Self Story

Values

Deep Motivation

The personality-informed behaviors and attitudes that someone, like a leader, exhibits each day are surface-level indicators of the deeper motivation I mentioned earlier with that question, What do I really seek in this situation? The part of the iceberg above the water line is what everyone sees—how we behave, respond, communicate, decide, or not—those visible and characteristic personality traits.

What is true for everyone, including leaders, is that, like icebergs, the deepest parts of us are sometimes hidden, even from ourselves. But those deep motivations for what we seek, such as significance, security, and control, ultimately drive your leadership's visible actions. For example, if a leader's drive is for significance, then meeting the target, beating the competition, and looking good while doing so can overshadow seeing one's impact on the frontline staff, realistic timelines, and not cutting corners. If a leader's drive is for security, then micromanaging and hoarding information may seem like necessities. Not that these deep motivations can't also be used for good—you've likely heard the statement "Our greatest strengths are our greatest weaknesses." It's true for personality too.

Your leader personality, or persona, can become disconnected from your deeply personal core potential by way of keeping the more, well…unsavory parts of self hidden beneath the surface. The first order of business is busting the belief that hiding it is possible. It isn't! The unsavory parts of our personality deep below the water line leak out in lots of creative ways, like mis-interpreting situations, reacting impulsively, or losing sight of the big picture. Colleagues and your team may experience this unaware and disconnected part of your leadership as inauthentic or they may not know which "version" of your leadership will show up on a given day. A leader's disconnection from self and lack of awareness also results in overusing their strengths in an effort to hide the unsavory (but-not-as-well-hidden-as-we-think-they-are) parts of leader self. Our attempts to keep the unsavories hidden, in psychology speak, are called defenses, which you can also see at the water line on the iceberg picture. Defenses may take different forms like humor, denial, rationalization—or my personal favor-ite— intellectualizing. It comes in handy for someone who needs to have the right answers at the ready!

> " The unsavory parts of our personality deep below the water line leak out in lots of creative ways.

PERSONALITY SCARIES

For all of us, as humans who happen to be leaders, the fear is this: if others know our deep motivations and desires or our vulnerabilities and personal weaknesses, they will never respect our leadership or choose us for the role, let alone want to share work life with us. Or they will take advantage of that deeper-level knowledge. The awareness phase will help you recognize those deeper level motivations.

Refusal to look at what's below the water line has a hurtful impact on the leader's fulfillment and flourishing. For example, the disconnection experienced when a leader is pressured by themselves or someone else to lead from someone else's script. I see this often with new leaders and supervisors—or with experienced leaders in situations that are especially uncertain or complex. The do's and don'ts, definition of success or failure, tools to use, even what to wear become attempts to replicate a former or current boss's leadership style despite fundamental differences in values, personality, and mission.

FROM THE CADRE

A woman in my business coaching group shared how, over the years in her software company, the impact of their visionary CEO's bold ideas and unshakable confidence rocketed their start-up success. But his decisiveness turned into unchecked impulsiveness, and his charisma, which had appealed to venture capitalists, morphed into arrogance. Dismissing dissent as weakness, he surrounded himself with yes-people, mistaking control for leadership. As pressure grew, his relentless drive led to reckless overreach. He took critical risks that were financially irrecoverable. His approach alienated top talent, who tired quickly of not having real input. By the time he saw the cracks, his once-thriving empire had already begun its collapse.

I want you to use your gritty honesty to look deep at your self-as-leader iceberg before those cracks ever show up for you!

SELF-AS-LEADER IDENTITY

Leader identity is a piece of your overall identity and, again, is simply defined by how much you've internalized your view of "leadership" into your foundational sense and story of self. Your leader identity also consists of the roles you play and the labels you adopt formally or informally: manager, CEO, mentor, coach, team lead, strategist, innovator, or achiever. These roles are influenced internally by your leader story of self. They are also externally influenced by perceived expectations, past experiences, and social systems. Leader identity also expands beyond work. Leading is inherent to your life outside work too—you are likely leading in other organizations, as a volunteer, in your community, and within your personal network. Back to that discrepancy of showing up differently depending on the situation, a solid and clear leader identity keeps you more integrated across all of the facets and domains of your daily leadership life!

Your leader identity is constructed and reconstructed over time. As our marble sculpture metaphor illustrated, identity overlaps with your sense of self and your personality. And leader identity is not solely explained by your various roles. It also depends on how other people experience you. Research indicates that the emergence and endurance of leaders is based significantly on others' perception of the leader's traits and attitudes. This makes sense, doesn't it? Higher levels of responsibility and bigger roles are granted based on the perception of others that this person has great capacity to influence others.

I'll illustrate the social aspect of identity formation with a personal example. I was one of the tallest people in my rural high school. I'm 6'1", which at the time was a lot closer to freak status than it is today. My identity story-of-self assumed labels like "the tall girl." As a teenager highly sensitized to how others perceived me, this morphed into seeing myself as awkward and out of place. As I got older, I realized people's perception was actually the opposite of "freak." I began to see that those few comments I had deeply internalized locked in a negative and untrue narrative. I began to notice the confidence of other tall women, heard women tell me they wished they were tall, and I started rescripting my physical identity story. It also helped that clothing stores started carrying tall sizes! Now I confidently refer to myself as "the tall psychologist you met" when I follow up with someone after a conference or an event.

As I worked on reshaping the narrative, I first had to become aware of the negative script. Then I started reconstructing negative thoughts of my appearance to neutral—"People are all shapes and sizes"—and then to a more positive mindset—"Tall women are confident, like you." My innocuous but impactful example also illustrates how deeply our formative years can impact our identities for a long time, especially if left unchecked.
In coaching, many leaders cite the experiences of their younger selves as what built or shattered their ability to see themselves as leaders.

FROM THE CADRE

I was working with a highly relational leader committed to a coach-leader paradigm. He had a successful career as a project manager and was hand-picked for a leadership opportunity. In one of our early coaching sessions, he noted two distinct moments "when the imposter voice started talking to me." One of these was when he chose a career path that was very different from what his parents had envisioned for him. Now in his fifties, this leader's epiphany was that "they lived through me vicariously and saw my choice as a mistake. I took this to the worst possible extreme and seeded the belief that as long as I'm in this industry, I'm doing it wrong."

No wonder his leadership identity was being held back.

IDENTITY IMPACT

Again, the importance of a leader's strength of their self-as-leader identity is so important for the leader, their followers, and their organization. Leaders with a clearly defined and internalized leadership identity demonstrate greater motivation, resilience, and consistency in their decisions and actions. When leaders see themselves as legitimate and capable, it impacts followership too, shaping how others perceive them and contributing to stronger organizational outcomes.

Leadership development opportunities, like this book, strengthen a leader's view of their leadership by building awareness and intentionally reconstructing their leader identity. This translates to greater effectiveness in just about any leadership competency or key performance indicator that you put on the table.

A well-known leader selection and development assessment I use, the-Hogan,[9] is based on this two-fold reality of identity formation using both the leader's and others' perceptions of the leader on the analysis of a leader's identity: Those who know and are being influenced by the leader also define the leader's reputation. Assessments like the Hogan— and I would include the Enneagram assessment here—similarly illuminate what Hogan refers to as "the dark side of leadership," which helps leaders recognize how the same positive leadership traits, which contribute to their success, under stress, become what Hogan calls "derailers" for a leader.[9]

When we shed light on and get honest about these deeper levels of self-as-leader motivations beneath the water line of the iceberg and how these drive the good stuff and the unsavories, it can certainly be uncomfortable—but isn't that why you're here?

SELF-ASSESSMENT AND REFLECTION

With the personality iceberg and your leader story-of-self identity in mind, I invite you to consider how well you know your unsavories, the deep parts, and how these inform your leadership. The following one-question self-assessment is a means to capture your honest thoughts today around how much you confidently embrace seeing yourself as a leader. Additional reflection questions for deeper exploration of your self-as-leader identity follow.

To what extent do you see yourself as a leader today? In your current situation?

$$0 \longleftrightarrow 10$$

0 = I'm pretending.

3 = I've got some things down.

7 = I'm pretty settled in this.

10 = I confidently identify as a leader.

IDENTITY DEEPER DIVE

- With your rating in mind, list all of your current personal, professional, and leadership roles. It's helpful to consider all of the places and contexts where your self-as-leader is present. As you review your list, answer each of the following. No rush here. These are time-involved deeper dive questions.

- How differently do you show up in these roles? When you look at your list, is there a small difference in how you present in these various situations? A large difference?

- What specifically prompted your response to the self-assessment? What do people see above the water line in these different contexts and situations?

- Why do you think the difference in your self-as-leader happens in these various personal and professional roles?

• When you think about a more aligned identity across your various roles, what do you see? What do you hear? What do you feel? (Did you really think you would read a book by a psychologist and *not* do some business with your feelings?)

• What words do others use to describe your leadership style?

• Are there aspects of your leadership personality that you're working hard to keep on lockdown? Are there traits you want to refine? Strengthen? Allow to surface freely with intention?

• Do you have a sense of the deeper core motivation drivers of your leadership? Why do you lead?

CLARITY IS COMPETENCY

Similarly to your assessment above, we can measure leader identity clarity by asking leaders to rate their confidence in statements like "Yes, I am a leader," "I see myself as a leader," and "Being a leader is important to me."[10] Leaders who participate in leadership development and are exposed to new ideas about leadership will continue reconstructing their leader identities. This deepening of one's leader identity is connected to the growth of specific leadership competencies like challenging status quo, valuing diversity, and creating commitment.[11]

The takeaway is that building identity clarity, one of the two dimensions of the Leading Becomes You framework, supports any leader's effectiveness and fulfillment. It also means that organizations should prioritize leader identity in their training programs!

_____ THE GORILLA GLUE OF IDENTITY AND SELF _____

Personal agency describes the reality that we can influence our own life and leadership—"I have agency of my life." Self and identity are agency cousins.

And the gorilla glue holding them together are your personal and professional values.

Your values influenced your responses to the earlier reflection questions and they are a key contributor to how you answer the meta questions of this book:

- What keeps me from becoming my best and most authentic self-as-leader?

- What do I need to do to sustain my flourishing meadow leader land-scape?
- How can I realign, repurpose, and recover my self-as-leader through identity clarity and connection?

Values are the bedrock of your personal identity, and thereby your leader identity. They can greatly contribute to your effectiveness within your role if you know them and intentionally apply them. Values are the guiding principles informing your sense of right and wrong and your life and leadership choices. Your leadership flourishing stems directly from the alignment between your daily leadership decisions and your deeply held values.

Your values are internalized from the many past and present influences in your life—family, society, culture, personal experiences, religious and spiritual beliefs, education. Cultures and societies reflect value differences.

For example, whether a culture prioritizes the group or individual plays out in lots of ways, like who gets rewarded—the team or the individual? Whether emphasis is on fast decisions or decisions by consensus. How belonging is prioritized. Establishing team-focused and individual performance targets. Other examples of value differences may show up in directness in communication, gender egalitarianism, competition, timeliness, and what and how to celebrate.* Earlier, we looked at the impact of being unaware of your deep iceberg motivation that gets translated into those visible above-the-water-line personality attributes.

* Scholars have long shown that cultural values shape how leadership, teamwork, and organizational behavior unfold. In highly individualistic cultures (e.g., the United States, Germany, Australia), performance rewards often go to the individual, and direct communication is the norm. In collectivist cultures (e.g., Japan, South Korea, India, Mexico), recognition is shared, and decisions tend to be made by consensus. Leaders who recognize the implicit "rules" their culture brings to work— and especially how these may differ from those of their colleagues— are better equipped to navigate conflict, set fair performance targets, and build inclusive teams that thrive across geographical, relational, and shared leadership borders.

A leader's values shape their leadership in profound ways, especially decision-making. Your choices for resource allocation and which projects you champion are influenced by your deeply held value-informed judgment. When you pursue a particular role or career path, do you prioritize achievement, stability, independence, work-life balance, or helping others? Purpose or profit? The team's well-being or individual interests? Long-term growth or short-term wins? Corporate consciousness or the bottom line? It's not that you don't value the other option, but one value rings *more* importantly.

Values aren't inherently right or wrong—their priority simply reflects your unique self-as-leader perspective. A leader who values integrity builds trust by making ethical decisions, such as refusing to cut corners on safety regulations even when it would save the company millions. When community is central to a leader's core values, they create an inclusive environment—like adjusting a team member's workload after parental leave to ease their transition. A leader who prioritizes courage makes difficult but necessary choices, such as advocating for ethical artificial intelligence (AI) development despite investor pressure for faster albeit less regulated growth. These values not only define leadership but also influence the culture and success of the team or organization.

Values are integral to our personal lives too. Families, for example, have shared values such as honesty, respect, and kindness. Individuals in families have unique values. With a new teen driver in our family, we got the phone app called Life360, which allows you to see where your family members are on your phone via GPS. It shows when they are driving and how fast they're going (so I need to watch my speed too!). If you look at our family Life360 profiles, you can see that each family member has, *ahem*, a value difference for speed and efficiency. Beyond driving, our family personalities are also a blend of introverts and extroverts who more highly value social interaction or solitude. This means that Friday evenings look different too, with some of us at home and others with friends or attending social gatherings.

Finally, values are also critical to your deepest leadership motivation. From an organizational perspective, the values are more than words but are evident in everything the organization and its leaders do. Not surprisingly, leaders' commitment to their organizations depends on mutual goodness-of-fit for their values.[12]

If your leader values are being honored, you will experience flourishing, success and fulfillment. When your values are challenged or compromised, you will be frustrated, disappointed, or anxious. Values are a key factor in leader burnout. If the work doesn't connect to what you care about, or worse, contradicts your personal beliefs or purpose, inner tension and cynicism will take center stage. I worked as an internal consultant for a large organization during a reorganization. As months of limited communication, rumors, gap-filling with no strategic or succession plan stacked up, high performers predictably left in droves. A recurring theme in those exit interviews noted that senior leaders' invalidation, disrespect, and refusal to acknowledge frontline emotional and psychological impact created value incongruence. It's important to have value clarity when big change happens. This informs your non-negotiables for career decision-making. You'll also make connections to value-informed emotional awareness in phase one of the four As.

Sometimes values shift. These changes may be influenced by meeting someone new, a life-stage transition, or hard experiences. You may keep some core values in every season. Maybe their order of importance changes. The reality of shifting values reminds us that leadership growth, flourishing, and self-as-leader development is a lifelong process and another reason that I highly encourage you to keep revisiting this process year after year.

Team and peer relationships also depend on a base level of shared values and alignment. When core personal and professional values align, then priorities, strategies, and pursuits are easier to rally and collaborate. The values of the organization, if known and prioritized and practiced, attract people who want their work and career investment to reflect those values too.[*]

Personal value differences can show up on teams in lots of ways too. For example, if one person on a team highly values efficiency and another person prioritizes flexibility, we have two different approaches to a project.

Let's call one team member "The Efficiency Valuer," who finishes their part of the project two days before deadline. Most organizations positively reinforce this value with the assumption that high efficiency equals more productivity.

Another team member, "The Flexibility Valuer," prioritizes autonomy and flexibility—of schedule, time, and project completion. This can be frustrating for "The Efficiency Valuer" because inevitably one day before the project deadline "The Flexibility Valuer" says, "What if we add this idea?" Neither is right or wrong per se, but values inform working styles. And leading a values-diverse team requires the leader's insight of their own values in the mix.

FROM THE CADRE

An executive nurse leader held mentorship as a top professional value, much to the benefit of her nurse managers. In a leadership coaching session with me, she compared her leadership approach to a house: "When you begin a leadership role, you are the roof—protecting staff and helping them build and design as a team. You make sure they have what they need and buffer them

---

* Research in organizational psychology consistently shows that shared values are a foundation for trust, collaboration, and team alignment—and that value clashes often surface as work style differences rather than outright conflict.

from unnecessary elements. As they get the house in order, your role shifts to the foundation of the house, hidden from sight, leading from behind, holding steady as they build their own roof."

As her coach, I noted that her leadership approach prioritizes relationships with her staff. Her metaphor illustrated how her leadership also values scaffold-

"...your role shifts to the foundation of the house

ing—a progressive and intentional shift to delegating more responsibility and leader independence. She also highly values her role in developing people and respecting each individual leader's autonomy. Perhaps you have a metaphor to capture your own value-centered leadership approach.

YOUR TURN

I've provided a values exercise in the back of the book. Getting clear on your values greatly informs your flourishing meadow leader landscape and sets up your work for the first phase of awareness. Sometimes values get buried under ill-fitting contracts, outdated scripts, and others' expectations. Or they're trapped in the sludge of inner conflict and tension, lack of awareness, or unresolved debris of painful experiences. We will work through all of this step by step. You may even discover new values over the course of the Leading Becomes You journey. Now that you've busted your self-as-leader out of your too-tight container, let's see what values show up front and center.

In the **Resources section** on pg. 339, you will find the leader values exercise with instructions. Don't worry if you find yourself deliberating over your top five values—*re*-rooting work is our life's work. The deliberating *is* the journey!

Once you've identified your top five leadership values, write them below and take some time to reflect and capture your thoughts.

My top five leadership values are:

1.

2.

3.

4.

5.

_____ FOR REFLECTION: _____

- How do I embody these values in my current leadership role?

- In what areas of my work can I express my core values more?

- Are there areas of my work where I am holding myself back from expressing or leading from my core values?

- Is there anything or anyone keeping me from value-aligned self-expression?

- How can I better integrate these values into my day-to-day leadership consistently?

- How can I use my values in my decision-making?

- How are my values impacting my leadership performance?

This is a great exercise to share with your team—to gain insights into who they are, what motivates them, and how you can support and empower them more effectively.

Knowing your values will help you communicate your vision, inspire others, influence authentically and more effectively, and wrangle complexity—earning you less stress and a healthier environment.

CHAPTER RECAP

☐ *Leader identity is shaped by self, personality, and identity:* Your leadership approach is expressed from your core values (self), roles and how others perceive you (identity), and outward traits and patterns (personality).

☐ *Fragmentation of leader identity causes misalignment:* Authenticity, burnout, and feeling like different versions of yourself signal a need for deeper leader identity integration (which you're doing here!).

☐ *Values are foundational to leader-becoming authenticity:* Your values work will enhance your leader fulfillment and influence.

☐ *Leader identity is influenced by internal and external factors:* Your upbringing, life experiences, and organizational expectations shape how you define your approach and how others experience your leadership.

☐ *Long-term leader success requires ongoing awareness:* Leader becoming is a continual process essential for your personal and professional sustenance.

LEADING BECOMES YOU BREAKTHROUGHS

In the following space, take a few moments to write notes for what resonated with you from this chapter.

How might your self-as-leader be trapped in the marble?

Considering how you rated your belief in your self-as-leader earlier in this chapter, what hopes do you have for the journey ahead?

"We are each other's harvest; we are each other's business; we are each other's magnitude and bond."

– Gwendolyn Brooks

"The soil is the great connector of our lives, the source and destination of all."

– Wendell Berry

CHAPTER 3

LEADING IS NOT A SOLO TREK

People Need You and You Need Them

A t the core of every human life is a quiet, persistent longing to belong. Our belonging and our identities cannot be built in isolation. From infancy, we construct our sense of self through seeing ourselves in others' eyes.* Leadership identity, too, is relational. We become who we are as leaders, in part, through our impact and presence in communities of teams, workgroups, committees and organizations. Leaders rooted in authentic connection are more likely to lead with congruence between values and behaviors, recover more quickly from failure or criticism, and build cultures where others feel seen and safe. Connection is not about being extroverted or "social"—it's about being seen and supported in ways that affirm one's humanity and leadership purpose.

When leaders lose connection to or don't prioritize connection with others, their identity clarity becomes fragile. They may double down on performance metrics, over-identify with their role, or chase approval instead of alignment. This is why the two dimensions of the Leading Becomes You approach, connection and identity clarity, are interdependent.

Connection isn't a nice-to-have—it's fundamental to our well-being, even our survival. Not only does it shape our identity, as we unpacked in the last chapter. But connection is wired into our biology. Neuroscience backs this up too. Brain imaging studies show that social pain—that ache we feel if we are picked last for the team, left out on the group chat, ignored by a loved one, or betrayed by a colleague friend for the promotion—activates the same neural pathways as physical pain.[13] From our first moments in the world, our safety

---

* Psychologist D.W. Winnicott's concept of mirroring describes how a caregiver's attuned emotional responses help form a child's sense of self. Applied to leadership, we also come to understand and clarify who we are through how others reflect us back. In healthy relationships, this builds confidence and identity clarity; in their absence, leaders may develop fragile self-concepts and seek excessive external affirmation. See: Winnicott, D.W. (1960). The Maturational Processes and the Facilitating Environment. International Universities Press.

and development depend on the presence of others. And across a lifetime, the depth and quality of those connections shape how we live, love, and lead.

Our lived experience shows us that strong connection to others boosts well-being and buffers anxiety and depression to support greater life satisfaction. The Harvard Study of Adult Development found that close relationships were the most reliable predictor of happiness and health across the lifespan. Loneliness and chronic disconnection, on the other hand, carry health risks on par with smoking or obesity.[14]

And this isn't just true for life—it's true for leadership!

Connection is essential for leaders—but often more complicated. The higher up you go, the fewer honest sounding boards you may have. The social pain shows up when trust is broken, when feedback dries up, or when your position sets you apart from the very people you're supposed to support. Leadership roles demand relational intelligence—but can subtly discourage true relational presence. This leaves many leaders surrounded by people but feeling alone. This is also why one of our foundational premises is: No Solo Treks.

> **"Without the real nourishment of connection, you won't grow. And without others' reflection, you can't know who you truly are.**

The good news is that respectful, balanced, and intentional connection fuels leader flourishing and follower flourishing. It increases motivation, buffers against burnout, deepens engagement, strengthens teams, and even boosts performance.

So, this journey of repotting yourself as a leader—moving into your one-of-a kind approach, realigning values with choices, setting new boundaries, rewriting old scripts—is the work, but it isn't enough on its own. You can upgrade your container, but without the real nourishment of connection, you won't grow. And without others' reflection, you can't know who you truly are.

Let's make the metaphor real. And edible!

Cacao trees—the ones that give us chocolate (which, let's be honest, is a strong motivator for keeping ecosystems intact)—are famously fussy. They need just the right combination of humidity, shade, and soil. But most importantly, they require biodiversity. A cacao tree cannot pollinate itself. It depends on midges—tiny insects that only thrive in biodiverse forest environments—to move pollen from one flower to another. Without the right mix of trees, fungi, insects, and undergrowth, there is no pollination. No fruit. No chocolate.*

A cacao tree can be alive but unproductive. Like a leader.

Repotting your leadership without relationship connection is like growing cacao in a greenhouse monoculture. It might look good on paper. But the fruit won't come.

Flourishing leaders, like flourishing cacao groves, need diverse ecosystems—people who challenge them, support them, think differently than they do, and invite discomfort alongside growth. They need cross-pollination. Not just professional acquaintances, but real relationships—those who ask good questions, reflect back who you are, and carry insight from one part of the forest to another.

Connection is the fertilizer for your journey to renewed flourishing—rich with empathy, feedback, and shared perspective. The work you're undertaking to move through the Leading Becomes You process and repotting your self-as-leader also requires proper nourishment. Connection fertilizes and pollinates—moving creativity, emotion, and energy through your relational network. You

---

*Chocolate is a personal staple. If you're not a fan, just substitute your personal favorite treat when I reference it— which is more than a few times!

can upgrade your title, your calendar, your boundaries, and your mindset—but without connection, your fruit won't set.

And none of us will get the chocolate.

_____CONNECTION AND LEADERSHIP OUTCOMES _____

If you aren't convinced, here are some research-backed direct links between connection and leadership. Leaders who foster meaningful relationships are more likely to engage their teams, retain talent, and create psychologically safe cultures. Connected leader-follower relationships enhance ethical decision-making and organizational citizenship. Leaders who themselves experience connection—peer support, mentorship, a sense of team—are more likely to be resilient, satisfied, and effective.[15]

Are you convinced that connection is a self-as-leader essential??

While some traditional leadership models treat relationships as a secondary focus to prioritizing tasks, delegation, and pace-setting, the most effective and human-centered leadership approaches understand that connection is central to leading effectively. This is not to say that autocratic, transactional, and task-focused aren't important and efficient in some high-risk and high-stakes contexts. But the best leaders balance both and different contexts require different facets of a leader's aptitude. And when leaders have capacity for empathy, trust, collaboration, and co-creation, their relational focus and results affirm what we know intuitively: leadership isn't something you do alone—it's something that happens between people, teams, and organizational life. Connection isn't just a leadership skill; it's the medium of leadership itself.[16]

Hopefully, cacao and I have convinced you that connection naturally and essentially strengthens your leader identity clarity—the internal story leaders tell themselves about who they are and why they and their leadership matter. And research unequivocally proves that deepening of leader identity clarity in combination with leader connection increases resilience, adaptability, and performance.[17]

Unless...

CONNECTION CAUTION

Connection gets carried away. Leader connection is not simply a matter of presence or absence. Like many of the concepts we will look at together—flourishing, burnout, awareness—connection exists on a spectrum, with risks for extremes at both ends. Like any powerful force, connection can be distorted.

FROM THE CADRE: DISCONNECTION DESERT

Marcus, a senior project manager in a global construction firm, had risen from site engineer to overseeing multimillion-dollar builds. But as his team expanded, so did the layers of insulation. By year four, Marcus found himself in back-to-back strategic meetings but could not name the last time someone offered him feedback that wasn't filtered through admiration or fear. His team respected him, but no one really knew him anymore. He felt increasingly numb and disconnected from the mission he once lived for. When a close advisor finally told him, "You've built a castle but locked yourself in the tower," Marcus realized that proximity was not the same as connection.

This extreme of leader invulnerability is isolation, the dried-up, stagnant well of disconnection and superficiality. Leaders may be surrounded by people and yet experience profound loneliness. Senior-level roles are often structurally isolating due to heightened confidentiality requirements, decision-making burdens, and role-based boundaries that can lead to a significant sense of separateness.

While some leadership isolation is part of the territory, disconnection can easily be reinforced by a leader's own behaviors and beliefs. Disconnection isn't always something that happens to leaders. Sometimes it seems to be the safer option. In Part Two, your journey through the four As of the Leading Becomes You process will help you recognize any potential disconnection habits or beliefs holding back your leadership best.

Another example of leader disconnection is a particular version that looks warm on the surface—but underneath, it leaves others feeling unsettled, unsure, and unwilling to follow. When behavior is too polished and too polite, it feels like contrived performance to those on the receiving end. It may seem to pass as relational leadership but lacks the depth to support deep trust or team and leader transformation. It's like Wi-Fi with one bar—you're technically connected, but nothing's getting through. I worked with a tech team whose leader appeared positive and encouraging in meetings with senior leadership or the whole team, but her pattern of abrasive and critical defensiveness showed up in one-on-one conversations with her team members leaving them confused, distrusting, and divided.

On the inside, this desert disconnection sounds like:
- "I don't have time to deal with people's feelings."
- "I've learned not to get too close—it just makes things messy."
- "If I get too personal, I'll lose credibility."
- "Connection is nice, but delivery is what matters."
- "People should be able to do their jobs without needing that from me."
- "I keep things professional for a reason."

- "I keep work at work and life at home."
- "Team building feels like a waste of time."

It can also feel confusing and disingenuous when people hear:

- "Let's circle back!" (but it's never scheduled)
- "I've got your back!" (but the leader is not available when the meeting, conversation, conflict is happening)
- "The door is always open!" (but it doesn't feel safe to walk through it)
- "How's the family?" (without listening for the answer)

These patterns may not be intentionally deceptive—but they can become the default for leaders who are intimidated by authentic relationship and too insecure to receive honest feedback. Leaders often maintain these surface-level dynamics because they're time-efficient, emotionally safer, or culturally reinforced. But in reality, shallow connection is emotional distancing in disguise.

Disconnection doesn't always feel like emptiness; sometimes, it feels like exhaustion. A leader who no longer feels seen, known, or understood may still attend every meeting, lead every initiative, and smile for every photo—while internally fraying at the edges.

FROM THE CADRE: THE FOG OF OVER CONNECTION

Leila, a nonprofit executive director, was revered for her emotional and relational intelligence. Her team described her as the heart of the organization. But behind the accolades, Leila was quietly frustrated. She couldn't separate her own sense of worth from her staff's morale. She answered emails late into the night, mediated personal disputes, and absorbed every disappointment. Over time, her identity became so wrapped around being needed that she forgot how to ask for what she needed. When she collapsed from exhaustion mid-quarter, she was forced to realize that trying to hold everyone and everything else together resulted in losing herself. She didn't even realize it was happening.

At the other extreme from disconnection desert is enmeshment—too much connection, without boundaries. Leaders who overly identify with the needs, expectations, or emotions of others can lose themselves in the process. This often presents as people-pleasing, emotional over functioning, or chronic empathy fatigue—when someone loses their ability to care.*

Enmeshment occurs when an individual's sense of self, emotions, and identity become excessively intertwined with another person, group, or their job. Enmeshed leaders struggle with saying no, fear disappointing others, and often conflate their value with their availability. They've built a reputation, but buried their essence of self-as-leader identity.[18]

Too much connection can lead to role confusion, decision paralysis, and burnout from carrying emotional weight that isn't the leader's to hold. It can also distort leader identity: rather than leading from internal conviction, enmeshed leaders lead from external validation.

Most leaders don't intend to become disconnected—or enmeshed. It happens slowly, subtly, through the accumulation of experiences, roles, and unspoken expectations.

On the inside, the fog of over connection sounds like:
- "If they're not okay, I can't be okay."
- "Saying no feels selfish."
- "If I'm not available, everything will fall apart."

---

* Compassion fatigue, emotional overfunctioning, and burnout are well-documented risks in helping professions, where high-empathy individuals face chronic emotional labor, blurred boundaries, and identity strain

- "I'm responsible for how everyone feels at work."
- "I know I'm doing a good job if everyone is happy with me."
- "I'll deal with my work later—right now, they need me."
- "I'll take care of it."

THE SUBTLE ISOLATION AND
DISCONNECTION EROSION

In addition to those examples of the inner dialogue of under-connection or over-connection, there are additional internal and external factors that can lead to the subtle but slippery slope of leader disconnection. Check any that resonates with you:

☐ Promotion and elevation have led to distance from peers and former collaborators.

☐ Role-based boundaries create structural separation (e.g., confidentiality, power dynamics).

☐ Success myths, often reinforced by organizational culture, reward independence, stoicism, and decisiveness—traits often considered at odds with relational transparency.

☐ Self-protection inhibits connection after betrayal, criticism, or failure—leading to guardedness and mistrust.

☐ Blurry boundaries develop in relational cultures that prize harmony over clarity.

☐ Heroic leadership myths encourage self-sacrifice in the name of team cohesion.

☐ Unresolved identity work leads leaders to seek connection not as an expression of self, but as a replacement for it.

☐ Digital overload creates the illusion of connection without depth, driving constant communication but little authentic relating.

☐ Fear of rejection or vulnerability: Leaders avoid connection to avoid pain.

☐ Shame and impostor syndrome: These internal narratives convince us we don't belong.

☐ Cultural conditioning: Messages about self-sufficiency, hierarchy, and emotional restraint resist relational authenticity.

☐ Power differentials: Employees may withhold honest connection from those they perceive as evaluators.

☐ Time scarcity: Leaders often prioritize urgency over intimacy, tasks over people.

☐ Identity diffusion: Leaders unsure of who they are may adopt roles or masks that hinder connection.

☐ Mistrust of others' intentions: Especially in competitive or politicized environments, connection may feel unsafe. This may be heightened for leaders who have unresolved personal histories including trauma.

BUTTER AND POPCORN

Identity clarity and authentic connection are not separate pursuits—they are fundamentally interdependent. Without connection, identity becomes distorted, rigid, or performative, shaped by external pressures rather than internal truth. And without a clear sense of identity, connection to others and purpose lacks depth and direction, setting leaders up for codependence, superficiality, or reactive responses. True leader identity emerges not in isolation but through intentional relationship: we come to know who we are by how we show up with others, and we refine our self-as-leader through reflection and feedback.

Likewise, meaningful connection with peers, mentors, and mentees depends on a leader identity that is anchored, honest, and self-aware. The clarity of who you are as a leader and the quality of your connections form an ecosystem—each nourishing and requiring the other, like the cacao tree and the midges. Like popcorn and butter.

The four As in Part Two will walk you through the process that supports both identity clarity and capacity for balanced connection. The Leading Becomes You approach uniquely integrates relational connection with identity clarity—it is the full-spectrum map for your self-as-leader field guide.

Coming up in the next chapter is a recommended and time-tested packing list for your Leading Becomes You trek—just like going to camp! You won't be surprised to find that one of your packing essentials includes a trek-mate, someone who knows you and whom you can trust to talk about your trek. I'll share ideas for how to identify someone.

You need someone to drop chocolate as you trek.

Flourishing leaders learn to cultivate connection with wisdom and discernment. They lead not just from authority, but from authenticity. Not from isolation, but from integration. They do not lead alone—not because they can't, but because they know that the most human work requires the most human presence.

_____ FOR REFLECTION _____

- When do I feel most connected in my leadership? What relationships or conditions contribute to that?

- What subtle signs show up in my life or leadership when I'm experiencing disconnection?

- In what ways might I be unintentionally contributing to my own disconnection?

- How do I tend to show up at each extreme—emotional distance or over-involvement?

- What beliefs or internal narratives hold me back from seeking or sustaining meaningful connection?

- Who are the people in my life that act as midges—those who pollinate my thinking and reflect back who I really am?

- What intentional practices would help me lead from connection with clarity rather than connection instead of clarity?

CHAPTER RECAP

☐ *Connection is foundational—not optional—for leadership and identity.* Just as our personal identity is shaped in relationship, so too is our leadership identity. We cannot become who we're meant to be in isolation.

☐ *Disconnection damages clarity and culture.* When leaders lose authentic connection, their identity clarity erodes, performance becomes performative, and organizational health suffers.

☐ *Connection is both a survival need and a strategic advantage.* Neuroscience and leadership research show that meaningful relationships increase resilience, engagement, and well-being—for both leaders and teams.

☐ *There are two extremes to connection: desert and fog.* Leaders can suffer from too little connection (isolation, emotional distance) or too much (enmeshment, blurred boundaries)—both distort identity and deplete vitality.

☐ *Authentic leadership grows in relational ecosystems.* Like the cacao tree, leaders flourish when they're embedded in rich, diverse, reciprocal relationships. Connection fertilizes insight and pollinates growth.

LEADING BECOMES YOU BREAKTHROUGHS

What version of connection am I performing—and what would authentic connection cost me or give me instead?

If I believed I didn't have to lead alone, what would I do differently starting this week?

"No matter how prepared you are, you're never ready."

– Jacqueline Lapidus

"It does not do to leave a live dragon out of your calculations, if you live near him."

– J.R.R. Tolkien

"A goal without a plan is just a wish."

– Antoine de Saint-Exupéry

CHAPTER 4

A
PACKING LIST

Essential Tools for Your Journey

Great leaders know that good planning differentiates thriving from scrambling. Your Leading Becomes You trek, like any journey, requires intentional packing. And I've created your packing list.

I've learned a lot about packing from my 16-year-old daughter, who loves organization. To be honest, she did not get this love from me. In fact, I'm willing to consider that her Queen of Tidy *might* be a response to my habit of stacks and sticky notes. Days before a trip, she methodically launders and lays out her clothes using travel cubes to create a perfectly organized suitcase. Me? In my best moments, I pack the night before, flitting from bedroom to closet to bathroom grabbing things as I go. A few items stuffed into the bag and my nightstand charger shoved into my running shoes. Done.

Not surprisingly, a consistent result of my approach is forgetting a basic essential. Multiple times, I've arrived at the hotel, unzipped my mound of hastily stuffed madness only to discover that I have not packed the simplest item—my underwear.

This chapter ensures you do not forget your Leading Becomes You essentials. Like any journey, leadership requires intentional preparation. Otherwise, you risk carrying unnecessary baggage and, at worst, missing essentials that make a difference—like underwear. The short form of your Leading Becomes You packing list includes:

- Permission Passport
- Guts
- Gyroscope
- Coordinates
- Realistic Expectations
- Pacer and SAG Team

_____ESSENTIAL #1: PERMISSION PASSPORT _____

When I work with groups or teams, I start with a key question: Are there any barriers to making the most of the session? We tackle break times and room temperature and then get to deeper concerns about sharing openly in the group, depending on the situation. Sometimes leaders and direct reports are in the workshop together and I'm sensitive to necessary boundaries. Then I probe a little more deeply to inquire about internal authority and permission. I ask, "What do you need in order to take personal permission to engage and wrestle with the content individually and collectively?" Establishing psychological safety is an important foundational agreement.

Consider the idea of permission in everyday life. We need IDs to board flights and enter other countries. We need licenses to drive, buy wine, vote, and open a bank account. These are external stamps of permission. Leaders are often so focused on the team, stakeholders, and organization, they often set their own growth aside.

Take a few moments and reflect on the following questions.

When it comes to your Leading Becomes You journey:

1. Do you have permission from yourself to do this work?

2. What barriers block you from fully engaging in your own leadership growth?

3. Whose expectations or limits might you be holding on to? Yours? Someone else's?

4. What's the cost of not claiming permission and your own authority to grow?

5. Have you given yourself permission to fully engage in this growth process?

FROM THE CADRE

An insightful mid-level leader hired me for personal coaching after I did a workshop for her company. As she shared her goal of building a brand new department, she paused abruptly.

"Natalie, I have deadlines. I need this, but now I'm feeling guilty about taking this time out of my week."

I listened to her recount the reasons she should not continue coaching with me. Then I asked, "How does your own growth impact your team?"

"I don't know... I guess I feel like I'm taking time away from them," she began. "They need support, not a leader who's focused on herself. I worry they'll think I'm checked out or prioritizing myself too much."

"That makes so much sense," I responded. "It sounds like you care deeply about how your team experiences you. When you're growing—learning and gaining clarity—how does that affect how you lead them?"

"Hmm… Well, as I think about it, when I take that time, I do feel more grounded. I'm less reactive. I listen better. I'm clearer."

"So your growth doesn't take away from them—it sounds like it shapes the way you show up *for* them."

"Yeah… I hadn't thought about it that way. A better version of me is a better leader for them. Maybe it's not selfish—maybe it's actually responsible."

We spent the rest of the session from this reframe, specifically applying what she will gain to tangibles like long-term buy-in, confronting complacency, boosting morale, and supporting others' pursuit of their potential.

Later in the book, we will look at the internal and external contributors to a leader's unhealthy inner terrain. Others' influence may try to convince you that you don't have permission or authority. It's often unconscious. Bringing it to light may sound like: "What would _____ think of my commitment to re-flourishing?" Or: "Maybe I should start my leader re-becoming after I've _____."

To be honest, not giving yourself the authority to do this work may be a significant contributor to your rootbound self-as-leader.

Not packing your permission passport risks undermining many miles of hard work. Keep your permission passport close to you.

Here is a personal permission statement if you need to sticky this to your bathroom mirror or computer screen:

I, _____ [your name], am taking personal authority and permission to invest in my leadership growth by entrusting this process to myself. I will set aside dedicated time, remove distractions like _____, block my calendar, and allow myself the time, space, and freedom to my leading-becomes-me journey.

If you didn't block your calendar before, this reminder is for you! Get out your phone, planner, wherever you keep track of your appointments and schedule a recurring meeting with yourself for the next six weeks.

While we're on the subject of logistics, I do believe that permission-taking includes establishing your favorite thinking spot and stocking this place with your favorite coffee or tea or other beverage, pen, notebook, and chocolate bar. Mine is a dark chocolate bar with orange bits, a medium-tip gel pen, and a notebook with those little dots instead of lines.

When you've completed this packing essential, check here:

☐ Permission taken.

☐ Thinking spot stocked.

ESSENTIAL #2: GUTS

You can check this one off right now. I know you have this packing essential because you picked up this book with the courage to look at your leader self honestly. You signed up for a growth process written by someone with some practice in asking hard questions. When I think of your self-as-leader, several leadership attributes come to mind—courage, inner fortitude, and fiber of heart, mind, and soul.

In positive psychology, "leadership grit" refers to the character of a leader who demonstrates unwavering perseverance toward long-term goals, despite challenges and setbacks.[19]

I think you're gritty.

Your guts and grit brought you here. Go ahead and check off this essential from your packing list:

☐ Acknowledgment of my guts and grit.

_____ ESSENTIAL #3: GYROSCOPE _____

Every airplane pilot movie has a scene when the plane gets hit by an enemy rocket, suffers engine failure, or flies into a swirling dark storm. The plane spins and careens, and the pilot either ejects or miraculously navigates to safety. We see the pilot's flight deck, what used to be called the artificial horizon, with a spinning device called a gyroscope. The gyroscope keeps its orientation, allowing the pilot to see the artificial horizon when the actual horizon isn't visible.

What is a helpful indicator for _your_ leadership when it's stormy and you can't see the horizon line of direction or purpose? Perhaps your gyroscope is fresh perspective from a trusted other, taking a drive or a walk, listening to your favorite song, taking off your socks and shoes, looking at a favorite picture, or simply shifting your attention to the sound of someone's voice, the drone of the refrigerator, or the office hum happening around you.

Do you know the personal early indicators that your own actual horizon is getting hard to see? Maybe it's an emotion that moves front and center for you—sadness, fear, anger, embarrassment. Or sneaky self-doubt or a no-permission statement creeping in. In Chapter 7 on emotional awareness, I'll show you more specific ideas for recognizing your early indicators.

For now, you might consider your gyroscope as sticking with your current self-care plan. If you don't have one, maybe start there. It doesn't have to be elaborate. Going to bed a little earlier, drinking water, adding a vegetable to your sandwich.

Leader re-becoming and re-flourishing takes a lot of energy, so be sure you're restoring yourself consistently along the way.

☐ My personal gyroscope is _____.

_____ESSENTIAL #4: COORDINATES _____

Coordinates remind you how far you've come and how you did it. Looking back helps you chart the course for today and forward. Here are some questions for your starting coordinates check. Jot your responses below.

1. Where were you in your leadership journey one year ago?

2. Three years ago? Ten?

3. What were you doing and thinking?

4. How were you growing? Were you facing a challenge?

5. What's different about you now? How would you describe what's working for you? Or not?

6. How did you get here?

7. Where do you want to be in the next stage of your leader journey?

Your leadership and life journey likely includes both mountaintop summits and some washed-out basecamps. Starting coordinates pinpoint the beginning of the trail so we can accurately plan the route ahead. Leaders know how essential it is to define the current state when preparing for big change. Your leader path to flourishing needs the same attention.

A helpful tool for considering starting coordinates is the Leader Becoming Compass pictured here. The center of the compass is the true north target for aligned leadership.If a domain or multiple domains move away from center, the compass is pulled away from equilibrium. If some domains are centered and others are off-center, life and leadership is misdirected. The domains I included reflect identity clarity and relational leadership, such as the authentic leadership approach.[20] You can add or remove domains based on your leader preferences and domains most important to your current situation. Place an 'X' on each domain section to indicate if that domain is close to center or misaligned. You can use this as an on-going quick self-assessment for you and your team.

Like all the tools I'm sharing with you, make it your own!

THE LEADER BECOMING COMPASS

©Dr. Natalie Pickering

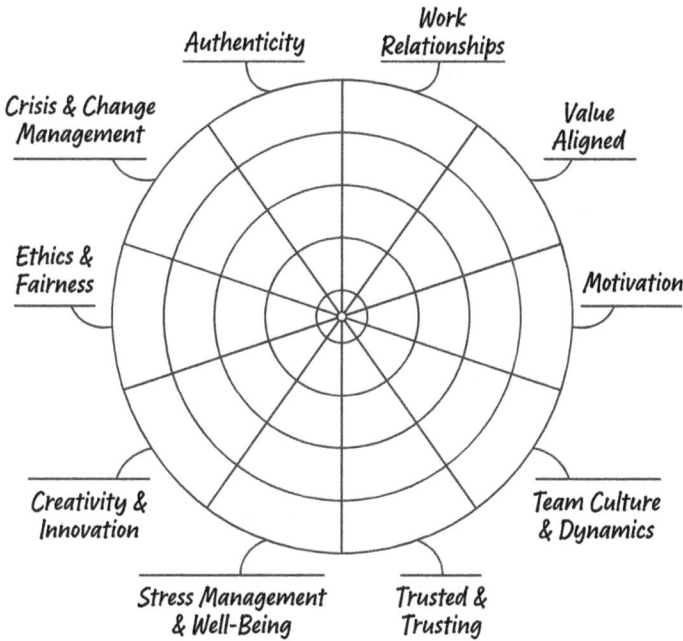

☐ I have reviewed my starting coordinates.

_____ESSENTIAL #5: REALISTIC EXPECTATIONS _____

Ten years ago, our family moved to east Tennessee for my job. Like many who have relocated there, we were captivated by the natural beauty. We were also made aware that there were some new cultural norms for us to learn.

This true story is a parable of expectations. A farmer asked to let his cattle graze on our land. We agreed, with naive win-win expectations of fed cattle and no need to bushhog the acreage. We soon learned that our handshake agreement actually left out some unstated expectations, such as watering the cattle from the pump in our barn (connected to our water bill) and our liability for any accidents caused by loose cows.

One Sunday morning as we were leaving for church, the farmer's brother called to report a stray cow on his property next to ours. Little did we know that the handshake had also positioned us squarely in a family feud with sibling neighbors who were not on speaking terms and expected us to run the go-between complaints. Ultimately, we told the farmer we thought it best to let fences make good neighbors.

Expectations can get muddy in lots of ways, often with two extremes. If a leader has a swampy, petrified, or wasteland inner terrain, the leader has likely reduced their expectations to very few for survival. On the other extreme, even in the flourishing meadow, it's easy to expect that things will always stay positive, challenges minimal, and the work will move forward.

Wherever your own situation lands between few to many expectations, here are some reminders:

- Even flourishing meadows always need weeding.
- Clear expectations of self and others must be communicated.

- These clear expectations can restore respect of self and others.
- Hidden costs and unintended consequences are still realities that impact any terrain type. They can be reduced with clear expectations.
- Your recovered leadership expectations may also redefine relationships.
- Choosing just 1 or 2 domains on The Leader Becoming Compass is a realistic start to clarifying expectations.

☐ I have double-checked my expectations.

_____ ESSENTIAL #6: YOUR SAG TEAM _____

In long-distance sports, there are two kinds of support that make endurance possible: the pacer and the support and gear (SAG) team.

The pacer runs or rides beside you—not to push, not to fix your form, but to match your rhythm and remind you: *You're not doing this alone.* They stay steady when you wobble, help you recalibrate when you rush, and quietly reflect your strength back to you.

The SAG team is less visible but just as vital. They're the ones who show up at the rest stop with fuel, fluids, dry socks, and a word of encouragement when you're questioning everything. They hold the tools, supplies, and backup plan so you don't have to carry it yourself while you're focused on the finish line.

My family and I hiked the Camino de Santiago together. It's an ancient system of walking paths with different starting points all leading to Santiago de Compostela, Spain, which is believed to be the resting place of the apostle St. James. The Camino, which means "way" in Spanish, dates to the Christian monastic tradition and is visited by thousands of "pilgrims" from all over the world each year.

My husband, 16-year-old daughter, 10-year-old son, and I each had only a pack and two sets of woolen garments for handwashing and quick drying. (I did remember underwear, in case you were worried!) In our pilgrim newbie-ness, we noticed that each late afternoon when we reached our village stop, people carrying only water packs and hiking poles retrieved their backpacks from a van. We looked at each other with realization (and admitted jealousy) that SAG support shuttled pilgrim luggage to the next stop.

I strongly encourage you to enlist a pacer for your journey. Consider at least one person and ideally two or three trusted people you can intentionally share your progress with consistently. They can get their own copy of the book and do it with you!

Loneliness is a challenge for many leaders and some mind it more than others. This packing essential might be the most challenging aspect of your detangling and re-rooting process. I get it. Solo is safer. Hurtful betrayals, mis-understandings, and wrong assumptions along the leadership journey make it challenging to connect, especially at a deeper level.

But remember, leader identity clarity *depends* on how others see us and how we think they do. The journey to flourishing depends on connection. And the only way to test out new ways of thinking and responding is in rela-tionship and conversation with other people. My own SAG team honestly tells me when I'm out of bounds or a blind spot has resurfaced. Ask a peer, another leader, maybe a coach, to walk your leader re-becoming journey with you.

Your pacer also helps solidify what you are discovering, which locks it in. You can test drive new layers of vulnerability and new ways of being with safe, trusted others.

FROM THE CADRE

One of my SAG team members, Val, is a friend and fellow business owner. We talk about business and life stuff. One morning in a coffee shop, we were chatting about our upcoming opportunities. She pulled out a small round purple notebook with a smiley face and the words "Be Happy" on the front and flipped to a clean page. Then she looked at me and said nonchalantly, "You should have one of these notebooks for your meetings so people aren't intimidated by you."

Now, I have a loud inner critic (named Edna)* who is highly committed to ensuring that Natalie—and everyone else— sees Natalie as right and good. When Edna noted potential criticism in Val's off-handed comment, she issued a red alert, which led to my sort of defensive response to Val, "I don't think I'm intimidating... am I?" In further defense of my innocence, I awkwardly pulled my leg out from under the table and lifted it up. As Val looked at me curiously I said, "See?" with my leg still in the air, "I really can't be intimidating. I wore yoga pants to this meeting!"

Um.

She laughed graciously and slid the notebook over to me. "Just keep it!" she whispered. Later as I drove back to the office, Edna persisted with chattering justification. It went something like: *I'm a psychologist so I must have self-awareness.* (I know.) *I can't be intimidating because—er—strangers start friendly conversations with me...and my 360 assessment describes me as approachable.* And in a burst of Edna inspiration came my crowning justification: A-ha! *I'm an introvert— introverts cannot be intimidating.*

Glowing with my foolproof rationale, I pulled out my phone to search "introvert intimidation," giddily awaiting pages of documented reinforcement. And there, in search engine-optimized first place was the article titled: *"Are You an Introvert? Here's 5 Ways You Intimidate People without Doing a Thing."*[21]

Blimey, Edna.

I need Val and others who care about me enough to say, "No performance here. The real you, with your quirks, shortcomings, and kinda judgy, is safe here." They celebrate the good stuff too and love me in all of it—leadership.

---

* You can meet Edna in my TEDx talk titled "Saying Yes to True Self: Lessons from Dolly, Edna, and Moonshine."

Research confirms that even if we *think* we are looking at ourselves with our most open, honest, get-real lenses, they are called blind spots for good reason.

SIDE NOTE TO THE INTROVERT

My justification attempt reminds me of the research on introversion in leadership which challenges the long-standing bias that extroversion is the ideal leader personality trait. In fact, introverted leaders can be more effective than extroverted leaders, for example, when leading proactive self-starters. Introverts listen closely to detailed feedback, support autonomy, and naturally foster deep-thinking environments.[22]

Fellow introverts, if you're reading, I know this "invite others to the journey" packing essential idea may tempt you to close the book. Stay with me. And extroverts and ambiverts (if you're reading the introvert note for fun)—your resistance to inviting a leader trek mate is equally understandable. But this is a non-negotiable for the best leaders—those who surround themselves with learning communities and peer mentors make better decisions and pivot more effectively.[23]

PACERS ARE PEATLANDS

To keep our terrain metaphor alive, you might liken your pacer or SAG team to a terrain type called peatlands. These lands are critically important for climate health, just like a pacer or SAG team is important for your leader health.

I did some extra research on the features of peatlands, which just so happen to be the features I recommend prioritizing for your pacer or SAG team. Next to each feature, write the names of one or two people who come to mind. The name that shows up the most by the end of the list will be a great candidate to call at the end of this chapter!

Feature 1: Healthy peatlands capture carbon dioxide, a key contributor to global warming, like a pacer catches your toxic thoughts or attitudes. This sounds like _____ (name) and _____ (name).

Feature 2: Peatlands have a wide variety of rare plants and insects. A pacer would have lots of new ideas and a growth-focused approach to life and leadership. This sounds like _____ (name) and_____ (name).

Feature 3: Peatlands reduce flood risk by slowing water flow. A pacer helps you slow your roll when needed. This sounds like: _____ (name) and _____ (name).

Feature 4: Peatlands source safe drinking water. A pacer offers you safe presence. (They know your favorite chocolate and beverage too.) This sounds like: _____ (name) and _____(name).

Feature 5: Peatlands filter water and treat wastewater. A pacer helps you sort out the smelly stuff from the good stuff. This sounds like: _____ (name) and _____ (name).

Feature 6: Peat softens water. A pacer knows how to help you soften the hard stuff. This sounds like: _____ (name) and_____ (name).

Feature 7: Peatlands provide a record of the past landscape, people, and vegetation of a place. A pacer has known you a while. This sounds like _____(name) and _____ (name),

OK, whose name shows up more than once? Close your book and reach out to that person. Ask if they would join you for your journey. Better yet, buy them the book.

- The pacer I will contact within the next 24 hours is:

  _____

Share your coordinates with your pacer who is now your backup on the trail.

They need to know exactly where to drop more chocolate.

CHAPTER RECAP

This recap is one last double check of your essentials list (no forgotten underwear on my watch).

☐ *Your permission passport* is your first growth essential: Block the time so you can fully absorb the process.

☐ *Guts* fuel your journey: Embracing self-reflection and honest growth will gain you long-term leader payoff.

☐ *Your gyroscope* keeps you steady: Your personal grounding habits help you maintain clarity and steady direction.

☐ *Coordinates* ensure you're starting on the right path: Reflection on the past brings clarity for your current trek and where you want to go.

☐ *Realistic expectations*: Clarity on what is realistic for your leadership right now might be your top takeaway.

☐ *Pacers and SAG support* sustains leaders: Your pacer and SAG team help you navigate blind spots, maintain perspective, and stay accountable.

LEADING BECOMES YOU BREAKTHROUGHS

In the following space, take a few moments to write notes for what resonated with you from this chapter.

- Which of the packing essentials feels the most challenging?

- Are there other packing essentials you need that aren't included here?

"Manners are a sensitive awareness of the feelings of others. If you have that awareness, you have good manners, no matter what fork you use."

— Emily Post

"Owning our story can be hard but not nearly as difficult as spending our lives running from it."

— Brené Brown

CHAPTER 5

YOUR SELF-AS-LEADER STORY FOUNDATION

Rediscover the Good Stuff
and Confront the Hard Stuff

A wareness is the foundation of change.[24] We cannot change what we cannot see. Sometimes the ability to notice, observe, and reflect on what is happening in life and leadership is very intentional—like your work in this book. Other times, awareness crashes through as a profound "a-ha" moment of insight. It's a sudden awareness—like the moment you realize you sent a vent text to the wrong person. Or you wave enthusiastically to a friend only to realize it's a stranger waving back awkwardly. Or your highway exit was five miles back.

A sudden awareness happened to me one weekend morning. I sauntered out to join my early-risers family at the kitchen table. One by one they smiled, giggled, and pointed at my pajama top. I looked down to see that at the bottom of my shirt sat a small but suspicious brown stain. Rifling through my non-caffeinated memory banks, my sudden awareness pinged. The rogue chocolate chip from the stash in my nightstand I had not-so-secretly eaten in bed the night before was discovered via embarrassing sudden awareness.

Deep-level awareness brought you to this journey. Deeper awareness helps you realize building frustration when someone interrupts you during a task, or that bottling up your emotion under the guise of self-control is actually unhealthy shutdown. Studies show that 95% of people think they have self-awareness but only 10 to 15% do.[*/25]

A cousin of awareness, named attention, defines a tighter focus than awareness. Bigger picture awareness directs the more narrow attention. For example, you use attention to define your daily priority: What is my single most important task today? Think of attention as a laser pointer on your priorities compared to the wide-angle lens of awareness taking in the whole room. Awareness is your laptop screen full of apps and open windows.

---

* This has always been one of those "Yikes- and makes sense!" statistic to me.

Attention is the one page you are looking at right now. Awareness and attention can both be hijacked and can both be developed.

They are also both crucial for personal and professional success. Attention supports focus not only on priorities but for skill development and task follow-through. Awareness reads the situation so you can choose an attentive response.

We are focusing on the big picture lens of awareness. The following two chapters will unpack two critical aspects of leader awareness: mental and emotional. Awareness is the key first phase of the four As of your Leading Becomes You process.

Leader self-awareness is phase one for building identity clarity and flourishing. Awareness opens the door: Until leaders can see themselves honestly—both their patterns and blind spots—they cannot do the deeper work of phase two and three—accepting and assimilating their inner terrain identity. Research links self-awareness with more effective decision-making and greater trust from others, but its true power lies in how it sets the stage for transformation. In the Leading Becomes You model, awareness initiates the shift from fragmented or distorted inner self-as-leader terrains (like the swamp, wasteland, or petrified forest) to the integrity and vitality of the flourishing meadow.

Identity clarity—and all that follows—begins with your gritty courage to become aware.

Self-as-leader awareness is correlated with effective decision-making and the ability to inspire trust in your team. On the flip side, for some leaders, excessive focus on self leads to self-doubt, overthinking, decision paralysis, or inauthentic self-absorption. The tools I'm sharing in phase one, awareness, will help you strike your personal balance.

_____ YOUR LEADER STORY TIMELINE _____

Before you can fully step into the work of building your flourishing meadow inner leader terrain by defining an integrated leader identity, you must first trace the steps that got you here. Your Leader Story Timeline is your surveyor for awareness-building. It's the tool that guides your intentional looking back—not only at career milestones, but at the narratives and influences that have shaped how you learned to lead, follow, protect, strive, and perform. Leadership research consistently shows that self-reflection on one's life story is foundational for authentic leadership.[26]

This Leader Story Timeline will become a cornerstone for your one-of-a-kind leadership approach and will guide your philosophy of leadership. You will use it to anchor your work through the other phases of the four As. Your leader identity story has multiple purposes:

- Respectful acknowledgment of big challenges and hard situations that have been bypassed in the hustle and how these have impacted your current leadership. Sometimes the Leader Story Timeline is the means for leaders to realize where old debris is impacting them in ways they were not aware of.
- Reflecting on your previous versions of leader self and what they remind you, such as skills, strengths, lessons you had forgotten.
- Intentionally translating what you rediscover for your maximal leadership effectiveness now.

YOUR STORY

The goal in this section is to review your entire life and leader story to date. There is no right or wrong here. You can start wherever you want in terms of past or present to document your story, but it's important to put it all on paper (real or digital) so you can go back and reference it. Time is required, but you've already blocked your calendar, right?

_____ LEADER STORY TIMELINE: STEP ONE _____

Here are some ideas for how to format and approach this step. Choose what feels most natural for you, and as always if there's another method I haven't listed, go for it!

- Chronological structure: Simply track your life and leadership story in a linear way. You might include headings for this approach, such as:
  - *-Early Life and Influences*
  - *-First Leadership Experiences*
  - *-Major Life or Leadership Challenges*
  - *-How Challenges Grew Me*
  - *-Current Leadership Influences and Challenges*
  - *-Self-as-leader Looking Ahead*
- Reverse chronological format: Start with today and review in reverse.
- Leader lessons and themes format: Organize by the following example themes:
  - *-My Leadership Premises—what defines your current approach? Why? How did you come to learn these?*
  - *-Stories and Experiences for Each Premise—who and what shaped your premises?*
  - *-Leader Daily—how do the premises show up and shape your day-to-day now? What are some examples? Who and what continues to influence you?*
- Metaphor format: For my fellow creatives, you could choose a central metaphor (e.g., river, bridge, compass, garden, the house metaphor my coaching client used, etc.) Each phase of your Leader Story Timeline could

be reflected as a stage in your chosen metaphor. For example: *"The small stream of influence in my life started with my early years in* _____. *My little stream grew with tributaries of (person)_____ and (situation)_____. These made me stronger by _____ / polluted my stream with _____."*

Just start writing.

I would suggest a fresh notebook section, separate from the reflection question responses for this book, or a new digital document or phone note. Choose an option that you already use regularly. Once you settle on your format, write about one season, theme, metaphor element, or leadership life "chapter" at a time—maybe one per day. Some chapters will have more to capture than others. Whatever comes to mind is worth writing down. Don't worry about missing things. You won't capture everything on the first pass through your story. The four As will ask you to revisit your Leader Story Timeline a few times from different angles. You can always add additional highlights to your timeline. Remember, leader becoming is an ongoing life-as-leader work in process!

If you're feeling stuck, here are some more prompts to get the juices flowing:

I never saw myself as a leader until one day when…

I used to think leadership was all about …

I wasn't ready for leadership but got thrown in…

If you had asked me ten years ago what leadership meant, I thought I knew.

I've learned that life and leadership is very different when…

One big leadership lesson happened when…

When I look back at my earliest experiences as a child or teenager, I see my leadership story there…

There have been _____ defining moments in my life and leadership that have significantly impacted my leader identity.

My own best reflective thinking happens when I'm in motion. Both my memories and my new ideas are more accessible when I'm walking or jogging. I will often start an email to myself on my phone and push the microphone icon and start talking. I might narrate a current situation from my life or work, intentionally capturing my thoughts and what I felt. Then I press send to email it to myself. I keep a folder in my email workspace titled "Personal". Sometimes I realize that the same type of situation or thought or emotion keeps resurfacing and I need to do some deeper business with it. I may use the folder to define goals for the next year during my annual December personal retreat.

FROM THE CADRE

For her Leader Story Timeline, one of my coaching clients bought a pad of extra large poster-sized sticky sheets. She hung nine sheets in a line along the wall of her basement labeled by her age: one sheet for ages 0 to 5, another sheet for ages 5 to 10, and up to 40 to 45. She spent time brainstorming events and memories, moving back and forth across her posters. When satisfied, she sat in front of the posters and typed her Leader Story Timeline straight from those sheets.

When I work with people one-on-one for intensive personal coaching retreats, they talk and I write their leader timeline on the big whiteboard in my office. Your pacer could do this with you—even better, take turns writing for each other.

_____ LEADER STORY TIMELINE: STEP TWO _____

When you're finished outlining the main events, themes, or seasons, this next step provides a framework to organize your story. Think of it as building your self-as-leader story highlight reel!

In your notebook, or right here in your book, make some notes for each of the following leadership story elements. These may be positive or negative.

- How you came to leadership (or how it came to you)?

- Leader breakthroughs and challenges (what has shaped your leadership)?

- Your leadership beliefs and values (what do you stand for in your leadership)?

- Your leadership re-flourishing (how are you growing)?

LEADER STORY TIMELINE: STEP THREE

Now that you have completed your Leader Story Timeline and some initial reflections to tie together your timeline with values, influences, and perhaps some new realizations, we're going one step deeper. The following questions are intended to shift the focus of your reflection from *"what impacted me"* to *"how"* the events on your timeline impacted you. The big picture questions we are asking here are:

- How are those moments, people, situations, decisions continuing to impact my leadership and influence—for good or bad?

- Is it debris or fuel for leading differently?

The focus for your review in this step is rediscovering forgotten gems, *the good stuff*, of personal strengths, proud moments, right responses that you may have forgotten! The default focus lens for high performers like you often tends toward improvement, what can be better, and pushing high standards higher. This is how you got to where you are! But it's easy to forget the good stuff, and I'm inviting you to intentionally bring it all to mind. These hard-earned personal and professional strengths and capacities need to be intentionally infused into your current leadership. Let's not overlook them.

> " But it's easy to forget the good stuff.

How was your leadership identity and approach impacted by:

- A specific conversation?

- A hard decision?

- An early challenge?

- A big win?

- A disappointment?

- A moment of significant change, one that you chose or one that happened to you?

- A surprising reaction you had to something or someone?

- A loss?

Where in your Leader Story Timeline do you see *Good Stuff* like:
- Personal and professional strengths that show up consistently over your life and leadership?

- Leadership potential you didn't realize at that time?

- Challenges that you have already repurposed?

- Mindset shifts?

- Capacities that others have noted, recognized, appreciated?

- Strengths you've overlooked because they come easily to you?

- Three moments over the course of your career that you are most proud of?

- Wins that felt aligned with who you are more so than external validation?

———— LEADER STORY TIMELINE: STEP FOUR ————

In this final step of your Leader Story Timeline, we are distilling all the work you've done in this chapter in a way that makes your story more portable for your next three phases of the four As. Whether you chose life season chapters, themes, or metaphors, bring it together into a *one-to-two-sentence summary of the key lesson or takeaway.* If you have five seasons or sections, you will write five one-to-two-sentence summaries.

As an example, I'm going to share a few of the summary statements from one of my own Leader Story Timeline exercises to illustrate. I used the chronological method for my timeline.

Early Years: Growing up in a small Midwest farming community with strong Protestant influence, I internalized deep rules about work ethic, responsibility, and "pulling yourself up by your bootstraps." I was protected from unhealthy gender norms as men and women in my family worked together baling hay, butchering, pulling weeds, and hanging laundry.

Young Adult Years: My leadership approach was developed via traveling internationally, playing collegiate sports, and attending a service academy. While these opportunities opened my aperture of the world, they also reinforced my high, exacting standards of self and others.

Career Season One: I transferred colleges and pursued an emotionally complicated goal. Despite some achievements, my shaking confidence was falsely fueled by a belief that following other people's ideas for my life would work.

Career Season Two: My professional burnout, losing my mom, medical challenges, and starting graduate school culminated in personal reckoning. This season taught me the non-negotiable of intentionally inviting others into my story.

There are more sections to my story, but those are the first few to give you an example of summary statements. Your last step is to put the summary statements you wrote for each section into one final takeaway.

Here's an example based on my earlier summary statements:

Growing up in a rural Midwest farming community, I was shaped by strong values of work ethic, responsibility, and strong women. Later, sports, international travel, and military training sharpened my worldview and leadership but also reinforced a wasteland waterlogged with perfectionism and over-responsibility. My early career path, influenced more by others' expectations than my own clarity, left me misaligned and unsure. A heartbreaking season of upheaval forced a pivot and taught me that healing and wholeness require the courage to invite others into my story, especially as a leader.

If you're someone who uses AI, I loaded my section summary statements into an AI program to get me started on distilling and crystallizing and then reworked it into my own words for the final version. I've also created some templates to get you started, but feel free, of course, to use your own. This is Mad Libs for your Leader Story Timeline! Here's my personal example in a template (with the blank template for you to use following):

From [*early years on a Midwest farm*], [*Natalie*] journeyed through [*hard work, family first, responsibility*] and experienced [*sports, military, working internationally*], ultimately discovering [*limits of other-dependence, falsity of bootstrap-pulling, importance of vulnerability*], and her leadership identity started to prioritize [*realistic influence, breaking unhealthy vows, learning to depend on others, internalizing her own confidence*], which shaped her [*desire to lead from behind, strategic influence, problem-solving strengths, and people-first value*] as a leader.

Here's the blank template for you to use if you'd like for your own story:

From [*early challenge or beginning*], [*your name*] journeyed through [*key experiences*], ultimately discovering [*lesson, purpose, insight*] and impacting their [__] and their internalizing of [__] as they vowed to [__], held tightly to [__], and learned [__]. Ultimately [__], which shaped their [*current situation, ability, strength, value*] as a leader.

Here's another template option to try out:

> Born with a passion for [*interest or talent*], [*your name*] navigated [*specific challenges*] and realized [*positive or negative experiences*] to transform that [*experience and its lessons, challenges*] into [*mindset or beliefs*], becoming [*leader attributes*] and shaping their leadership non-negotiables of [__].

And if you want the ultimate distill—short and sweet:

> My story has taught me that leadership isn't about [__]. It's about [__].

TWO-LEVEL AWARENESS

As you worked through your Leader Story Timeline, you may have noticed two lenses of awareness. I want to put words to this because it frames up your next phase of the four As. One lens is your *mental awareness*—remembering the facts, details, places, people. It's amazing what details may come to mind once you start mentally time-traveling.

The second lens is your *emotional awareness*. Revisiting these chapters may have surfaced different emotions—probably a mix of positive and negative—as you remembered scary challenges, painful disappointments, and frustrating circumstances, as well as instances of overcoming, succeeding, learning, and growing.

Maybe a section brought a literal smile to your face or tears to your eyes. Or both.

FROM THE CADRE

A mid-career entrepreneur in the healthcare space reached out to work with me as she was pivoting her business. She had done some great work in recognizing attitudes that had previously held her back. Her training in health-care got mixed up with the role her family of origin had unconsciously put her in—namely, the emotional caretaking of the grown-ups—and reinforced her belief to an unhealthy degree that helping should happen at all costs, even to self. As we worked through her Leader Story Timeline, she easily noted the mindset awareness level and recognized her thought and belief traps. But something shifted as she spoke those beliefs, and I wrote them for her on the big whiteboard in my office. As she looked at them all together, tears welled up in her eyes. The emotional awareness was catching up to her mental awareness. Together, we started clearing the bog of emotional pain that had been holding her back as she recounted the cost to this point of prioritizing others over herself in her professional life.

It's important to make space for both levels of awareness. If it gets rough, don't forget your gyroscope.

Take a break.

Care well for yourself.

Gritty requires rest too.

ZOOMING OUT

Excellent work! You're doing it—your self-as-leader is brimming new aware-ness and clarity. Outlining your Leader Story Timeline is foundational to the next phases of your journey, which focus on specific muscle-building of mental and emotional awareness. Before we set your Leader Story Timeline aside for now, let's zoom back out by answering the following reflection questions. These questions are specifically designed to start shifting your gears to the next two awareness-building chapters.

_____ FOR REFLECTION_____

In your review of your life story to date:

• How did you decide what to include or not include?

• What story do you tell yourself about your leadership and your self-as-leader based on the events and experiences you included?

• Were you thinking of anyone else who would look at your story time-line? What would they think?

• Did anything surprise you?

- What accomplishments from any of these chapters or life seasons are you most proud of?

- What strengths do you see in yourself during these seasons that you didn't realize before?

- Has your view of yourself or your identity shifted in any way?

CHAPTER RECAP

☐ *Awareness is a cornerstone of your leader identity*: Honesty meets awareness to root out hidden patterns, strengths, and challenges impacting you.

☐ *Capturing your leader identity story provides clarity*: Mapping the past reveals key themes, lessons, and areas for intentional growth.

☐ *Self-perception shapes leadership effectiveness:* The story you tell yourself can reinforce growth or perpetuate limiting beliefs—we're going for growth!

☐ *Emotions play a critical role in leader awareness:* Revisiting leadership experiences often surfaces emotions tied to past successes, failures, and defining moments, which require acknowledgment and integration.

☐ *Honest reflection fuels transformation:* The Leading Becomes You process refines your leadership philosophy and moves you toward a more authentic and flourishing self-as-leader terrain.

LEADING BECOMES YOU BREAKTHROUGHS

In the following space, take a few moments to write notes for what resonated with you from this chapter.

How was the experience of putting your Leader Story Timeline on paper?

Do you see connections between your Leader Story Timeline and the current state of your leadership terrain?

PART 2

"We are what we believe we are."

– C.S. Lewis

"We just may be the most well-informed yet least self-aware people in history."

– Norman Lear

"Many people in this world are still so identified with every thought that arises in their head. There is not the slightest space of awareness there."

– Eckhart Tolle

CHAPTER 6

AWARENESS 1.0: WHEN LEADERS RETHINK

Know Your Traps and How
to Navigate Them

Some people have a knack for things. My coworker can remember every name on a 40-person Zoom call. My friend has a gut instinct for spotting the checkout line that will move the fastest, even at Costco on a Saturday. Another friend of mine can open the fridge, throw together three wilted ingredients, and end up with a gourmet lunch. My sister can disarm any uncomfortable moment with one sarcastic comment and shift the mood to a room full of laughter-tears. And me? On some days, I'm celebrating that I remember where I parked!

Lest Edna get out of hand, I do have some knacks. I'm pretty good at reading the room and getting to the root of something fast. My ability to get to the point is important for the work I do, but sometimes it gets carried away. I take on too many challenges to fix at once, and if I'm not careful, my fast conclusions are premature. My deep below-the-iceberg water line motivation is to get it right but sometimes I overdo it and forget that not everyone wants my input!

Like you, I'm a work in progress.

Leaders have knacks too. Some have a knack for hiring, some for coaching talent, some for vision-casting, and some are guru strategic planners.

Like our knacks, we tend to default to what comes easiest in our thinking and mindset. It takes extra effort to slow down, examine and determine layers of thinking, how you perceive situations and make sense of complexity. Your mindset directly influences your leader identity clarity—how you perceive your ability, your potential and your response to challenges.

As we focus on building mental awareness, I'm sharing some frameworks and strategies to address mental traps that can plague any leader's unique approach. Some of these mental habits are easier to spot than others. Once you learn strategies for clarifying mental habits, then you can intentionally redevelop them for your maximal effectiveness and fulfillment. I'll show you that too!

First, let's look at the relationship between mindset and emotion habits. Emotional awareness will take center stage in the next chapter but they go hand in hand.

THINKING, MEET EMOTIONS

When you look at your mental and emotional habits together, you can get to the core reason for almost every leadership action or inaction you take.

Some people find it easier to bring awareness first to what they're thinking and then move to consider the related emotions. Others find it easier to label their experience of emotions first (we will practice that in the next chapter) and then figuring out the associated thoughts and beliefs.

Here is an illustration of the relationship between thoughts, emotions, and behavior.

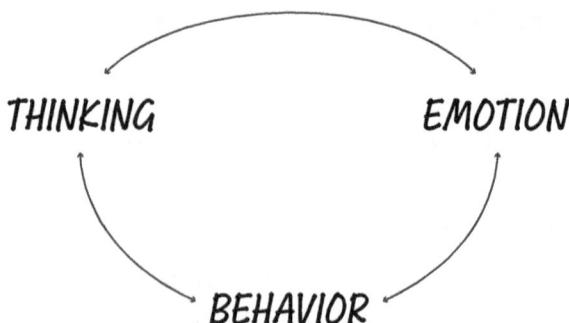

THINKING   *EMOTION*

BEHAVIOR

As you can see, there is a bidirectional arrow between thinking on the left and emotion on the right. Earlier I mentioned that some people start with thinking and move to emotion while others start with emotion and move to thinking. Then we add the label of behaviors—the action or inaction— to form a circle with thinking and emotion. I've added a bidirectional arrow between thinking and behavior and between emotion and behavior to illustrate the interdependent relationship between these three elements of a leader's response.

Sometimes thinking can get hijacked by feelings—and feelings can get locked out by thinking. A common example of this is "thinking your emotions" rather than "feeling your emotions." Even if you recognize an emotion connected to a belief tentacle, finding resolution requires you to experience the emotion. More on that in the next chapter.

I wanted you to see the big picture for this two-chapter awareness phase.

AWARENESS, MEET MINDSET

All leaders (and people) fall into patterns of thinking and conclusion-making that they've learned work for them. Layer onto those well-worn habits the fact that the brain loves efficiency, with the average adult firing approximately 6,200 thoughts per day.[27] It's easy to see how thoughts, beliefs, and attitudes quickly become ingrained habits.

Without intentional consideration, we fall into auto-pilot and the ruts and traps in default thinking lead to default behaviors, responses, and views of our current reality that may or may not support our leader identity clarity and connection.

Here are the mindset awareness categories I will be referring to in this chapter:

1. *Deep beliefs:*[*] Enduring, core convictions about ourselves, others, and the world that shape how we make sense and meaning of our lived experience. Strongly related to those values you identified earlier. They hang out with core motivations at the base of the iceberg and are mostly out of awareness (until now!) Deep beliefs fuel the next type of mental habits, reflex thoughts.

2. *Reflex thoughts:*[28] Automatic, fast mental shortcuts our brains use to interpret situations quickly, often without conscious awareness. Involved in day-to-day decisions.

3. *Identity thinking traps:*[28] Habitual, inaccurate thought patterns that reinforce negative emotions and misinterpret reality about your self-as-leader.

DEEPER BELIEFS IMPACT LEADERSHIP

Deep beliefs—true to their name are the deeply held assumptions you hold about yourself, other people, and the world in general. They are also the bedrock for the values you identified earlier. These deep beliefs may range from the nature of truth to how the world works.

Our focus is spending time looking at your deep mental engine, which is essential for your leader identity clarity.[29]

Deep beliefs can be positive or negative and likely got their start earlier in your life. Without delving too deep here, they impact low self-worth, ability to trust, or holding onto a role you had to practice a lot as your younger self. If leaders don't recognize how their deep beliefs show up, they can wreak havoc.

[*]Psychologists sometimes call these core beliefs or schemas—mental frameworks often formed early in life that quietly run the show. Research in schema therapy shows that when they go unchecked, they can fuel patterns that chip away at confidence, trust, and clarity (Young, Klosko, and Weishaar; Beck).

Let's look at an example. A leader may have a deep self belief that they "are not enough." Without awareness, this deep belief may lead to isolating, overworking, or not delegating. Tentacles of this deep belief show up as reflex thoughts or identity thinking traps like, "I have to prove myself in this position" or "These people do not want to be on my team" or "This project must be perfect."

FROM THE CADRE

The chief marketing officer (CMO) of a large healthcare organization gave my name and phone number to the leadership team of a partner hospital. The CMO's take was that a conflict between two of the team members was negatively impacting their respective clinical directors. One team member called me requesting individual coaching. He seemed to genuinely desire resolution, having pursued it with his colleague. As we coached, another issue became clear: The leader of the team was so insecure in her position, she could not make a decision without the entire team's input. The conflict between two of her members paralyzed operations because she would not decide without consensus. The leader was oblivious that her professional insecurities and some deep beliefs were contributing to a destructive cycle.

REFLEX THOUGHTS

It's easy to see how those deeply grooved deep beliefs inform the reflex thoughts happening in seconds over the course of an hour and a day.[30] Default thinking patterns are necessary for making quick decisions and we can't deliberate every single thought. But our mental shortcuts have patterns and it's good to consider whether the patterns are helping or hurting. Negative impact can narrow your capacity for mental agility.

Here are some examples of reflex thinking traps that can lead to judgment errors when efficiency wins:

- *Confirmation reflex*: Only seeing information and data that confirm your existing belief or attitude. Not seeing information that challenges your beliefs. Example: A leader only listens to team members who agree with their decision and ignores dissenting opinions.

- *Anchoring reflex*: Over-reliance on the first piece of information received. Example: If a leader hears that an employee is "difficult" before meeting them, they may unconsciously look for signs to confirm that anchored perception.

- *Overconfidence reflex*: Assuming your ability, knowledge, and expertise is higher than it is, leading to short-circuiting discussion and new information. Example: A leader insists on making all decisions without input because they believe they know best.

- *Negativity reflex*: More focus and attention is given to potential loss than possible gain. Example: A leader focuses on one critical performance review instead of the overall positive feedback from their team.

- *False consensus reflex*: Overestimating how much others agree with one's beliefs or decisions. Example: A leader assumes their entire team supports a new policy just because no one speaks out against it.

- *Recency reflex*: Giving more weight to recent events rather than long-term patterns. Example: A leader gives a year-end promotion based only on the last few months' performance, ignoring prior achievements.

- *Halo effect reflex*: Assuming someone is good (or bad) at everything based on one positive (or negative) trait. Example: A leader assumes a confident employee is also competent in all areas, even without evidence.

- *Groupthink reflex*: Prioritizing group harmony over critical thinking or dissenting opinions. Example: A leadership team agrees to a risky decision because no one wants to challenge the CEO's idea.

- *Sunk cost reflex*: Continuing with a failing course of action because of past investments. Example: A leader refuses to pivot from an unsuccessful project because they've already spent so much time and money on it.
- *Attribution error reflex*: Judging others more harshly than oneself for the same behavior. Example: A leader views their own missed deadline as "due to workload" but assumes an employee's missed deadline is because of laziness.

Which two of these thinking reflexes sound familiar? Circle them and see if you can catch them this week. Perhaps you can think of others. Your leadership mindset has been honed over time and you come to your reflex thinking habits honestly due to prioritizing efficiency over accuracy. Mindset awareness requires attention, intention, and practice to ensure your leadership maximizes your mental agility and mindset.

IDENTITY THINKING TRAPS

We also have reflex thoughts specifically related to our leader identity. The reflex thoughts above may show up as biases and quick judgments about anything—most likely whatever threatens core motivation and values. Next I'm sharing examples of a reflex thinking subset that I call identity thinking traps, beliefs that are usually negative and often exaggerated about yourself. They are often tentacles of a deep belief.

You'll see the name of the trap followed by an example, the negative leadership impact, and an example of how rethinking shifts the trap to a healthier place.

IDENTITY THINKING TRAP	LEADERSHIP EXAMPLE SELF-STATEMENT	IMPACT	RETHINKING
CLIFF THINKING	"If this project fails, my credibility is ruined."	Solid ground or off the edge—no middle ground. Fear of risk-taking and innovation paralysis.	"Every setback is a learning opportunity for long-term success."
TRAIL WASHOUT	"My team never meets deadlines."	One storm ruins the whole path—this route is always inaccessible. Creates frustration and damages morale.	"This deadline was missed; let's assess why and improve our process."
FOGGY FILTERING	"No one appreciates my leadership."	Only seeing a shadowy path—missing sunlight and vistas. Leads to disengagement and resentment.	"Some people have acknowledged my leadership; I should focus on their feedback."
GEM TOSSING	"They said I did a good job, but they were just being polite."	Tossing unearthed gems right off the mountain. Undermines confidence and motivation.	"I worked hard, and their feedback is valid."
FALSE TRAIL FORK	"My boss didn't reply to my email—she must be upset with me."	Path looks right—but it's not on the map. Unnecessary stress and miscommunication.	"She might be busy; I'll follow up for clarity."

IDENTITY THINKING TRAP	LEADERSHIP EXAMPLE SELF-STATEMENT	IMPACT	RETHINKING
SUPERSTORM FORECASTING	"If I don't get this promotion, my career is over."	Turning clouds into worsening tornadoes at every bend. Creates anxiety and limits resilience.	"There are multiple paths to career growth."
COMPASS CONFUSION	"I feel like an imposter, so I must not be qualified."	Charting the course by mood with no map. Leads to imposter syndrome and self-doubt.	"Feeling uncertain is normal; my track record speaks for itself."
SOLO TREK MINDSET TRAP	"If my team is struggling, it must be my fault."	All detours, delays, washouts are my sole responsibility. Unnecessary guilt and micromanagement.	"I play a role, but external factors also contribute."

THINKING OVERLOAD

I see this so frequently in leaders, I wanted to include this topic simply to validate your experience if it resonates. Cognitive load refers to the very real limit of our brains for how much information we can process at any given time. More specifically, cognitive *overload* is when we exceed our brain's capacity to process information. When this occurs, leaders feel overwhelmed, burned out, and anxious. Limited focus and concentration negatively impact a leader due to decision fatigue, increased errors, and avoiding challenges that require deep-level brain power.

Female leaders often carry a heavier cognitive load—not because they are less capable, but because they are managing more layers of invisible labor.

Beyond the demands of the role itself, many are holding the emotional climate of their teams, anticipating needs, and coordinating responsibilities both at work and at home. Add to that the tightrope of "likability labor"—the unspoken expectation to be both strong and agreeable—and the mental load compounds. When you factor in the double bind of leadership identity for women, where being direct can be seen as harsh and being warm can be seen as weak, it's no wonder many high-capacity women feel exhausted not just from what they do, but from the constant calculation of how to be.[31]

This reality may account for much of your mental load, perhaps more than the beliefs or thinking habits we have considered.

———————— MINDSET EXCAVATION ————————

Now that you've organized your mental habits by deep beliefs, reflex thoughts and identity thought traps, what next? Roll up your sleeves and put on your boots. I'm showing you options for excavating the mental habits landscape of your inner leader terrain! I'm sharing a range of strategies—some will resonate with you and others won't. I've included options from wading in more shallow waters to the polar plunge (the only way to *really* see the base of the iceberg!)

Here is a warm-up list to get you started. Remember, this is a process. Depending on your season and situation, wading may be the very *best* option for your bandwidth right now. Don't forget your realistic expectations.

Some strategies for building awareness of reflex thoughts and identity thinking traps include:

1. *Use a beliefs and attitudes audit:* Regularly challenge your own long-held assumptions about yourself, your leadership, your team, your industry, etc. Write down the beliefs and then list two different, even oppositional, beliefs. See what happens!

2. *Pause intentionally:* Keep a tally list of your thought/emotion ratio. Start with capturing emotions. See if you can find the thought or belief that goes with it. This strategy really is best in the moment. Ask yourself: Is an emotional response driving a thought? Is overthinking shutting down emotion data?

3. *Ask your pacer:* What are other beliefs, thoughts, interpretations, and perspectives from your pacer, an objective source?

4. *Use a mental buffer:* Take a walk; go do something else and come back. See if the intensity of the thought or belief changes.

5. *Try mindfulness to buy time between the event and your response:* Mindfulness simply means paying attention and not missing the right now. One way to try this is shifting your awareness to an approach of curiosity rather than quickly locking in on the right, wrong, or next. Be willing to ask silly questions. Ask "why," "how," and "what if." If emotion is driving a thought or belief, curiosity makes space to ask yourself: Am I considering data, facts, and reality? Have I fallen into a reflex thought?

6. *Shift the data default:* This strategy goes deeper and connects your Leader Story Timeline with your mental awareness and habits. Your Leader Story Timeline can help you identify deep beliefs, reflex thinking, and identity thinking traps. Your mental filters are running your identity in the background. Without awareness, we automatically filter *in* the thoughts and beliefs that confirm our story (whether true and accurate

or not) and we filter *out* the thoughts that don't match the interpretation we have about our identity story (including the true and accurate). Overfiltering and underfiltering can both be problematic. Part of our default mental habits are the years-long result of over-identifying with true parts of our story that are hogging all the mental airtime. For example, someone who has endured harrowing and traumatic experiences often come to the understandable belief, "no one can be trusted." The very real data of those experiences locked in a necessarily protective belief. But years later, when those experiences are no longer happening, the locked in belief is still working overtime in the background. And trusting no one is not an effective leadership strategy. The solution is not to swing to the opposite belief that "everyone can be trusted," which is equally disastrous. But once awareness identifies the trap or unhelpful ingrained belief, the next step is considering a healthier attitude that filters in other parts of the story, something like:

> "All relationships have some risk, but I do remember when [*someone in your life*] followed through on a promise and when [*someone in your life*] kept my confidence."

7. *Sprinkle with positive.* One more strategy for your mental awareness toolkit is optimism, expecting positive outcomes. Optimism is a big picture mindset focused on solutions and viewing challenges as temporary setbacks rather than impossible obstacles.[32] This capacity is a leader quality-essential and requires balance. All positivity with no tough consideration for real challenges keeps leaders trapped in behaviors of invalidation or maintaining the status quo. But an overemphasis on positivity can also keep leaders root bound. In fact, telling leaders that positive thinking is the exclusive path to growth is a classic overfiltering thinking trap. It

ignores the reality of challenges, real barriers, and the work involved in the sometimes-tedious detangling. The leader sounds tone deaf to the team and organization. Balanced optimism accounts for negative realities and keeps a lookout for ways to celebrate.

The reflex thinking and deep beliefs, left unchecked, keep us trapped and tangled in our rootbound version of self-as-leader. The takeaway here: Examine your thoughts.

YOUR TURN

Let's pause and take some time to consider the ground you've covered on mental awareness so far.

Which of these thinking traps do you recognize in your own mental patterns?

Can you think of some specific examples when your thinking traps are particularly noticeable?

What makes them challenging to notice or find?

How do these thinking traps hold back your most effective self-as-leader?

CATCH THEM TO CHANGE THEM

For many high-performing leaders struggling with the imposter phenomenon, there is often a deep belief that sounds something like "*Any* mistake is shameful." That is a slippery slope to the deeper deep belief "*I* must be shameful."

If someone carries deep beliefs that they are bad, shameful, unlovable, [your label], then reflex thought tentacles might be "Success is impossible for me" or "No one would promote me." Below is a list of harmful deep beliefs and identity thinking traps from other leaders I've worked with, in case you're struggling to find your own. It takes time and practice to recognize them. Be patient with yourself.

Perhaps an example in the list is similar to yours, but you have your own variation. Just write it down at the end of the list right here in your book. You've caught it. Now you can change it. Check any beliefs that resonate. And if several resonate, the likely reason is that they are tentacle thoughts connected to one deep belief. The good news is when you sort out the deep belief and start weeding that patch to health, the tentacle beliefs go with it. Look for themes and overlaps.

- ☐ If I feel mad or reach my limit, I'm a bad boss/leader.
- ☐ I cannot work or lead with this issue, problem, reality, person.
- ☐ I'm trapped.
- ☐ Her anger must be my fault.
- ☐ It's my fault.

- ☐ Awful feelings mean I'm an awful person.
- ☐ Vulnerability is dangerous and weak.
- ☐ I cannot be honest.
- ☐ If I'm honest, it will be bad.
- ☐ If I don't fix this, it will be bad.
- ☐ I have to rescue.
- ☐ I have to protect.
- ☐ My loyalty will eventually be honored.
- ☐ If I don't step up 100%, I am a bad employee/leader/boss.
- ☐ I don't deserve to be successful.
- ☐ I cannot tolerate criticism.
- ☐ If I'm not in control, bad things happen.
- ☐ I am just a number, an object, or a cog in the wheel.
- ☐ I'm not as talented as other people/leaders.
- ☐ If they don't respond, it must be bad.
- ☐ If someone knew the truth about me, they would never like me, hire me, or collaborate with me.
- ☐ I'm too old to do that.
- ☐ I'm too young to do that.
- ☐ I'm not ___ enough to do that.
- ☐ I don't have time.
- ☐ I can't.
- ☐ I've got to state this as politely as possible.
- ☐ Succeeding in this is beyond my control.
- ☐ No one in this place has my back.
- ☐ I can do all of it myself.

☐ I should be able to do this all by myself.

☐ What other people think of me is so important, I must anticipate it at all times.

☐ I can't break free of their expectations.

☐ I read in a book that this person's leadership approach works, so I should follow it closely.

☐ If I don't lead like _____, I will fail.

☐ Changing my leadership approach means I was wrong before.

☐ Others: _____

What do the multiple options you've checked have in common?

Do they connect to a chapter, season, theme on your Leader Story Timeline?

BELIEF CONTAGION

Many leaders I work with recognize that one big reason their self-as-leader identity is rootbound because they've been following, at some level, someone else's ideas, rules, or script for *their* leadership. And often, these co-opted deep beliefs account for several acres of harmful inner leader terrain.

> "And often, these co-opted deep beliefs account for several acres of harmful inner leader terrain.

Here is our previous illustration with the bidirectional arrows showing the relationship between thinking and emotion and action or inaction, labeled behavior. I've added the deep belief: "My worth depends on what people think of me." I also labeled likely connected emotions of sadness and bitterness—and a potential behavior, which in this example is giving more, doing more, and showing up all the time, any time.

My worth depends on
what people think of me.

Sadness, Bitterness
(which is anger)

THINKING   EMOTION

BEHAVIOR

Give more. Do More.
Show up all the time, anytime.

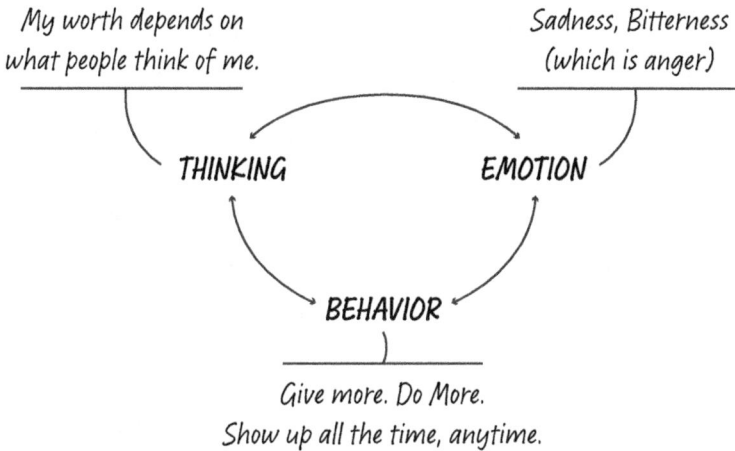

Beliefs and attitudes rooted in deep dependence on what others think are usually the culprit for the inner leader terrain of the wasteland, where this belief leads to a leader's overfunctioning for others and not for themselves. They have lost connection to their own purpose, needs, and preferences.

A NOTE ABOUT THE REALLY DEEP STUFF

Sometimes when we dig around and start excavating inner terrain we come to unexpected and extremely deep belief and emotion sinkholes. Beyond your pacer, these may require an equally deeper level of expertise to support your clearing for transformation.If your gyroscope horizon line gets too tough to find or you're feeling overwhelmed, please don't hesitate to connect with a trained mental health professional equipped to support you. There are lots of options for heavier equipment for those big sinkhole experiences, but it's helpful to have someone show you how to operate it safely.

Getting another set of eyes and ears on your situation can be incredibly reassuring.

BRING BELIEFS TO LIGHT

Using the space in the first column below labeled "Beliefs I'm Rooted In," list the leadership-related beliefs that you may have inherited or co-opted from others. These can be positive or negative! They may reflect the influence of individuals, teams, or even an organizational culture. They may also have been learned from teachers, family, religious leaders, or an athletic coach. Our work is two-fold, clearing out what's not working and intentionally repurposing what does.

In the right column labeled "Beliefs Chosen by Me," write the beliefs and attitudes you choose to lead and live by. You might have some beliefs in both columns. This exercise helps identify beliefs and attitudes you may have taken in unconsciously but, with new awareness, have realized they don't actually suit your self-as-leader. It also becomes a handy reference for the hard days when you need a reminder of the deep beliefs that are your very own. I've included some examples to get you started.

BELIEFS I'M ROOTED IN (FOR GOOD OR BAD)	BELIEFS I'M CHOOSING TO ROOT IN
Leadership means being the smartest person in the room.	Leadership means creating a space where everyone's intelligence, strengths, and perspective are valued.
Good leaders never show vulnerability.	Authentic leadership includes appropriate vulnerability to build trust and connection.
Success is measured solely by promotions and titles.	Success is defined by impact, growth, and integrity.
Leaders must have all the answers.	Leaders ask powerful questions, foster collaborative problem-solving, and acnowledge when they don't know.
Authority must be maintained through control.	Authority is earned through respect, service, and consistent values.

BELIEFS I'M ROOTED IN (FOR GOOD OR BAD)	BELIEFS I'M CHOOSING TO ROOT IN
High performance is more important than team well-being.	Sustainable performance is built on a foundation of psychological safety and well-being.
Conflict should be avoided to maintain harmony.	Healthy conflict is necessary for innovation, growth, and team strength.
Mistakes are failures that must be hidden.	Mistakes are opportunities for learning, resilience, and transparency.
Leadership is about meeting external expectations.	Leadership is about aligning actions with internal values and purpose.
Leaders must be available 24/7 to prove commitment.	Leaders set and model healthy boundaries to protect energy and creativity.

Write your thoughts related to the following questions:

Which "Beliefs I'm Rooted In" still serve my personal leadership approach? Are there any that I've realized are, in fact, root-binding?

Do I need to shift more intentionally and bring tighter focus to the leadership beliefs in the "Chosen by Me" column? What does this look like?

Choose an action and an accountability plan to implement it—your pacer would be a great reference here. Identify a leadership behavior that reflects one or more of the beliefs you listed in the "Chosen by Me" column. Some examples might be:

- Rewrite your self-as-leader mission statement to reflect a healthier belief you've chosen.

- Test the belief through real-world actions. For example, if you believe, "My team will think I'm weak if I admit uncertainty," test it by saying out loud to the team, "I don't have the answer yet—what do you think?" and observe the response.

- Initiate a redemptive conversation (i.e., acknowledgment or relationship repair based on new insights).

- For a season, redesign a daily, weekly, or quarterly rhythm focused exclusively on mental awareness.

- Run beliefs through the filter of your top five values (*on pg. 59*). Does the belief align with your most important values? If not, how can you adjust the belief to align?

- Name a "no more"—a habit or attitude you're done with—and a "new yes"—a practice or boundary you're committed to honoring.

A FINAL STRATEGY: USE YOUR NEUROPLASTICITY

The fascinating reality of neuroplasticity is that the brain grows, learns, and changes.[33] Every time you mindfully shift to a healthier, more aligned deep belief or positive reflex thought, your brain is literally building a new pathway—and weakening the old one. As you keep repeating shifts to those new thoughts, your brain will more easily and consistently choose those. Neuroplasticity weeds your inner leader terrain. Like weeding for the first few times, the mental rewiring can seem never-ending as you tug at stubborn, deep-rooted, pesky unhelpful

> "Neuroplasticity weeds your inner leader terrain.

thought traps popping up everywhere. But just like regular weeding, the more you remove them, the less they return. And eventually, new growth—healthier beliefs—take over the terrain.

Here's why: awareness is noticing what's happening—your thoughts, emotions, body sensations—like pulling back branches to see what's growing underneath. Adding mindfulness goes one step further. Mindfulness is awareness plus curiosity, asking the questions in the section above. After you lift the branches, mindfulness keeps you kneeling there long enough to look closely before yanking. It's slowing down and observing the thought or belief closely. It buys time and breathing room for you to choose a response.

If we put it all together, here are the practical steps for incorporating mindfulness meets neuroplasticity for your healthiest leader mindset.

YOUR TURN

1. *First, write down one mindset trap* you would like to change. It could be a deep belief, reflex thought, or identity thinking trap.

Mindset trap:_____

_____

_____

2. *Next, write down a cue* that happens when this trap shows up. Cues help you spot the first thought weed sprout so you can yank it out by the root. The cue might be something that happens in your body. Perhaps you experience tightness in your chest, shallow breathing, jaw clenching, or shoulder tension. Maybe your heart races or your face flushes.

The cue may also be an emotion. Every time this belief or thought shows up you feel irritation, self-doubt, a sense of urgency, or defensiveness. These sensations and emotions are your mindful signals to pause, take a slow breath, and observe the thought or belief before responding. You can interrupt those arrows between thinking, emotion, and behavior. Write your cues here.

Cues for this mindset trap:_____

_____

_____

These cues are your signal that you can interrupt that seemingly automatic bidirectional arrow between the negative mindset trap, emotion, and/or your typical response to the mindset trap. Cues help you spot the first thought weed sprout so you can yank it out by the root.

3. *Finally, choose a reframe*—a new thought or belief that is more helpful and true. We've looked at lists of examples throughout the chapter. I'm sharing more ideas below. You might also choose one of the beliefs from your earlier reflection on page 151 titled "Beliefs I'm Choosing to Root In" list. Pick the statement that gives you a little pick-me-up on the inside. You're looking for your very own believable beliefs. Once you choose, hold the belief in your attention for 20 or 30 seconds to help reinforce that new neural pathway.

☐ I can handle this challenge.

☐ This challenge is tough, but I am capable of getting through it.

☐ I have succeeded at ___ before. I can succeed again.

☐ I am worthy of respect [integrity, care, growth, connection].

☐ I see this as a growth opportunity, even if I mess it up.

☐ This mistake has taught me _____.

☐ I have been supported by someone else. An example is _____.

☐ I'm giving my best work.

☐ New opportunities happen.

☐ I can control my response.

☐ Asking for help is a normal part of living.

☐ I can grow and change today.

☐ One small example of joy right now is _____.

☐ A small way I can have a positive influence today is _____.

☐ I can trust myself with _____.

☐ I've found fulfillment when I _____.

☐ A fear I have faced before is _____.

☐ I have grown resilience when I _____.

☐ My personal resources include _____.

☐ Changes I have navigated before were _____.

CHAPTER RECAP

☐ *Mental awareness is key to busting unhelpful mindset patterns*: Re-rooted leaders recognize biases, core beliefs, and distortions that shape their decision-making and influence.

☐ *Biases create mental efficiency traps*: Common biases like confirmation bias, overconfidence, and negativity bias limit your ability to rethink and adapt.

☐ *Core beliefs influence leadership identity*: Deeply ingrained beliefs about worth, control, and vulnerability can empower or limit your leader re-becoming.

☐ *Rethinking builds resilience*: Developing the ability to challenge assumptions, adopt new perspectives, and rewrite limiting beliefs strengthens your leader mental agility and flourishing.

LEADING BECOMES YOU BREAKTHROUGHS

In the following space, take a few moments to write notes for what reso-nated with you from this chapter.

What is one singular takeaway from this chapter that you would like to focus on?

How will addressing your thinking and belief traps support you in becoming a more effective leader? A more fulfilled leader?

"We are dangerous when we are not conscious of our responsibility for how we behave, think, and feel."

— Marshall B. Rosenberg

"I am not afraid of storms, for I am learning how to sail my ship."

— Jo, *Little Women*, Louisa May Alcott

CHAPTER 7

AWARENESS 2.0: WHEN LEADERS FEEL

Emotional Intelligence How-To for
Essential Leader Performance

A kidney stone converted me.

If you've never experienced this horror, pause here to count that blessing. If you have, you know the feels-like-forever rolling around on the floor *pain*! The experience converted me from "Coffee is water, right?" to a consistent starting the morning with a large glass of plain water (before the coffee).

Pain changes behavior.

Do we talk about what leadership feels like? No one tells you that leadership is an emotional experience. That rush of excitement meets wrenching anxiety. That intense discomfort precedes growth. Whether it is unexpected team conflict, personal stress, or an organizational crisis, distress moments and the emotions that accompany them are the potentiators for significant change—if leaders have the emotional agility to navigate them.

EMOTIONAL INTELLIGENCE: MAXIMAL LEADER ROI

Similar to the mental agility you just planted and grew with new seeds of awareness, emotional agility refers to how well we adapt to emotionally charged situations. A related term, emotional intelligence, includes our good friend awareness—now specifically applied to emotions: What's the feeling? Why is it there? Emotional intelligence includes four domains: self-awareness, other awareness, self-management, and other management.[34]

With emotional awareness in place, leaders can intentionally choose their emotional management course of action—what will I do (or not do) in light of the emotion I'm experiencing and that person is expressing? How will I respond (or not)? Do I send the snarky email or pause and reconsider until tomorrow? (That one's easy, right?)

The two dimensions of emotional intelligence, self and other, ask the same questions: What feeling am I/are they experiencing? What might be some reasons? How can I support, respond, coach, lead, mentor in the most effective way so I/they have the opportunity to respond effectively?

As a leader, your capacity to engage and intentionally respond to emotions—your own and those of your team—translates to more effective decision-making, psychologically safe cultures, and long-term success.

Your personal gains include growing flowers instead of weeds—like increased resilience, stronger relationships, greater adaptability, sharper strategic vision, and of course, flourishing!

EMOTIONAL AVOIDANCE: A HIDDEN LEADERSHIP LIABILITY

If all this talk about emotions has you looking for good options for movie night or ordering pizza, you're not alone! Leaders often shove emotions away like unfiled papers stacked in boxes. I was meeting with a senior manager and his team consulting with me to design a new supervisor program for their operations staff. As I took my seat, he told his team that his personal leader approach was simple—give people the tools and, as a leader, you will never have to deal with emotions.

Gulp.

And no.

Many leaders believe that staying neutral and detaching from emotion is the means to composure and professionalism. And the higher leaders climb, the associated stakes make it more tempting to shut down emotion to maintain credibility.

The reality is that "unemotional" leaders do feel. The difference is how much they might be stacking up boxes of unfiled papers. But unacknowledged emotion can leak into a leader's inner terrain, contributing to blind spots, difficulty receiving feedback, reactive choices, and limiting influence and connection. Your healthy relationship with self and others requires emotional input for deeper understanding, trust, and a sense of belonging.

Sometimes leaders recognize the emotions but would choose anything (maybe not a kidney stone) other than explicit discussion of them.

The reality is that strong leaders with true followers harness and utilize emotion wisely.

A friend and colleague provides mental health care to not-for-profit healthcare professionals working in difficult places around the world. He finds that these high-powered medical professionals are leaders who are often resistant to emotions-dabbling. In part, it's been trained out of them. They also work long hours, so it's easier to stuff the emotions into boxes and add a layer of duct tape to keep those lids of boxes in place. Maybe you can relate.

He compares building emotional awareness to having a wound on your arm. When the cut happens—like when a mentor abandons you in a crisis, you are forced out, or feeling good lasts only as long as your last win—there isn't time in the moment to bandage the wound well. Grab some gauze, wrap it up, and keep going. But the gauze on emotional wounds gets dirty too, so you add more layers until one day, you wake up and realize something stinks. The infection is undeniable and must be treated.

Sometimes the realization is that the cut is deeper than you thought—like some of the things that may have resurfaced in your Leader Story Timeline.

If you discover a deep wound, consider connecting with professional support. Old life stuff can wreak havoc and toxify leader inner terrain in short order.

Another reason high-achieving professionals in most every industry I've worked with have been conditioned to set emotions to the side is the belief that logic should exclusively determine decisions. But as research reveals, emotions also have a critical role in rational thought.[35] Leaders who avoid or suppress emotions are operating with incomplete data—and often have some fears related to digging around in those emotion boxes.

YOUR TURN

Here are some common fears I hear from leaders like you. Are any similar to your own fears? If yours isn't listed, add it.

- If I allow emotions on the scene, I will lose control.
- I'm not sure I want to know what emotions will tell me.
- If I show vulnerability, people will not respect me.
- I'm going to discover something I just can't stand about myself.
- What if the emotions illuminate I need a big change in my life?
- I'm not sure I want to know if these are linked to some buried painful memory.
- I don't know how to make sense of them.
- I do not want to be needy or realize I've been lying to myself about something I want or need.
- I'm pretty fond of my emotional boxes and unsorted files, thanks.
- Others: _____

These concerns may be connected to the deep beliefs or reflex thoughts you identified in the previous chapter. Our families of origin had rules for emotions, like which ones are acceptable or not. Our teams and organizations and workplaces have spoken and unspoken rules about emotions. For example, some systems have an unspoken rule that anger should never be shown, while in other systems anger is the emotion that shows up for everything. As your Leader Story Timeline may have illuminated, you don't leave your story at the office door. And sometimes your office family system follows you to your home. Those emotional rules you learned when you were young are very sticky and—without awareness—may be shaping how you interact in your personal and professional life—and they follow you into your leadership.

Many courageous high-impact people like you bravely allowed me to hold the metaphorical flashlight while they peeled duct tape from their tightly packed and shelved boxes of unexplored emotions. Sometimes they laughed. Sometimes they cried. But they always shared relief for the insight, release, and recovered energy. This chapter is inspired by them—and you, my gritty and growth-minded leader comrade.

CHOOSE ONE BOX

Let's capture some initial reflections about the role of emotions in your leadership today and how they've shown up—or not—over the course of your life. Like beliefs and thoughts, our relationship with emotions is strongly influenced by our formative years. Start with one box and one emotion.

In my family, expressing negative emotions, such as anger, sadness, or fear, meant _____.

Growing up, if I was having a hard time emotionally, the response by my family was usually _____.

When my feelings were hurt, the expectation was for me to _____.

Did my family value control or expression of emotion? How does this show up in my leadership today?

Some examples for the last question might be:
- Difficulty asking for help
- Admitting you don't know
- Dismissing the emotions of others on the team, which leaves them feeling unheard
- Avoiding difficult conversations because emotions may show up

This emotional exploration might feel messy. And don't be surprised if you bump into discomfort—memories that are tough to revisit, realizations about choices or habits, or feelings you've kept boxed up. When you lift the branches, take a closer look, and name what you see there's also relief as you lighten hidden weight and clear out inner terrain to make it freer, more breathable, and open for exploration.

EMOTIONS, FEELINGS, POTATO, POTAH-TO

Emotions. Feelings. I won't spend a lot of time on this, but the distinction does matter. The words "emotion" and "feeling" get used interchangeably, and I'll continue do so in this book, even though they're two different things. *Emotions* are raw data—which is why they are important for considering decisions. They are brain and nervous system-prompted automatic responses to something happening to us, internally or externally. They are fast and instinctual. Think of your response to stubbing your toe. That physical pain generates the emotion of anger and probably a verbal expletive in response.

When I'm feeling "hangry," my word label of my experience is irritability in response to physical hunger. My behavioral response is a shorter fuse and impatience with others, but I could choose a different response to the instinctual signal that my body needs fuel.

Emotions are the rapid, primal indicator lights on your dashboard of life. They arise before conscious awareness and feelings come after, as you process and label what's happening through your senses. You can't stop emotions from firing, but you can work with the feeling—reframing and regulating. It all happens at lightning speed, but feeling is the interpretation of the sensation your emotion prompted. Then add newly aligned interpretations from your mental awareness in the last chapter.

Emotion sensations and feeling labels give you information and each feeling has its own job. Anger prompts you to act, be assertive, or set a limit. Sadness directs you to ask for help or consolation. Sometimes a feeling may lead us to stop or withdraw. Fear may cause you to act, like launching an initiative or presenting to senior executives. It may also cause you to freeze, like not pursuing a new role for which you feel unqualified.

In the same situation, people may have different emotional responses. Here's an example: You're at a party and suddenly your chest feels tight. Your breathing gets faster and shorter and your stomach locks up with an emotional response. For one person the sensation translates to "I feel awkward because I don't know anyone at this party." Someone with the same physical sensation realizes, "I feel disgusted because the boss who fired me is pretending nothing happened."

Feelings are more accessible to self-awareness and verbalization, while those unconscious emotions drive behavior if we don't slow down to see the patterns. Understanding both allows leaders to reflect more clearly and respond more intentionally. They also remind you that others' responses are following the same process. Feelings are connected to your leader identity story in how you interpret the emotionally-related events from your Leader Story Timeline. Your identity story includes the real data and experiences from life—memories and beliefs and the related emotions that get stirred up, and how you've come to label and interpret those feelings. Avoiding them may dilute or distill versions of the story rather than repurpose it for good, allow it to metabolize, not hold you back, and make inner terrain space for you to intentionally respond to situations now in the most self-respecting and other-respecting way.

EMOTIONS HAVE JOBS

That raw data of emotions serves important life and survival purposes. Here's a chart summarizing the jobs of each emotion and their feeling labels. I gave them trail names too!

EMOTION	JOB OF THE EMOTION	EXAMPLE IN LEADERSHIP
FEAR *TRAIL SCOUT*	Alerts you to potential danger or risk; prepares you for caution or action. Appears at cliff edges pointing to danger and demanding alertness.	A leader feels fear before a big decision, prompting careful risk assessment.

EMOTION	JOB OF THE EMOTION	EXAMPLE IN LEADERSHIP
ANGER *BOUNDARY BLAZE*	Signals that a boundary has been crossed or an injustice has occurred; motivates action. Alerts when trail is trespassed.	A leader experiences anger when team values are violated; motivates to address the issue directly.
SADNESS *MOURNING FOG*	Allows for processing loss and change; signals the need for reflection or support. Rolls in when something is lost, slows your pace, draws others close.	A leader feels sadness when a valued team member resigns, prompting reflection on team morale.
JOY *SUMMIT GLOW*	Signals alignment with values and goals; fosters motivation and connection. Lights up the trail when you're aligned— motivating, connecting, why the journey matters.	A leader celebrates a team win, boosting morale and reinforcing positive behaviors.
GUILT *MISSTEP ECHO*	Encourages repair of mistakes; signals the need for accountability. A stumble reminding you to course correct.	A leader acknowledges an error in strategy and takes responsibility, earning trust.
SHAME *SHROUDED SHADOW*	Protects social bonds by discouraging behaviors that may lead to rejection. Can be trouble when even in the clearing you feel shadow hidden.	A leader feels shame after dismissing an employee's concern, leading them to correct their behavior.

EMOTION	JOB OF THE EMOTION	EXAMPLE IN LEADERSHIP
SURPRISE *WIND SHIFT*	Enhances readiness for unexpected events; helps in rapid learning and adaptation. Sudden signal something is changing.	A leader is surprised by an unexpected challenge and quickly pivots their strategy.
DISGUST *POISONOUS PLANT*	Protects from harmful influences; signals avoidance of something toxic or wrong. Alert to toxic, off-track, unsafe.	A leader senses discomfort with a proposal that lacks ethical integrity and speaks up.
LOVE *TETHER LINE*	Drives connection and belonging; encourages collaboration and care. Linking partners on exposed ridges.	A leader builds strong relationships with their team, fostering trust and loyalty.
HOPE *HORIZON LINE*	Encourages perseverance and belief in positive future outcomes. Moving toward unseen peaks, trekking to better.	A leader remains hopeful despite setbacks, inspiring the team to push forward.

If you've never seen the Inside Out movies, this is your homework![36] *Inside Out* and *Inside Out 2* are emotional intelligence masterclasses, taking us inside the brain of an adolescent girl whose emotions are personified in a compelling way. The movies do a great job illustrating the jobs of our emotions, the importance of both negative and positive emotions, and how they all work together.

Understanding that emotions are automatic responses and feelings are the conscious labels we assign to them gives leaders a critical advantage: the power to pause, interpret, and respond intentionally. Emotions act like internal messengers. Fear signals a threat, anger signals a boundary, joy signals alignment—but without self-awareness, those signals can be misread.

Feelings are where interpretation happens, and that's where leadership begins. For example, imagine you walk into a team meeting, see the person who canceled your project, and sense irritation rising within yourself. The automatic emotion is *anger*, triggered by an action of invalidation or dismissal. The feeling that follows might be *disrespected* or *undervalued* or *hurt*. An unaware leader might snap with a verbal retort or disengage from participating in the meeting. But an attuned leader recognizes the emotion, names the feeling, and redirects the response: "I'm disappointed in the decision, not feeling engaged, but will work to stay present." This moment of awareness shifts a potentially reactive spiral into a constructive conversation. The spiral is understandable but would not earn you any leadership credibility. When you learn to track both emotion and feeling, you build emotional intelligence and leadership trust, clarity, and presence.

Creating cultures where this can happen is also a leader's responsibility. This work requires an abundance of psychological safety—an environment in which people feel comfortable and supported to express differences, ideas, opinions, and concerns without fear of negative consequences. The investment is worth it! Engagement, performance, innovation, and creativity will follow—along with better decisions and well-being for the leader and the team.

EMOTION AWARENESS SELF-ASSESSMENT

Your own comfort with emotional experience and expression exists on a spectrum. Let's do a quick self-assessment to bring this connection to practical life.

On the far-left side of the spectrum indicated by a horizontal line below, you can see the label "I never express emotion." And on the far-right side of the, the label reads "I always express emotion."

Where would you put yourself on the spectrum? Place an X along the spectrum. Ask your pacer or someone who knows you well to weigh in on this too.

I never express emotion, no thanks! ├───────────────────┤ I always express emotion; no problem!

Extremes on either end of the spectrum are not helpful, and both extremes will keep you from flourishing. Extreme emotional avoidance and resistance, keeping the boxes shelved, and refusing to consider the emotional data will keep you rootbound, distrusted, and disconnected.

The opposite extreme of over-prioritizing emotion as absolute truth and overexpressing emotion as a means of making things happen or manipulating situations is also harmful—to yourself and others. This leads to emotions running the show, which breeds a different type of distrust in relationships, as well as the risk of not being taken seriously.

The goal here, like much of leadership life, is—you guessed it: balance.

Sometimes leaders are more comfortable stepping into emotional awareness for others than focusing awareness on their own interior terrain.

Below is the same rating scale as above. This time, how would you rate your emotional awareness for others—colleagues, teammates, direct reports, friends?

Rate your comfort level with others' emotions on the same scale below with the left side reading "No, thank you" and the right side reading "Bring it."

Place an X to indicate this.

No, thank you. |——————————————| Bring it!!

Compare your X on this line with where you placed the X on the line earlier. Did your rating change on this scale when considering emotional awareness for your relationships?

Now, where would you have placed yourself on the spectrum of comfort with emotions for yourself and others *prior* to the Leading Becomes You journey you've undertaken so far?

Indicate that place on the line above with a +.

No matter where you placed your X or your + on any of the spectrums, simply taking time to do this exercise is building emotional awareness and bringing that mindful meets neuroplasticity to the relationship between emotions and thinking. You've just increased your ability to identify and verbalize your own and others' emotions. Your becoming is in process!

Finally, think about where you want to place your X by the end of the Leading Becomes You process.

Put a nice big X on that spot on the line now. Consider any barriers or trek provisions you might need to get there.

WHAT ABOUT EMPATHY?

You might be thinking, "Good, I'm glad she's covering empathy!" or you might be rolling your eyes and looking ahead to see how long is this section. The truth is we can't talk emotional intelligence without it. Empathy is a key component of the awareness of others' emotions dimension. It's an important trait for leaders and also explains why women are typically rated as more effective in some leadership situations.[37] Their empathy-infused relational focus specifically supports consensus-building and maintains followership in unpopular decisions.*

Too little empathy can lead to leaders:

- Mired in low connection capacity
- Dismissing of others' emotional needs
- Focusing only on performance or results
- Having difficulty picking up on interpersonal cues
- Being cold, unapproachable, or intimidating

---

*Research shows that, on average, women often score higher in empathy, interpersonal sensitivity, and relational attunement—strengths that can boost effectiveness in emotionally intelligent leadership, collaboration, and trust-building. In practice, this means women leaders may be especially effective in contexts that require navigating complexity through relationships, building team cohesion, and fostering engagement. These patterns aren't universal, but they underscore relational intelligence as both a critical leadership strength and a skill worth cultivating for all leaders (Eagly and Carli; Bass and Riggio).

Too much empathy may result in leaders:

- Overdoing connection capacity on behalf of others
- Over-identifying with team members' stress or pain
- Avoiding hard feedback conversations to spare the feelings of others
- Taking on others' emotional burdens, which leads to overwhelm
- Not asserting their own needs and preferences

Revisiting the model, you can see how emotional awareness brings balance to the connection and identity clarity dimensions. It is only in relationship that you recognize and recalibrate your self-as-leader emotional presence.

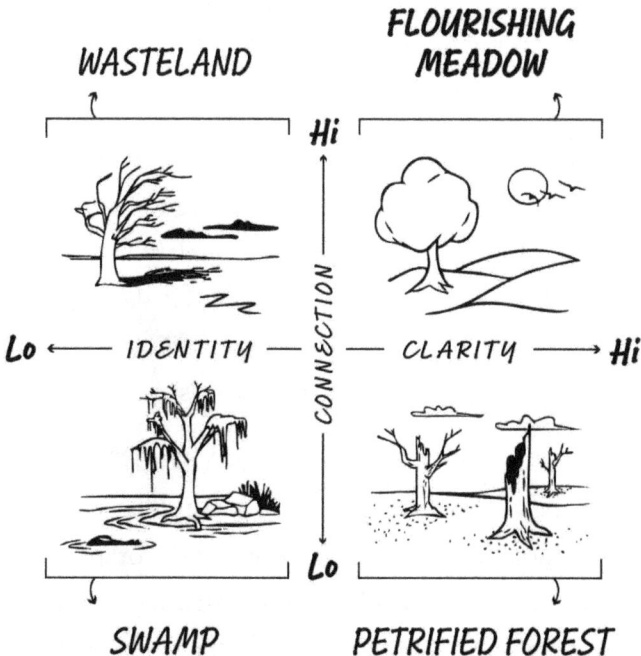

LEADING BECOMES YOU MODEL
©Dr. Natalie Pickering

DON'T FORGET YOUR GUT

Leadership culture prioritizes rational thought and logic, which is important. However, this emphasis often excludes other kinds of knowledge sourced in a leader's emotion-heart and instinct-gut. We're sometimes trapped by Descartes' enlightenment-era mantra, "I think, therefore I am." Separating mind from body elevated reason as the most important path and focus, even for leader identity.

This chapter has made the case for the importance of a leader's emotional intelligence, and I'm taking it one step further to ask: What about gut, body, instinctual intelligence? We even have language for this, "I knew it in my gut!" We looked at the nervous system's role in firing emotional responses. It also delivers fast, physical gut signals from tuning into the environment that say, "Pay attention." Gut signals influence emotional regulation, decision-making, and even perception of risk.[38]

Intuition and gut instinct are vital elements of a leader's hiring, strategy, and crisis decisions. But gut intelligence also depends on your self-as-leader awareness.

In *The Extended Mind: The Power of Thinking Outside the Brain*, Annie Murphy Paul draws on neuroscience and cognitive science to argue that cognition is extended across our bodies, surroundings, and relationships. She writes,"[T]hinking doesn't just happen in the brain—it happens in the body, too."[39] She goes on to emphasize that gut, heart, and physical sensations are part of intelligent decision-making, especially in complex, high-stakes situations.

Paul's thesis validates the Leading Becomes You model by reframing leadership not as a purely internal trait but as identity that is context-sensitive, embodied, and shaped through team dynamics and workplace environments. Her insights show that leader identity is co-constructed through trusted peers (aka your pacer), learning communities, and connection. She writes, "People who need to think together should learn together. People who need to think together should train together. People who need to think together should feel together." That's what we do in my team retreats and workshops, by the way!

MAKING EQ PERSONAL

Let's bring back your Leader Story Timeline. With your new emotional awareness superpowers, let's go back to those leader story chapters you wrote. This time, I want you to look at the full sections or lists you created, not just the summary statements. Re-read each section, this time from an emotional awareness lens. Some chapters will be easier than others. As you review each section you wrote, the goal is to try to keep your awareness on what emotions show up for you in a particular scene, situation, or season of your Leader Story Timeline.

Two different perspectives of emotion will surface as you review each section. One perspective is the younger "then you" leader experiencing the very moment that your "right now you" is revisiting—the younger leader you (even if it was last week) experienced specific thoughts and emotions connected to that moment, experience, and place in time.

Your "right now you"—your present leader self looking back is noticing and observing that previous experience. Don't be surprised if your "right now you" has a different emotion, a different gut response, and/or a different thought or perspective in looking back.

When you review your chapters or sections, capture the emotions for both perspectives side by side or together in a way that makes sense for where your timeline is written. You could use two different colors of pens, one for "then you" and one for "right now you." The goal is to record the emotion for any moment in your timeline that prompts some sort of emotional charge for you. Some situations may only have an emotion for "then you" and others for "now you"—that's ok. Just see what happens. No matter what, you're building emotion awareness muscle!

Go with your gut here! Practice that new emotion and body awareness and listen to yourself. Don't *Descartes* it. Overthinking lets those rational rules sneak in to "edit" your emotional response.

I picture you crouched low to the ground of your leader terrain, hands in the dirt, pulling up what doesn't belong and pausing to notice what does. I see you opening boxes you had forgotten, and naming and sorting the feelings you found there. It's hard work—seeing what's tangled, what's thriving, what's stunted.

But your raw clarity is essential for the next phase of your journey. You'll use these insights in the next chapter, next month, and maybe even today.

Emotions are the color for your leader becoming.

Wholeness.

Authenticity.

Depth.

Real.

You're doing it.

_____ FOR REFLECTION _____

In your notebook or below, write your responses to each of the following 12 questions. Consider working through two or three questions each day this week.

- For which section(s) did I notice the strongest emotional experiences?

- Where did my "then" and "now" self-as-leader have different emotional responses?

- How did I handle those moments of stronger emotion in my life and leadership?

- Are there patterns? What did you do? What did you not do?

- What did you need but not have?

- Are there times in your life story when emotions impacted your decision-making?

- How? What was the outcome?

- What does consideration of emotions and gut look like for your decision-making moving forward?

- How did positive emotions or negative emotions impact your view of your self-as-leader?

- How did they impact relationships with others?

- Which emotions show up most consistently?

- Which emotions show up less often? Why do you think this is?

CHAPTER RECAP

☐ *Leadership is an emotional experience and necessitates a composed response.* Your commitment to recognizing the role of emotions—your own and your team's—gives you a major return on investment!

☐ *Sidelining emotions is a leadership liability.* Suppressing or ignoring emotions is tempting but doesn't eliminate them; instead, it can lead to blind spots, reactive choices, inauthenticity, and weakened influence.

☐ *Emotions provide critical leadership data.* Every emotion has a function and a feeling label. You can use this information to assess risks, set boundaries, celebrate wins, and navigate change.

☐ *Emotional intelligence strengthens leadership resilience.* Revived leaders who build emotional awareness and manage their feelings effectively foster psychological safety, trust, and adaptability.

☐ *Balance is key.* When emotions are available but not dictating, they offer strategic superpowers to your leader becoming you.

LEADING BECOMES YOU BREAKTHROUGHS

In the following space, take a few moments to write notes for what resonated with you from this chapter.

What is one takeaway that resonates most from this chapter?

What do you want to do with this takeaway?

How will you know you've gained some ground?

"Not till we are lost, in other words not till we have lost the world, do we begin to find ourselves…"

– Henry David Thoreau

"Of all deceivers, fear most yourself."

– Soren Kierkegaard

"The purposes of a person's heart are deep waters, but one who has insight draws them out."

– Proverbs 20:5

CHAPTER 8

MEASURING YOUR INNER TERRAIN

How to Project Scope Your Inner Leader Terrain

Remember those giant road maps—the ones you could never quite refold once you pulled them open? You could spread them across the kitchen table or the hood of the car and see the whole picture. The highways and backroads, the scenic detours, mountains, little towns, big cities. Growing up, we had a big road atlas book with all fifty states. My dad would highlight the routes for our family road trips.

GPS is great and I confess my dependence on it! But for its convenience, it doesn't show me the whole picture. This chapter is shifting from those micro weed patches of thoughts and emotions to a macro survey of your entire leader terrain plot. You're identifying the perimeter, zooming out and standing back to see the bigger map of your leadership life—noticing where exactly are the patches or swaths of wasteland, swamp, petrified forest, and flourishing meadow.

My personal self-as-leader terrain reclamation started when I removed the tarp I kept trying to stretch over my growing barren wasteland. Then I had to figure out where my erosion factors took over. My toxic terrain grew over several years of hard things in my life coupled with my well-honed avoidance strategy—which I'll briefly share in the next chapter. It seems easier in the moment to pretend the swamp, wasteland, or petrified forest is not getting worse, and to just get more tarps.

Early in my career, I moved to West Africa to work for a well-established and wonderful not-for-profit. They had a solid mission aligned with my own. The unspoken culture of the organization, like many not-for-profits, prioritized hardiness (my definition: "I can do hard things without complaining"). Now, hardiness[40] is essential to hiring people for hard things in hard places.* And

---

*Psychological hardiness is the blend of commitment (staying engaged), control (believing you can influence outcomes), and challenge (seeing stress as an opportunity to grow). Research shows these attitudes help leaders stay resilient under pressure, navigate change, and support

this was a very challenging place to live where electricity worked sometimes, you needed a special filter to purify drinking water, driving seemed like certain death, and my chocolate food group was not available (well, when I found it, it tasted like soap). Beyond and between the challenges, here I learned what human resilience, community, and faith during crisis really meant. I met women with the strongest minds and hearts I have ever known. And I learned that good and important work, like leadership, is inevitably hard.

I was also young and naively convinced that my 20-some years of life experience and keen eye for improving the world were plenty enough to tackle the challenge. And hardiness? Not to worry. Remember? I'm a farm girl who bailed hay, weeded gardens, painted chicken coops, and snapped beans for all-day vegetable canning marathons. But the bottom line up front: a perfect storm set up a wasteland that stretched into my next decade of life.

When I looked back on this season and my own Leader Story Timeline, I saw that my waterlogged and overexploited wasteland was one part organizational oversight and a larger part my youthful internal blind spots. With an open-ended job description, my penchant for perfection, and some approval-seeking boundarylessness in tow, the wasteland was inevitable. My barren and desolate inner terrain, like the parched Sahara a few countries north, built up quickly.

The organization provided all new employees a mentor and time to acclimate. My carefully orchestrated schedule (as much as possible in a time-flexible culture), empty spiritual life (one of my personal rooting and flourishing tools), and my well-practiced veneer of self working overtime led to burnout. My attempted tarping was fueled by self-doubting reflex thoughts of "I can't do this" and deep beliefs like "People can't know how much I hate this."

---

healthier, safer teams.

At the same time, my mom was fighting a decade-long cancer diagnosis, which had been deemed "in remission" before I left but then metastasized weeks after I moved across the ocean. Her remaining months of life were few. I came back to be with her. She died on Christmas Day. I was 30. I could not bring myself to finish the contract in Africa.

So I poured heaps of mindset toxins dosed with guilt and self-criticism onto the pile. Edna came into her own.

> " Scoping your leader terrain means opening that big, awkward map of yourself

Scoping your leader terrain means opening that big, awkward map of yourself to see the swamp or wasteland or petrified forest, the dead ends, the hidden trails—so you can choose where to lead from and where you don't want to end up again.

_____ 50,000 FEET _____

Tackling a desolate or overgrown inner self-as-leader landscape starts with using your new awareness insights to scope out just how much your inner terrain needs reclaimed. You might have features of multiple terrains in your landscape—that's normal. Your inner leader terrain is unique to you—just like your leader identity. The Leading Becomes You model illustrates the most common patterns of inner terrains holding back the leaders I support. When they stop to recalibrate connection and identity clarity, it's incredible to see the transformation of their inner landscape, fulfillment, and leadership influence.

Let's look more closely at the terrain types so you can determine what's in your own terrain perimeter. The wasteland, swamp, petrified forest, and flourishing meadow offer a starting point for your map.

INNER LEADER TERRAINS

Some common inner leader terrain types develop when a leader has too little or too much connection or identity clarity without the balance of the other. These inner terrains keep leaders from flourishing. In this chapter, you're becoming familiar with the terrain types. In the acceptance phase, we will unpack internal and external contributors to each of the terrain types for a next-level perspective. As you review each of the three terrain types, pay attention to factors you recognize as impacting your own terrain. If you don't fit squarely in one terrain type, don't worry! The map bridges your awareness and acceptance supporting your big picture view. As you learn and get honest about the type and scope of your terrain then you can see where you need to excavate, add fill dirt, drain, and rebuild for flourishing.

SHIFTING TERRAINS

This spring, my son tried his green thumb on a container garden. He carefully followed my master gardener father's advice for the layers of straw and dirt and fertilizer, planting his anticipated vegetables strategically. After a few days,we saw sprouts. He watered and waited. Then one morning, he ran in to the house calling me to come see his garden. Expecting to see new growth, I looked at the tears in his eyes and the empty soil. All the green was gone! Nothing visible in the dirt.

Decimated.

Terrains, and leader terrains, can be obliterated in one natural disaster. You wake up and everything you had been working for has been wiped out.

The bugs come in the night and steal it all.

Other times, terrain devastation is slow and years-long process. The terrain conditions change ever so slowly, barely noticeable in the moment.

I first visited Lake Nakuru in the Great Rift Valley of west-central Kenya in my twenties when it was home to a massive congregation of flamingos. When I returned years later for a work project, I was shocked to see the stark impact of industrial waste and deforestation from the fast-growing and non-infrastruc-tured neighboring town, leaving a few dots of pink on the shoreline. What once sustained life was now unfamiliar.

The inner leader terrain is the same. Our internal factors and external con-ditions shift and we must pay attention to them. Building awareness helps us recognize small changes well before the years-later devastation. Getting close to the dirt and pulling the weeds helps us see what type of bugs we are dealing with.

Scientists categorize a wasteland, swamp, or petrified forest based on how difficult it will be to reclaim. They determine whether the terrain state is emerg-ing, moderate, or severe. Maybe the landscape is strained with mild overload. Or at the other end of the spectrum, a severely hostile terrain is stagnant and eroding or completely overloaded.

Does your leadership land ever feel like a swamp, wasteland, or petrified forest? A once-flourishing leadership landscape can turn to emerging, moderate, or severely dangerous terrain when vision, clarity, and alignment erode. Maybe you've never experienced flourishing leadership yourself so it's hard to know what it is or how to build it.

As you keep working to scope your terrain size, I've given you the for-mula for the essential components: identity clarity and connection to others and purpose. Whether your terrain degradation is emerging or severe, you can

192 | LEADING BECOMES YOU

apply your new deep-level awareness to evaluating the complete picture of your current land of leadership.

My personal work with some wise and expert terrain renovators over the years (aka coach, therapist, and spiritual director) helped me navigate my Leading Becomes You reclamation in that season and others.. Later, in my own career as a psychologist, I have had the privilege of shaping the process and approach I developed to support others and that I'm sharing with you. I'm still tending my own self-as-leader land. Whether you are 22 or 72, the process of continued nurturing your leadership land of self is imperative. The factors you have reviewed for yourself like those deeply grooved deep beliefs, well-worn habits, the brain's love for efficiency, and those reflex thinking traps can quickly lure us back to inattention or "it's too hard," or "I don't have time," if we don't stay mindful and continually revisit the process.

PROJECT SCOPE YOUR TERRAIN

As you look across your inner leader terrain, maybe you see just one small, bare, muddy corner like a Midwest soybean field that's mostly green and lush, all but that little section on the end with no sprouts—what the terrain scientists would label emerging. The small patch may reveal a broken field tile easily remedied with a focused repair. Or maybe your terrain looks more like a decimated heap, charred from a raging forest fire of unhealthy workplace dynamics or corrupt and callous leader impact. The good news, leader friend, is that just like a megaproject can be completed with the right strategy, *even charred land can be reclaimed.*

And if, like me, you've been tempted to try tarping and just covering up those growing hazardous sections, I want to encourage you to put down the tarp! Pick up a land area calculator instead!

As you scope your terrain, write your thoughts in response to the following questions.

> Even charred land can be reclaimed.

Choose one or two of the following questions that resonate with your current situation.

As you consider the size and scope of your current wasteland, what or whom is being impacted?

Where do you see erosion? Loss? Overgrown sections?

Are you operating in survival mode? For how long?

Do most decisions feel like short-term fixes rather than long-term strategy?

Is your team motivated? How do you know?

Do meetings have energy? How do you know?

Are employees connected or distant? Why?

Do you feel uninspired? For how long?

Are you overcommitted? How do you know?

Are you under-supported? What would help this?

_____ TERRAIN TYPES IN REAL-LIFE _____

I'll illustrate each terrain type with a case study as a practical way to help you recognize terrain features in your own situation and experience. Note that there can be multiple ways a particular leader may look, sound, respond, and behave in one terrain type.

As we climb to higher ground also keep a lookout for parts of our terrain where you did not realize dumping occurred or where your personal needs were blown away—the dry, cracked places and where your potential was eroded from malnourished roots.

Don't be surprised if there are elements of multiple terrain types that match your experience. You might have some swamp bordering a strip of wasteland. The goal is to give you a starting canvas to build your map and growth path to flourishing.

LEADING BECOMES YOU FOUR As PROCESS
©Dr. Natalie Pickering

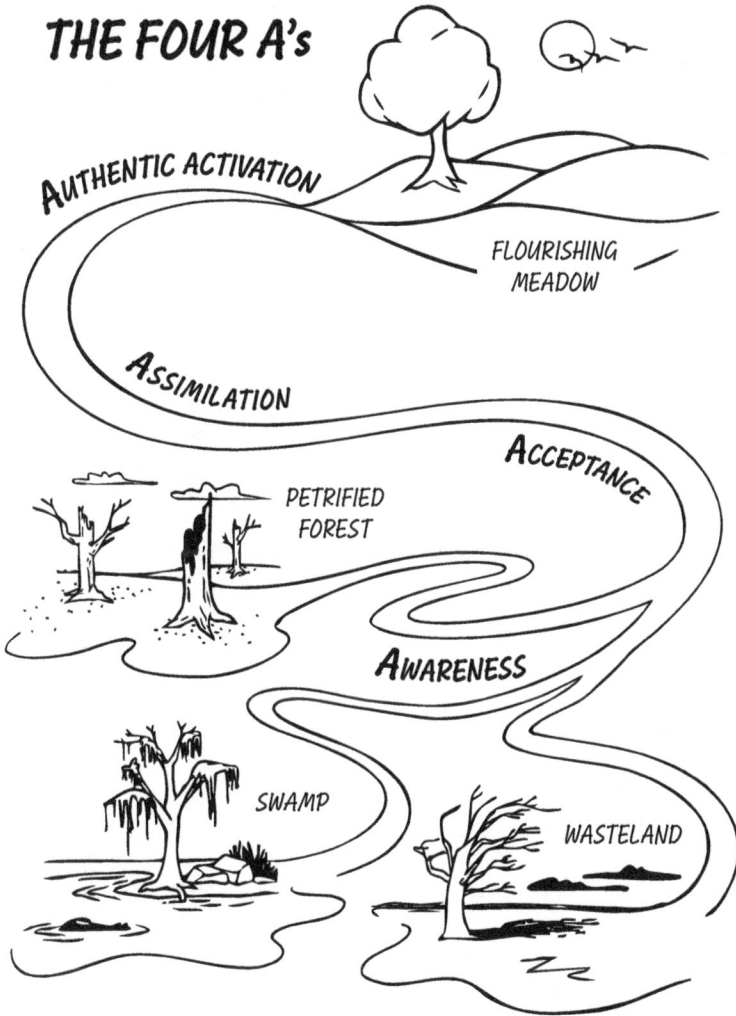

THE FOUR A's

AUTHENTIC ACTIVATION

FLOURISHING MEADOW

ASSIMILATION

ACCEPTANCE

PETRIFIED FOREST

AWARENESS

SWAMP

WASTELAND

The Swamp Terrain
Low Connection × Low Identity Clarity
The leader trapped here has no internal compass and no external anchors.

A leader who is low in connection and whose identity is unclear may find themselves trapped in the inner terrain called swamp—a slow, entangling terrain where clarity is clouded, values are submerged, and movement feels sluggish and aimless. For leaders here, disconnection from self, others, and vision leads to moral fatigue, emotional depletion, and a gradual sinking into resignation and spiritual stuck.

At worst, a leader in the swamp has collapsed inward or is trapped in little to no awareness that others are experiencing them as inauthentic. Their leadership energy may be drowned by burnout, not necessarily from workload but rather rootbound in low identity clarity. This leads to work as performance and always on the move for the next success hit. Leaders in the swamp are disconnected from self, which often leads to functioning from false self. They've lost sight of their own purpose and are internally disengaged from colleagues and the team, even though they appear friendly and likeable. While not necessarily evident to others, on the inside a leader in the swamp does not feel a sense of belonging, in their leadership role.

IDENTITY CLARITY DYNAMICS

- **The self is inauthentic**
- May function from different versions of self, like a chameleon
- Lacks a strong internal anchor to guide leadership decisions
- Shows up based on external circumstances, perceived pressure
- Self-view may be fragmented: "I'm surviving, not leading" (withdrawn) or "I'm adaptive and confident" (charismatic)

- Has lost their own convictions
- At a deeper level, driving for worth and significance

CONNECTION DYNAMICS
- **Connection is inauthentic and deep purpose has been lost**
- Struggles to create meaningful relationships because true self is deeply lost beneath the surface
- Withholds full presence to avoid vulnerable exposure
- Reluctant to assert deep longings, needs or truths
- Relationships feel disjointed or emotionally unrewarding
- Appears warm, friendly, dependable but lacks depth and vulnerability
- Avoidant, disengaged
- Adaptive to the situation and may shift language and tone based on who's in the room

PERFORMANCE AND INFLUENCE
- Role execution continues but lacks authentic inspiration or innovation
- Output is reactive, not proactive
- Prone to burnout from maintaining versions of self (versus workload-related burnout of the wasteland terrain)
- Lacks long-term credible influence
- Struggles to initiate or offer strategic direction
- Compliant to organizational dysfunction

Leaders in the swamp often "fade" rather than "fail." Their leadership deteriorates through erosion, not eruption.

> **Key challenge: identity confusion + relational detachment = invisible erosion.**

SWAMP TERRAIN CASE STUDY: JORDAN

Jordan was the charismatic founder of a boutique marketing firm known for its edgy brand strategies and loyal client base. He was the kind of leader who could light up a room—funny, magnetic, quick to pivot when things went sideways. Early in the company's growth, his adaptive energy and charm built a strong culture that thrived on collaboration, scrappiness, and creativity. Clients loved him. His team rallied behind him.

But three years in, something was off.

By the time Jordan came to coaching, revenue had plateaued, his team had lost momentum, and he was struggling to make even basic decisions. Initially, he seemed upbeat—he cracked jokes and called himself "a start-up guy, not a systems guy." But beneath the levity, there was a fog.

"The truth is, Natalie, I don't even know what I'm building anymore," he admitted one day.

The more we explored, the more the swamp came into focus.

Jordan didn't lack energy. He lacked center. His leadership identity had been built on momentum and appearances, not mission. He prided himself on being adaptable—"the guy who can read the room and shift"—but over time, that adaptability became chameleonism. His style changed with every client and every meeting. He didn't lie, but he often said what others wanted to hear. "It's just good leadership," he told himself. "Know your audience."

But behind closed doors, he felt increasingly hollow.

There was no stable voice. No internal alignment. His identity had been outsourced to whatever context he was navigating. His relationships with his senior team had grown thin—cordial but shallow. Team members were unclear on priorities. Jordan avoided difficult conversations, defaulting to vague praise and jokes rather than direction.

His connection to purpose was fading too. He couldn't articulate why the work mattered anymore—only that it needed to get done. When I asked what success looked like, he laughed. "Honestly? Just getting through Q3 without losing another account."

We named his terrain: the swamp.

His leadership identity and connection both had sunk—slowly, subtly, beneath the surface of charm and capability. Jordan wasn't in crisis. But he was disappearing—disconnected from "being," from others, and drifting without a vision that felt true.

In coaching, we began rebuilding his leadership identity from the inside out. He journaled responses to questions like "What do I want to be known for when I leave the room?" and "What's a decision I regret because I chose image over substance?" He began noticing how often he adjusted his tone mid-meeting based on others' facial expressions—a habit so reflexive, he hadn't realized it cost him authenticity.

Over time, Jordan began articulating a leadership voice that didn't shift based on applause. He initiated realignment conversations with his cofounders. He let his team see when he didn't have the answer—and was shocked they didn't run but, rather, leaned in.

"I thought my strength was being whoever people needed me to be," he reflected. "But I was disappearing. Now I'm learning to be one person, everywhere."

The Wasteland Terrain
High Connection × Low Identity Clarity
Leaders trapped in the wasteland function without flourishing, successful but soul starved.

The wasteland is a barren, overworked, overexposed landscape. Once fertile with ideas, energy, and possibility and still evidently visible, the leader's inner soil has been depleted by constant focus on external forces and relentless expectations. Imposter phenomenon and perfectionism often live in the wasteland as this terrain overprioritizes connection to others' agendas and perceived expectations at the expense of connection to self. Productivity overrides personal purpose—and erosion has replaced growth. The surface is active but nothing deeply new, meaningful, and significant can take root.

This terrain describes the leader who is compelled constantly by connection to everyone else's needs, opinions, and agendas—but untethered from their own internal compass, truth, and experience. Their identity is fluid, situational, and performance-driven. Whereas the swamp-trapped leader is self-focused with limited depth, a wasteland-trapped leader is deeply entangled in others' needs, expectations, and agendas—at the cost of their own voice and direction. They perform, achieve, and accommodate but have no internal compass. Work gets done but soul withers. Boundaries collapse, workload burnout brews, and the self erodes beneath chronic overfunctioning. Wasteland leaders aren't visibly dysfunctional. In fact, they're often admired for their reliability and stamina. But they're fueled by overfunctioning. Leaders here are stretched thin, pulled in too many directions, and often unsure who they are beneath the whirlwind of activity and connection. They've lost sight and anchoring of their own self-as-leader approach and mission.

IDENTITY CLARITY DYNAMICS

- **The self is blurry and dependent on others' approval**
- Sense of self is highly connected to performance
- Often feels overcommitted but doesn't know how to stop
- Functional but fragmented
- Other-referencing leads to loss of self-as-leader presence
- "I know what I do, but I don't know who I am in the doing"
- Over connection to others leads to hyper-responsibility
- Overcommitted, overfunctioning, over-responsible

CONNECTION DYNAMICS

- **Connection to performance and others' agendas is compulsive**
- Driven by approval, inclusion, or fear of disappointing
- Over-identifies with role as supporter or fixer
- Lacks boundaries, prone to enmeshment
- Highly responsive to others' emotional cues
- Often admired but personally isolated
- Struggles to delegate
- Adapts to meet others' expectations
- Says yes quickly, often lacks healthy boundaries
- Performs empathy but suppresses resentment

PERFORMANCE AND INFLUENCE

- Highly productive but directionless
- Workaholism, compassion fatigue due to substituting output for meaning

- Justifies staying in misaligned roles or systems
- Reactive execution with no pause for purpose
- Credibility can suffer from chronic overextension
- Long-term impact limited by burnout and misalignment

Key challenge: over-identification with external roles + constant output = internal depletion.

WASTELAND TERRAIN CASE STUDY: ELENA

Elena was the director of development for a large public university, responsible for cultivating major donors, securing foundation support, and leading a team of advancement professionals across multiple colleges. Known for her tireless work ethic, she had helped the institution exceed fundraising targets for five consecutive years. She was widely regarded as the glue that held the campaign engine together.

But when we met for coaching, Elena wasn't celebrating success—she was falling apart and petrified that anyone would find out.

In our first session, she habitually defaulted to convincing me of her performance outlining year-to-date gifts and upcoming board presentations. But when I asked how *she* was doing, she paused. Her posture softened.

"I'm executing," she said, "but I don't feel anything anymore."

Elena had led the university's development office through major transitions, staffing gaps, and an increasingly competitive funding landscape. Nights and weekends blurred into travel and events. Her phone pinged late into the evening. She kept showing up—always available, always competent. But she had stopped feeling connected to the work.

We named her terrain: the wasteland.

This wasn't visible burnout. It was a quiet erosion—the loss of internal vitality beneath continued output. She was still performing, still producing. But nothing was growing inside. Her creativity had dried up. Her sense of purpose had gone dormant.

She told me, "It's not that I don't care. I just don't know what part of me is left in it."

Through coaching, Elena began to trace the patterns: her belief that slowing down meant selfishness, her tendency to equate value with productivity, and the subtle but constant pressure to prove her worth through deliverables. She noticed how often her calendar filled the moment it opened, how rarely she said no, and how little space she left for reflection.

We started small. She reclaimed pockets of pause. She asked her team to run point on donor meetings she once felt she *had* to lead. She practiced not apologizing when she left early.

Gradually, she felt herself returning. Not dramatically—but quietly, like water seeping back into dry soil. She described walking out of a strategy session and realizing she had enjoyed it—really, fully enjoyed it—for the first time in months.

"I thought I had to do everything to be indispensable," she reflected. "But I had become a shell of the leader I wanted to be. I'm learning to lead in a way that leaves *me* intact."

The Petrified Forest Terrain
High Identity Clarity × Low Connection

Leaders trapped in the petrified forest resist change, co-creation, and humility—blocking the very relationships and purpose that keep leadership alive.

The petrified forest is an ancient landscape where trees have turned to stone. Time stands still. Though powerful in form, the leader trapped in this terrain is hardened and non-adaptive. The ecosystem is preserved, but it no longer breathes. A fossilized forest is anchored in the past or a safe identity but detached from human connection and deeper purpose.

This terrain reflects a leader who knows exactly who they are—or who they believe they must be—but is disconnected from others, feedback, and anything that might change them. Their identity has become fossilized: a fixed version of success, legacy, or ego-image. Emotional expression is avoided. The soul of leadership and deep purpose is resisted. The leader clings to control and certainty, while, like the swamp-trapped leader, connection to human vulnerability or transformational insight and meaning fades. The leader has stopped evolving, but remains preserved—impressive in stature, overly identified with self-as-leader confidence, and closed to change.

This terrain forms when a leader achieves recognition or mastery and then freezes their self-concept around what has worked in the past. Feedback is threatening. Adaptation is avoided. The leader believes they *are* their reputation or role—and any shift feels like an existential threat.

This is not incompetence. It's over-identification with a version of self-as-leader that is locked in the leader's hyperawareness and focus on their identity story. The leader operates from self-protection, relying on historical authority rather than present-moment responsiveness.

Leaders in the petrified forest remain "in charge" but disconnected—impressive in image but brittle underneath.

IDENTITY CLARITY DYNAMICS

- **The self is locked down**
- Strong but rigid identity
- Over-identified with role, past successes, or personal authority
- Clarity is unexamined and resistant to evolution
- Self-view is fixed: "This is who I've always been—and it works"
- Identity as armor with self-concept functioning as protection from vulnerability.
- Challenge to their identity story triggers overreaction.
- Self-trust overshadows self-flexibility

CONNECTION DYNAMICS

- **Connection is disregarded by preserved purpose and isolated identity**
- Controlling, directive, defensive
- Avoids feedback and collaboration
- Reluctant to share power or adapt to new leadership models
- May silence or override dissent
- Command-and-control relational stance
- Low psychological safety in team culture
- Keeps personal challenges private to maintain image
- Projects confidence but fosters relational distance

PERFORMANCE AND INFLUENCE

- Consistent performance but increasingly misaligned with context
- Influence relies on past authority rather than present relevance
- Team disengagement increases despite leader's perceived clarity
- Innovation stalls as relational trust erodes

Key challenge: Ego protection + relational detachment = leadership stagnation.

PETRIFIED FOREST CASE STUDY: CORBIN

Corbin had been the chief operating officer of a global logistics company for over a decade. He was revered for his sharp strategic mind and decisive leadership style. His reputation inside the company was legendary, "unshakable," as one colleague described him. With over 30 years in the industry, Corbin was the definition of seasoned.

Coach note: It takes a lot for a leader trapped in any terrain to reach out for coaching and personal support, but even more so for leaders trying to break free from the petrified forest.

Corbin came to coaching because the organization had stalled and the challenges were not responding to command and control.

The executive team was struggling to collaborate. Morale was low. Rising leaders had begun leaving. Meanwhile, Corbin insisted the company was "solid." He cited numbers, timelines, and benchmarks with ease—but the atmosphere was brittle.

In our early sessions, Corbin was guarded. He answered every question like a press statement—measured, practiced, unshakable. When I asked what he hoped for coaching he replied, "*I don't need help. I just need alignment. To sum it up, Natalie, it's my team that is the issue.*"

Over a few months it became clear: Corbin was no longer leading—he was preserving. He had built a powerful leadership identity over time, rooted in competence and control. But that identity had calcified. His strength had become his shield and it was not serving his team, organization, or himself.

Corbin was respected. But growth had stopped. His clarity was rigid. He rarely invited input and was threatened by innovation. He was known for "holding the line," but that line had become a wall.

As we worked together, small cracks opened. He admitted he no longer understood his younger directors. He scoffed at emotional intelligence and dismissed vulnerability as "self-indulgent." From his perspective, leadership was about certainty. Not presence.

But the cost was mounting.

Corbin's relationships with peers had eroded. He defaulted to unilateral decision-making, rarely asking for feedback. His team operated in silence, wary of speaking truth. Several capable directors had left under his watch—not because of what he did, but because of what he wouldn't change.

In one session, after a particularly tense board review, Corbin sat back and said quietly, "I used to feel proud of this work. Now I just feel like I'm holding up a system that isn't working anymore. But if I stop holding it up, what's left of me?"

I will never forget that moment the forest shifted to life.

In mapping his Leader Story Timeline and how he wanted to close out this career chapter, Corbin began to see how deeply his identity had merged with his position. We talked about the fear of stepping into unknown terrain, of loosening his grip on authority, and of trusting others' vision. He practiced letting his directors present their new strategies. He started asking versus telling in leadership meetings. He let himself not know, first for himself, and then in front of others.

He said, "I used to think leadership meant knowing. Now I'm realizing it means making space for others to know, too."

The Flourishing Terrain
High Connection × High Identity Clarity

Leaders in the flourishing meadow thrive in alignment, are rooted in a clear, evolving sense of self and lead with connection and purpose. Their identity clarity fuels their relationships; their relationships reinforce their growth

The flourishing meadow is not an arrival point—it is a cultivated landscape. Here the leader's identity is no longer split between role and story of self and others' perceptions. They lead from inner congruence, grounded clarity, and emotional presence. Connection flows in all directions: to self, to others, and to purpose. Values are clear and prioritized. But make no mistake:

the meadow is not idyllic ease. It is tended. Weeded. Watched.

Especially the cacao trees. It grows because the leader knows what to nourish—and what to prune.

Unlike the other terrains, the meadow is not defined by overdoing or hyper-attention but by balanced, consistent practice. This leader is not unfamiliar with the other languishing terrains and has even passed through seasons of swamp, wasteland, or petrified forest. They've processed the terrain of identity distortion and now lead from integration—one where boundaries protect energy, values filter decisions, and relationships are collaborative, not consuming.

Flourishing meadow leaders are clear but not rigid. They are emotionally available but not enmeshed. Their confidence doesn't come from knowing everything—it comes from knowing who they are, even when things are uncertain.

The flourishing meadow is not a destination but a constantly evolving and maturing ecosystem—one that requires attention, boundaries, and self-awareness to sustain because identity clarity and connection are prioritized, not passive.

IDENTITY CLARITY DYNAMICS

- **The self is known, content, and stable.**
- Leader identity is defined by purpose, not position
- "I am not the role—but I express who I am through it"
- Identity is rooted but open to feedback and growth
- Identity is reinforced by connection, not lost in it
- What others see matches what the leader feels inside
- Leads from inner clarity, not reaction
- Knows when to engage and when to pause
- Offers presence, not just productivity
- Balances truth and care in communication
- Nurtures others without disappearing in the process

CONNECTION DYNAMICS

- **Connection is a top priority but not consuming.**
- Leads from clarity, not control; able to flex without losing self
- Sets and maintains healthy boundaries with consistency and grace
- Delegates with trust, empowering others without micromanaging

- Takes time for visioning and meaning-making, not just delivery
- Communicates transparently and courageously
- Owns missteps without shame and adapts with integrity

PERFORMANCE AND INFLUENCE

- Practices sustainable rhythms of work, rest, reflection, and action
- Makes decisions aligned with both values and strategic priorities
- Leads with vision, intention, and integrity
- Work is both meaningful and impactful—driven by purpose, not performance alone
- Has credible influence grounded in authenticity and trust
- Makes values-based decisions, even under pressure
- Inspires others through coherence, not charisma alone
- Seen as both competent and deeply human—respected and trusted

THE FLOURISHING MEADOW CASE STUDY: NIA

Nia had led through seasons of nearly every inner terrain. Her 20-year career in tech had included burnout, reinvention, and more than one reckoning with identity. She'd learned to lead in environments that rewarded speed over depth and charisma over congruence—and she'd survived, often by overfunctioning. But when she stepped into her role as VP of Product & People at a global tech firm, she brought with her something different.

She didn't hustle for credibility. She didn't overexplain. She didn't perform. She arrived rooted.

Nia's leadership wasn't accidental—it was cultivated.

Note: I reached out to Nia after attending her session at a conference. I was impressed by her clear conviction that developing people is the heartbeat of an organization.

"I've done the other versions of leadership—the heroic one. The hustle one. The I'll-fix-it-myself one. I'm not doing that anymore."

Nia now led from the flourishing meadow—a terrain where identity and connection coexisted without distortion. Her presence was steady and available. On one of our virtual calls she told me, "I don't build for optics anymore. I build for alignment. And if I can't bring my whole self into the room, it's probably not a room I need to stay in."

She didn't say so but based on our interactions, I imagined that her colleagues would describe her as *calm but not passive, clear but not controlling.* I've attended meetings with leaders rooted in the flourishing meadow like Nia and would surmise that her team meetings include space for pause and she reminds others to hold calendar space for deep thinking time.

What makes Nia a flourishing meadow leader isn't perfection. It's *intentionality.* She had boundaries, but they weren't defensive. She had conviction, but she didn't cling to it when the data changed. She protected her own sustainability as a form of leadership modeling, not just personal wellness.

Nia had walked through the wasteland—she knew depletion. She had faced down the inner critic of the swamp. And she had done the excavation work so now she leads from wholeness.

She didn't view her position as proof of value. It was a platform for influence—and she treated it with stewardship, not entitlement.

"The meadow isn't easy," she reflected. "It just means I've done the inner weeding, as you call it. I know who I am, and I know what nourishes me. From here, I don't have to grip anything. I can grow and help others grow too."

YOUR TERRAIN TYPE

Do you see yourself and your leadership in the swamp, wasteland, petrified forest or flourishing meadow? Again, your terrain could be a unique blend of two types.

My current leader terrain most reflects the types:

_____ and _____

And maybe your inner terrain is a different terrain type all together. This is your journey, and you can use the tools however they work best for you!

MEASURE YOUR PERIMETER

We're project scoping so you'll know which materials you need for excavation and maintenance. We need a baseline so we can chart your progress!

Now that you've had a chance to consider your own inner terrain type and you're looking at your terrain from higher elevation. What do you notice about the scope and perimeter of your current leader terrain? Maybe you see a few dry or bogged patches and maybe the whole thing is fire-scorched.

Circle the word that best reflects the size of your current inner self-as-leader toxic terrain:

NONE	SMALL	MODER-ATE	FAIRLY LARGE	LARGE	MASSIVE

Circle the word that best captures how much work you estimate the clean-up process requires to recover your inner leadership terrain for flourishing:

EASY	NOT TOO DIFFI-CULT	SOME-WHAT DIFFI-CULT	DIFFICULT	VERY DIFFI-CULT	IMPOSSI-BLE

Even if your inner leader terrain is not completely wasteland-barren, swamp, or petrified, catching those overgrown patches of avoidance or waterlogs of competing demands as soon as possible gives you a significant advantage in preventing further damage.

Perhaps you circled "very difficult" or "impossible" because it feels like the entire landscape of your leader's soul and self is desolate, overgrown, or charred beyond recognition. Maybe you've forgotten your self-as-leader roots entirely. It's hard to imagine seeing sprouts of life anywhere because it's a mess. Far-from-your-best. And worse, far-from-your-hoped-for.

It might be that your current self-as-leader landscape lacks meaning and fulfillment. You even have "high producing yields" (farm girl speak) for performance and outcomes. Others would describe your leadership as empowering and collaborative with a foundation of integrity. Everyone seems happy with you.

Except for you.

You are not alone and all is not lost! Many other leaders have been in the exact same situation, afraid to talk about it, feeling alone. They used the exact tools I'm showing you next to start reclaiming their inner leader land.

I have some regrets about seasons of wasteland denial and how I attempted to tarp my growing barren terrain—which I'll share more about later. But I've chosen to let those fuel me forward. And this book is a product of that season— in hopes that my frenetic seed-scattering lessons coupled with the insights of the many leaders I have supported equip your Leading Becomes You pursuits.

As you gauge the level of your terrain reclamation, know that it's not going to stay that way. There's no job too big. There is no timeline.

And don't forget to honor the amazing work you've done so far! You stepped into the uncomfortable but important work of clarifying the magnitude and type of your inner leader terrain. Don't miss the good stuff. Your courageous, wholehearted, gritty leader self is getting stronger.

Nice job staying honest and digging deep.

I imagine you dragging your booted toe across the ground making a long line in the dirt.

While holding a chocolate bar.

Reclaiming your leader terrain.

No more waste coming in.

No more good soil going out.

Soren Kierkegaard said, "In the telling of our life stories, we become responsible for our lives." If you want someone to authentically follow you, you must follow your authentic leadership field guide.

Your leader becoming you is showing.

CHAPTER RECAP

☐ *Leadership terrain challenges emerge in different ways*: Overuse, neglect, misalignment. Just as environmental wastelands result from depletion or pollution, leadership wastelands form when clarity, vision, and authenticity erode over time.

☐ *There are four different types of leadership terrain challenges (two types of petrified forest, wasteland, swamp)*: Knowing your top type or two helps you focus on reclamation.

☐ *Denial fuels the toxic terrain contributors, but awareness starts the reclamation*: You're still here, which means you've kicked denial to the curb.

☐ *Measuring the scope of the terrain provides clarity for recovery*: Your self-as-leader has assessed if your wasteland is emerging, moderate, or severe and you know what is required to restore balance and flourishing. Nice job!

☐ *Every buried, scattered, petrified terrain can be revived with intentional action, namely the process I'm giving you*: No matter the size or severity of rocky or eroded terrain, you can reclaim your self-as-leader flourishing landscape.

LEADING BECOMES YOU BREAKTHROUGHS

In the following space, take a few moments to write notes for what resonated with you from this chapter.

What connections are you making between your mindset and emotional awareness and the terrain types that resonate?

Which internal terrain contributors do you recognize for yourself?

"The purpose of pruning is to improve the quality of the roses, not to hurt the bush."

— Florence Littauer

"…at the end of the day, you should smell like dirt."

— Margaret Atwood

CHAPTER 9

WHEN LEADERS ACCEPT

Is it Me? Is it Them?
Is it Us?

So far, you've taken a courageous look at the full terrain scope of your leader life. You've stepped into mindset and emotional awareness, and you've taken stock of where things flourish—and where they don't. Awareness alone doesn't change us—it simply lets us meet ourselves. Your thinking and emotional awareness was your first important phase, but if we stop there, awareness-only can easily turn into overthinking, avoidance, or a push to "fix" ourselves and perform even harder for the wrong reasons. The next phase, acceptance, gives awareness a place to land. It makes room for whatever the size of terrain might be—and the imperfections, contradictions, and growth potential it holds. In this chapter, we take acceptance to the next level. Acceptance allows your hard-earned awareness to take root. Acknowledging impact—on you. By you.

But it's not a chapter for blaming self or others. It's a chapter for bravery—that gritty fiber you've already been using to name internal beliefs, narratives, and behaviors that keep you stuck. Now we're focusing that grit on examining the external systems, relationships, and pressures that reinforce those patterns. This is where leaders begin to take full, fierce responsibility—not for everything that happened, but for everything that can change.

Acceptance: the phase where leaders allow themselves to see it all and pick a better pot with clear awareness why you can't stay where you are.

THE INVITATION

Acceptance is not passive. Nor is it letting yourself off the hook. It's looking your self-as-leader squarely in the eye and saying, *"This is what's here. And I'm not afraid or ashamed of it anymore."* Acceptance and awareness go hand-in-hand, but acceptance takes things—yep—a little deeper.

You will gain continued clarity and the freedom that comes from taking off the ill-fitting leader skin that doesn't belong to you and stepping into your own. You've gotten rid of the old pot, trekked your way to clear open space, and scoped the project of your inner leader terrain. Here, you will come face to face more specifically with what's been fueling the unhealthy terrain you've scoped. We just need to make sure you aren't planting your self-as-leader in pots that are still too small or trapped on some grocery store pallet with little chance of survival.

We're going to specifically acknowledge and map the two aspects of critical contributors that shape your self-as-leader terrain:

Internal contributors: You've gotten clarity on many of these including reflex thoughts, deep beliefs, stories, scripts, coping styles, hidden fears and emotion patterns, identity distortions. In this chapter we will match internal contributors to terrain types of wasteland, swamp and petrified forest for deeper awareness and informed acceptance.

External contributors: Outside influences in your work, role goodness-of-fit factors, organizational culture, inherited leader expectations, role pressures, and environmental constraints are terrain contributors that can erode and destroy a leader terrain or rather hydrate and nourish. You don't have control of most of these but they intersect with your internal contributors for languishing or flourishing.

Leaders land in stagnation, disillusionment, defensiveness, or burnout from a combination of contributors. When leader terrains are not intentionally and explicitly considered, it's not only the leader who is negatively impacted; the team and the organization lose too.

This acceptance phase applies not only to individual leaders but also to teams, and organizations, when they collectively acknowledges the ways they've adapted, masked, or disconnected to survive. Flourishing meadow teams and organizations create space for honest reckoning—opening the door to shared healing, deeper trust, and the possibility of rebuilding a culture where authenticity is not only allowed but expected and embraced.

For your self-as-leader, acceptance doesn't just soothe the unhealthy thinking and emotion traps—it keeps your self-as-leader identity organized. Psychological research links acceptance with greater identity clarity, because it allows individuals to integrate their full range of traits, emotions, strengths, growth edges, and contradictions into a stable self-concept.[41] This process began with your Leader Story Timeline. Your awareness to acceptance coherence becomes a touchstone for clarity in your day-to-day action and presence. Acceptance also fuels your connection dimension: leaders who welcome their own unsavories are more available to others, less reactive, and more trustworthy in relationship, personally and professionally.[42]

In the acceptance phase, the goal is figuring out where the leaks, toxins, or erosion are specifically sourced in your inner self-as-leader terrain so you can build your "stay rooted" prevention plan in the final phase of authentic activation. The interaction of internal and external contributors to your inner leader terrain can create lots of variation in challenging terrains. The framework of the Leading Becomes You approach prioritizes the three challenging terrains (swamp, wasteland, petrified forest) based on identity clarity meets connection because the internal contributors are within your control to change and grow.

Your terrain analysis from the previous chapter may have positioned you firmly in swamp, wasteland, or petrified forest. Or maybe your terrain felt more like a blend of all three. That's fine! I've given you a framework to personalize. Make it your own.

Your work in this chapter collects and acknowledges your deeper internal contributors in tandem with the mindset and emotional patterns you discovered in the awareness phase. Remember the iceberg. Those mental and emotional habits that you've identified are often reflected in your day-to-day mindset and impact your leadership effectiveness for good or bad or both.

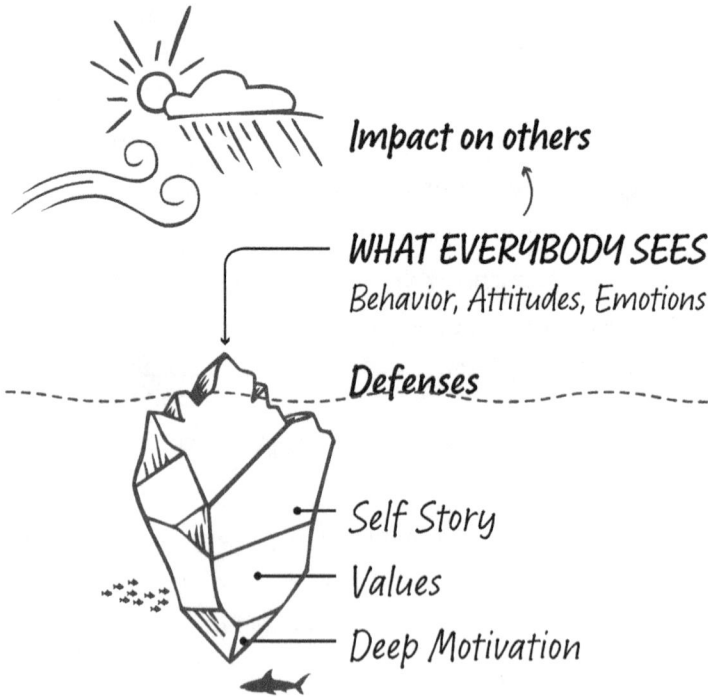

Impact on others

WHAT EVERYBODY SEES
Behavior, Attitudes, Emotions

Defenses

Self Story
Values
Deep Motivation

Your new mindset and emotional awareness inform much of what's above the water line. Those visible attitudes, behaviors, and responses are the *signals* that hint at what's going on below the surface. Beneath the water line is the interaction between your core motivations and those deeper inner contributors (those hard-wired and well-practiced deep beliefs about self and others based on personal history, traumatic situations, residual fears, and core motivations, which we also map to the terrain types). The external weather pattern and climate around the iceberg—culture, roles, demands, norms— both above and below the surface, impact the lifespan of the iceberg, (which, I learned, can be as long as 3,000 years!).

LEAD LIKE A TREE

Let's move from ocean-dwelling iceberg back to land. Imagine that you and your leadership are a tree. Your day-to-day mindset and emotion habits are the visible branches and leaves. Some may need pruned by awareness to allow others to grow. Some branches or limbs may be dead and need removal via the consistent neural rewiring thanks to the neuroplasticity I mentioned earlier. For your tree of self-as-leader, this chapter considers the deeper roots that ground the tree. Roots, like the unseen parts of the iceberg, are the source and foundation.

If the roots aren't healthy, no amount of trimming or pruning will bring health. Awareness allowed you to see yourself honestly, and acceptance will allow you to simply welcome what you see.

THE DEEPER

Now that you've identified your inner terrain type, I'm inviting you to excavate more deeply as we revisit each terrain and the more specific internal and external contributors for each. This is next level excavation. Just like the awareness phase, it doesn't mean that you won't have an internal or external contributor from multiple terrains that may have migrated to yours. Even if you identified one solid terrain type for yourself, I recommend reading through all of them to build your working contributors list.

For each terrain type deep dive, I'm including:

- Terrain impact
- Terrain-specific contributors
- Core Motivations
- Potential deeper debris for each terrain
- Emotional awareness takeaways
- Terrain specific reflection

Working backwards from contributor impact can also illuminate growth edges. Just like a 360-degree assessment, which includes performance feedback from various perspectives of an employee's work, looking at outcomes from internal and external terrain contributors, gives us another terrain baseline.

As you read each type, consider any resonance with your self-as-leader. Note those words or phrases in the space provided below each wasteland type.

The Swamp Terrain

RECAP

The swamp happens when low identity clarity meets low connection. A lower-severity inner swamp terrain indicates a leader with some sense of disconnection from purpose and authentic connection to self and others. At its most severe, the swamp swallows a leader's sense of self, leaving them adrift, masked, and performing from a hollowed identity. The swamp is murky with no clear path, only endless emotional maneuvering. Leaders here may not realize they are over-adapting to every situation to stay afloat Beneath it all, they don't know who they are or if or where they truly belong.

Some leaders in the swamp may present as disengaged or defeated, while others seem highly responsive—but only superficially. There is little true and authentic expression or conviction, and a lot of emotional and relational shape-shifting. Identity is either hidden, inflated, or eroded by lack of intentional deep inner business.

IMPACT

The swamp's toll is subtle but can be deeply corrosive. Teams led by swamp-trapped leaders struggle with inconsistency, vague direction, and mixed emotional cues. The leader may avoid conflict or authenticity, defaulting to emotional avoidance or passive compliance. Over time, teams grow unsure of priorities, trust erodes, and meaningful progress stagnates. Because the leader is caught in shape-shifting moral ambiguity, hyperfocus on self, or undetected systemic misalignment, their team operates without a stable purposed compass. At worst, the leader gaslights or splits team members. When values are consistently compromised or go unspoken, team members begin to question not only the direction of the work, but the integrity of the space itself. Silence becomes a survival mechanism.

An organization led by swamped leaders begins to normalize foggy expectations and diluted leadership, masking deeper issues with surface politeness or adaptive over-responsiveness. This terrain looks past unethical, disrespectful, and low-insight behavior to allow it to persist unchecked— eroding both internal culture and external credibility. Mission statements sound hollow. Conflicts fester unaddressed. Morale is often low but hard to measure because those still present have numbed themselves just to stay.

TWO SIGNIFICANT INTERNAL CONTRIBUTORS

1. **Emotional disorientation** arises when a leader lacks both an internal compass (identity clarity) and a secure sense of relational belonging (connection to others, values, or purpose). Without a grounded self-concept, leaders become prone to identity confusion, emotional volatility, or numbing—cycling between overreaction and performative, masked "all is well" veneering interpersonal shutdown.

The swamp-trapped terrain leader may find themselves internally fragmented—not because they lack skill, but because they lack stable self-referencing anchors for decision-making, integrity, or meaning. Their emotional experience becomes completely context-contingent. Leadership decisions feel reactive, often dependent on the leader's barometer of their success. Silence often replaces engagement, or they echo the loudest voice in the room because they are unsure of their own. This disorientation is not simply burnout—it is existential disconnection. The inner fog obscures values, boundaries, and vision, often leading to emotional exhaustion, disengagement, or internalized shame.[43]

My clinical specialization in trauma and Post-Traumatic Stress Disorder (PTSD) informs my reference here to the potential impact of relationship *attachment* on a leader's fragmented identity. Attachment theory explains how our early relationships with caregivers shape the way we connect with others, handle emotions, and seek security in our adult relationships—including at work. Secure or insecure attachment impacts a leader's capacity for both identity clarity and connection. Leaders who have not examined or integrated their early attachment experiences may unconsciously replay those insecure patterns—such as avoidance, overfunctioning, or seeking excessive validation—within their professional relationships.[44]

In leadership, this emotional fragmentation undermines not just the leader's presence, but trust in their own voice.

2. *Chameleonism* describes the swamp terrain leader's attempt to maintain influence and belonging through constant adaptation to others' expectations, rather than through anchored authenticity: "I just try to be what everyone needs. That's what a good leader does, right?" Lacking identity clarity, the leader constructs a flexible facade—changing tone, language, appearance, focus, or emotional expression to fit each conversation, meeting, event, or situation. On the surface, they appear charismatic, agreeable, or even well-liked. But underneath lies the tandem contributor of emotional disorientation mired in fear of rejection, insecurity, and self-betrayal.

This coping strategy often masks itself as emotional intelligence or diplomacy. And they likely have high emotional intelligence, but high emotional acuity doesn't necessarily translate to healthy use. Ponzi schemes and other scams rely on identifying and exploiting emotional vulnerabilities. In fact, I fell prey to one publishing this book. For leaders with high emotional intelligence, this capacity may serve as a protective survival strategy born from low self-insight and the overvaluation of harmony at the cost of alignment.

This leads to blurred boundaries, weak decision-making, and superficial relationships where team members feel manipulated, not inspired. The connection feels false and trust erodes quietly.[45]

The result is leadership that avoids confrontation, over-accommodates, over-promises and under-delivers, and shape-shifts, sacrificing belonging for approval.

Together, emotional disorientation and chameleonism trap leaders in the swamp terrain of uncertainty and relational distortion. Their leadership becomes fogged by ambiguity and performance, rather than rooted in self or truth. The leader may still be seen—but not truly known.

TOP 10 EXTERNAL | ORGANIZATIONAL CONTRIBUTORS

- Ethical fog: Values are vague, violated, or quietly abandoned
- Leadership gaslighting: Mixed messages or public praise with private blame leading to identity confusion
- Mission drift: Purpose shifts toward profit or optics with no explanation
- Emotionally toxic culture: Passive aggression, unspoken tension, triangulation, or avoidance
- Role ambiguity or scope creep: Constantly reassigned new tasks without clarity or recognition
- Suppressive norms: "Don't rock the boat," "Stay positive," or "Be loyal," even when harm is occurring
- Lack of feedback, recognition, or growth pathways: Leaders feel unseen and slowly emotionally disappear
- Ethical gray zones with no clear accountability
- Power dynamics that punish dissent or reward compliance
- Culture and tolerance of moral compromise framed as pragmatism

PROBLEMATIC DEEP BELIEFS IN THE SWAMP

- "I'm supposed to know who I am by now—so I'll pretend I do."
- "If I show doubt or struggle or don't perform, I'll be exposed as unfit."
- "My voice doesn't matter here—best to stay quiet."
- "I've played so many roles, I'm not sure there's anything real underneath."

CORE MOTIVATION

- To be seen and valued, recognized as relevant, craving validation
- To be seen as significant, authentic, deeply understood, connected to deep meaning and insight shared by others
- To maintain equilibrium both internally and externally, to avoid disruption

POTENTIAL DEEPER DEBRIS

- Attachment trauma or early relational inconsistency: Caregivers may have been emotionally unpredictable, overly enmeshed, or absent—leading to difficulty forming a cohesive sense of self.
- Role-shaped identity without reflection: The leader was molded to meet others' expectations (e.g., "the winner," "the reliable one") and never invited to ask, "Who am I beneath the role?"
- Repeated invalidation of personal needs: Environments that rewarded emotional suppression.
- Boundary violations: Situations where the leader was expected to carry emotional labor for others (e.g., in families with addiction or mental illness), creating chronic self-erasure.
- Workplace experiences of gaslighting, micromanagement, or moral confusion: These lead to inner paralysis and self-doubt or, with low insight, become adopted as norms.

SWAMP EMOTIONAL AWARENESS TAKEAWAY

Recognizing and validating grief, confusion, and suppressed ethical or misalignment tension. Learning to move from silence to honest naming.

SWAMP REFLECTION QUESTIONS

- Who am I when I stop performing?
- What would happen if I allowed myself more "being" versus "doing?"
- What part of me is lost, asking to be recovered, and what would it take to reclaim it?
- What would I say or do if I believed my values still had foundational meaning for me and my leadership?
- Who is modeling integrity that I can move toward or mirror?

The Wasteland Terrain

RECAP

Leaders in the wasteland terrain are overly attuned, more like hyperconnected, to others' agendas, feedback, and expectations—but lack a clear internal compass. This terrain is shaped by low identity clarity and high connection. Their leadership is shaped by performance and pressure, not presence. They are driven by the belief that any visible flaw will invalidate their worth. This leader doesn't trust that they can be fully human and still be respected. So they hide behind overfunctioning and over-preparing. The result is isolation: They are seen for their output, but not their own truth. A mild wasteland terrain resembles dry, cracked earth—parched but not yet barren. The leader functions, delivers, and connects, but vitality is diminished. The most severe wasteland is a scorched desert of overexposed, overcommitted survival. These leaders can keep up a polished and productive appearance—but are quietly ruled by fear, frantically tarping visible wasteland with their interior leader motivation, and trapped by performance pressure, approval addiction, and a persistent need for external validation. Their calendars are full, but their inner world is drained. They work hard to maintain credibility and trust—but underneath, they fear they're not getting it right or their faults and foibles will be found out.

IMPACT

On the surface, the wasteland leader looks ideal—productive, helpful, and engaged. But their team experiences emotional dissonance. Despite the leader's output, the team senses emotional unavailability, fragility, and a lack of grounding. Team members may mirror the perfectionistic culture, striving to avoid mistakes or to impress. This can set up unhealthy competition and insecurity. Psychological safety erodes—not due to hostility, but because no one feels safe to be human. Performance remains high until burnout from workload and impossible expectations takes hold. Quiet quitting, attrition, and simmering disconnection may appear.

At the organizational level, overfunctioning becomes the norm. Growth is unsustainable, and emotional health declines, even though there is lots of conversation and connection from endless meetings and well-intended initiatives, including development of the team. Direction has faded into a haze of busyness that isn't grounded in singular purpose and focus. Resources are scattered among varied priorities. Boundaries get blurred as leaders rescue without accountability and hard conversations don't happen. People depend on wasteland leaders to manage emotions. Resilience building opportunities get lost to caretaking and overfunctioning.

TWO SIGNIFICANT INTERNAL CONTRIBUTORS

1. ***Contingent self-worth and the productivity-performance identity trap:*** At the core of the wasteland terrain lies the internalized belief that one's value is directly tied to output and other-referenced approval. Leaders here

often exhibit contingent self-worth, a psychological pattern in which self-esteem fluctuates based on achievements or social approval. These leaders over-identify with their ability to meet others' expectations and suppress personal needs or emotions in the name of performance. The resulting pattern is overfunctioning, perfectionistic productivity, and emotional numbness. This is caused by low identity clarity (what do I need? what are my *own* foundational self-as-leader premises?) and hyper-connection to others' perceived agendas and purposes. All the while there is missed connection from authentic relationship due to performance-fueled burnout. This dynamic fuels unhealthy workaholism and leads to the "hollowing out of self beneath the armor of competence."[46]

2. **Imposter phenomenon, inner critic dominance, and perfection-ism-as-protection:** Many leaders in the wasteland suffer from impostor phenomenon—a persistent internal experience of feeling like a fraud despite significant external success.[47] Even when praised or promoted, a leader in the wasteland feels undeserving, anticipating exposure or failure. Their self-doubt fuels perfectionistic overfunctioning and an exaggerated fear of failure.

Recent studies have found imposter experiences to be especially prevalent among high-achieving professionals and organizational leaders. These leaders often develop a harsh inner critic, an inner "voice" keeping front and center the leader's strict self-evaluating deep beliefs and perfectionistic self-scrutiny. The inner critic thrives in performance-driven cultures, reinforcing anxiety, self-era-sure, and emotional exhaustion. Naming my inner critic Edna and personifying her (i.e., visualizing her putting down her loudspeaker and moving to the couch with a bowl of popcorn) has helped me navigate her overcommitted protection.

Perfectionism in this context is a defensive strategy (remember those defenses at the water line of the iceberg) to manage fear and avoid shame. Perfectionism-as-protection is common in environments where mistakes are punished or where leaders feel they must prove themselves continuously. As Brené Brown reminds us, perfectionism is not self-improvement but a shield to avoid vulnerability and judgment.[48]

This dynamic often originates from early systems—family, school, or early career cultures—that rewarded caretaking or overachievement. Over time, the leader's identity fuses with performance. Rest becomes synonymous with laziness, and delegation triggers guilt. There is no sustainable rhythm—only acceleration.

Neurologically, leaders operating from this mindset often override internal cues for rest or reflection due to a chronically activated stress response. Emotionally, the leader may feel increasingly numb or resentful but continue working harder, believing that exhaustion is the price of being enough.

Alternatively, a leader in the wasteland may resort to self-sabotage. It feels like a confusing disconnect between where you want to go and where you are but may explain why the terrain feels so desolate despite your attempts to cultivate it. The self-sabotage cycle is self-reinforcing—when you undermine your own success, it reinforces the negative core belief that success is not possible or you don't deserve it. Big awareness muscles are required, and you've been growing them!

TOP 10 EXTERNAL | ORGANIZATIONAL CONTRIBUTORS

- Workload normalization: Chronic overwork seen as standard or heroic, like a badge of honor
- Constant availability culture: Leaders are expected to be always on, emailing at all hours, no separation of work from personal life; "What are boundaries?"

- Invisible expectations of perfection: Excellence is assumed, support is absent
- Lack of psychological safety: Speaking honestly about struggles, workload, or burnout is taboo
- Recognition based only on output: Productivity replaces purpose
- No boundary culture: Self-sacrifice expected, rest seen as weakness
- Praise for overcommitment: Identity becomes fused with deliverables
- Reactive leadership cycles: Constant urgency displaces meaning
- Misalignment between team and organizational purpose: High external connection, no internal alignment
- Underdeveloped succession or delegation structures: Leads to chronic overload

PROBLEMATIC DEEP BELIEFS IN THE WASTELAND

- "If I'm not perfect, I'll lose credibility."
- "They only trust me when I perform."
- "I can't let others see my uncertainty, mistakes, weaknesses."
- "If I stop, everything will fall apart."
- "I am only valuable when I am useful."

CORE MOTIVATION

- To be essentially needed by others, known for what they do on behalf of
- To have solid ground and solid inner terrain, people, plans and systems to trust
- To have open possibilities, options, opportunities, expansion

POTENTIAL DEEPER DEBRIS

• Chronic people-pleasing or fawning responses: Often rooted in early relationships where love was conditional on performance, usefulness, or perfection

• Burnout trauma or cumulative moral injury: This shows up in caregiving, healthcare, nonprofit, or mission-driven professions where leaders feel they must serve beyond their capacity

• Unprocessed grief or loss of self: Career success that came at the cost of identity development, personal relationships, or meaning

• Traumatic systemic impact of always being needed: Leaders may have been cast in caretaker roles early on and learned to overextend to feel safe or included

• Betrayal trauma: Situations where the leader deeply invested in a mission or system that ultimately devalued or exploited them

WASTELAND EMOTIONAL AWARENESS TAKEAWAY

Recognizing shame, overfunctioning, and perfectionism as avoidance strategies rather than virtues. Reconnect to vulnerable authenticity and creativity.

WASTELAND REFLECTION QUESTIONS

• What would change if I led from wholeness rather than perfection?

• What's something I used to love about leading that I no longer feel connected to?

• How would I lead if rest were a priority, not a reward?

• Where am I managing perception rather than leading with true connection?

• When do I stay silent to maintain safety or polished presence?

The Petrified Forest Terrain

RECAP

The leader trapped in the petrified forest inner terrain is preserved in perceived success. They have a strong, often historic leader identity built on recognition, results, or power, but these are now frozen in that form. At a lower intensity, the inner terrain impact is a motionless grove—still, orderly, fortified by tradition. In its most hardened form, the forest is fossilized with trees turned to stone, growth halted, air stagnant. The petrified forest-trapped leader clings to an ossified identity, silencing questions with over-reliance on legacy authority and resistance to change. To grow would mean shedding old identity scaffolding, and that feels like loss.

These leaders may appear competent and decisive, but their rigidity stifles the organization. They confuse certainty with strength, and feedback becomes a threat rather than insight. They are rarely questioned—and often deeply alone. To grow would mean shedding their well-known and safe scaffolding of self, and that feels like loss, threat, or even betrayal of past success.

Like the other terrains, the leader trapped with a petrified inner self-as-leader may appear competent, decisive, and powerful, but their rigidity stifles the ecosystem around them. But beneath the armor of certainty lies a very human experience: fear of irrelevance, a loneliness of leadership, and the challenge to defossilize, replenish, and recover a green, responsive, and fluid self-as-leader that no longer fits.

IMPACT

The team learns to comply and color in the lines rather than contribute or challenge. They become cautious or disengaged, fearing that any deviation will be snapped back into line. Innovation slows because ideas that don't match the leader's mental model are dismissed outright. Minor decisions require layers of approval. People stop offering honest opinions and begin managing the leader instead. Culture is relegated to just getting the work done and psychological safety erodes.

Organizations with too much petrified leader influence lose morale and their adaptive edge and become out of sync. Policies are preeminent and projects stall because time is spent seeking permission more than making progress. The cascading effect shows up when departments start mirroring defensiveness of "this way" and silos are fortified. Talented employees underfunction or leave for growth-fueled systems. The organization becomes stagnant, the culture is brittle, and morale is non-existent, frozen by lack of adaptability and inspiration. What could have been an enduring legacy becomes a culture of fear, passivity, compliance, and eventually irrelevance.

TWO INTERNAL CONTRIBUTORS

1. *Role-identity fusion* occurs when a leader's sense of self becomes rigidly and exclusively defined by their position, title, or professional identity. This internal fusion creates a powerful attachment to authority and legacy— so much so that change, feedback, or humility can feel like personal erasure. The leader no longer sees their role as something they occupy—they see it as something they are.

Psychologically, role-identity fusion reflects what researchers describe as identity foreclosure. This term describes what happens when someone commits to a fixed identity someone else or the situation has assigned to them without meaningful exploration or evolution. Originally studied as a development process in adolescence, identity foreclosure also happens in adulthood, especially in high-stakes roles that have been socially rewarded but never consciously examined. In leadership, this results in defensiveness, control, and fear of irrelevance. Leaders operating from this mindset often reject new perspectives, overprotect their authority, and confuse leadership with dominance rather than development.[49]

This fusion is rarely conscious. It often forms over decades of affirmation, success, and cultural reinforcement. But eventually, the role that once offered purpose becomes a prison.

2. **Narrative control:** In the context of leadership, *narrative control* refers to the tendency of some leaders to maintain tight psychological and communicative control over the organizational story, strategic direction, or leadership narrative as a way to reinforce identity, preserve authority, and avoid vulnerability. This behavioral leader stance is linked to the psychological need to stabilize a self-image rooted in expertise or positional dominance. Leaders in this pattern often resist co-creation, downplay dissenting perspectives, and avoid admitting uncertainty. Sometimes the pattern is due to arrogance, but other times it is rooted in fear that disrupting the narrative threatens the other internal contributor of role-identity fusion.

Also in the mix is *self-enhancement bias,* which illustrates how high-status people inflate their own contribution and resist contradictory feedback to maintain esteem. This bias overlaps with identity foreclosure. Together, the combination hardens and petrifies the leader's identity and impact.[50]

TOP 10 EXTERNAL | ORGANIZATIONAL CONTRIBUTORS

- Hero leadership culture: Reveres individual authority, resists distributed leadership

- Rigid structures and hierarchies: Discourages feedback or bottom-up innovation
- Status-driven recognition systems: Rewards tenure and status quo over innovation and frontline expertise
- Legacy entrenchment: Prior successes overshadow new possibilities
- Low value on collaboration: Co-creation and diversity of thought discouraged
- Punitive or competitive peer culture: Risk-taking, new ideas, and vulnerability are perceived as weakness
- Over-reliance on one leader's authority: All roads lead through one gatekeeper
- Absence of feedback loops: Culture is too afraid or too reverent or too locked to challenge
- Micromanagement or narrative control: Subordinates feel stifled
- High formality, low relational warmth: Disconnect between role and relationship, unable to strike appropriate balance for both

PROBLEMATIC DEEP BELIEFS IN PETRIFIED FOREST

- "If I lose control, I lose relevance."
- "Being respected means not showing uncertainty."
- "I have to protect what I've built—no one else will."
- "They only value me for what I've done—not who I am."
- "To change now would mean admitting I was wrong."

CORE MOTIVATION

- To live and lead consistently, aligned from who they are and beliefs around how things should be
- To maintain self-sufficiency, capability, deep knowing and understanding
- To be strong and maintain control, limit vulnerabilities

POTENTIAL DEEPER DEBRIS

- Rewarded stoicism: Family systems, military, or masculine-coded environments that equated emotion with weakness and control with worth
- Post-success stagnation: Leaders who built careers around early excellence but now struggle to adapt as their environment or team changes
- Unresolved humiliation or shame events: Leaders who faced failure or betrayal and responded by armoring up, cutting off connection to stay safe
- Overidentification with legacy: Belief that changing course means erasing a valuable past, so the leader resists evolution
- Historical, personal, professional loneliness or power-induced isolation: They lead from above or behind a mask, unable or unwilling to allow vulnerability.

PETRIFIED FOREST EMOTIONAL AWARENESS TAKEAWAY

Recognizing that emotional detachment, irritation of others' emotional expression, and avoidance of vulnerability limits leader effectiveness and fulfillment. Leader reflection and evolving is essential for maximal impact.

PETRIFIED FOREST REFLECTION QUESTIONS

- What would it mean to be respected without being revered?
- When was the last time I truly changed my mind about something important?
- Where am I protecting my legacy at the expense of relevance or connection?
- Who do I trust enough to challenge me—and do they know that?
- What would happen if I led with curiosity instead of certainty?

The Flourishing Meadow Terrain

RECAP

Leaders in the flourishing meadow terrain do not perform authenticity but rather inhabit it. Their identity is rooted, evolving, and whole. They lead from clarity, connection, and calm authority, offering sustainable influence without sacrificing self. These leaders have typically walked through other terrains—burnout, disillusionment, perfectionism—and done the reflective work to realign. Flourishing is the result of intentional tending.

Rather than relying on role or output to define them, flourishing leaders lead from values and presence. They can move between strategy and empathy, directness and care, ambition and rest. The result is leadership that feels both strong and human—and teams that grow because they are trusted to.

IMPACT

The impact of leading from a flourishing terrain is felt in both performance and presence. Teams led by flourishing leaders are more resilient, more creative, and more psychologically safe. They are healthily challenged knowing they can bring forward bold ideas without fear and that these ideas will be held to meaningful standards. Mistakes are learning moments, not liabilities. Emotional range is welcomed, not suppressed because psychological safety is modeled. Meetings are purposeful.

Because the leader is internally coherent, the organization feels alive and expansive. The organization reflects the leader's coherence—in how decisions are made, how conflict is handled, and how sustainability is prioritized. Communication flows easily across levels and departments with cultural norms of appropriate transparency and trust. Long-term retention improves. Vision is clearer. Burnout is prevented, not just managed. Flourishing becomes a shared rhythm, not just a personal state. People know where they stand and have space to grow. Even missteps become learning soil and the organization evolves with resilience and purpose.

TWO INTERNAL CONTRIBUTORS

In the flourishing meadow, the leader's identity is cohesive, stable, and self-authored—not dependent on role, recognition, or relentless output. This form of integrated identity clarity allows the leader to adapt without distortion and lead without ego entanglement. Unlike leaders in the three toxic terrains, meadow leaders don't need titles or external validation to feel worthy. Their self-concept is strong yet flexible, capable of being challenged without collapse, and open to feedback without defensiveness.

1. ***Identity clarity: Self-concept clarity*** is defined as "the extent to which self-beliefs are clearly and confidently defined, internally consistent, and stable over time." High self-concept clarity is associated with greater emotional regulation, lower susceptibility to burnout, and increased leadership authenticity and presence. Psychologically, these leaders integrate their private and public selves, allowing them to lead with wholeness rather than fragmentation. They embody what Carl Rogers called congruence: being real, vulnerable, and aligned from the inside out. It sounds like leading from the inside out.

2. ***Relational-spiritual congruence: connection to others, values, and the soul of leadership:*** Flourishing meadow leaders exhibit high relational-spiritual congruence—a multidimensional connection to others, to purpose, and to what I'll call bigger-than-me (this may be a relationship with God, the greater human story, moral or philosophical principles). This may show up as dedication to a mission, a deep trust with the people they lead, or even an attunement to divine guidance. This is grounded in the leader's deep sense that leadership is

not self-serving but shared and meaningful. This connection is not codependence or performance for approval but rather rooted in integrity and humility.

I have heard many leaders talk about their experience of "bigger than me" when, for example, they witness the collective achievement of their team accomplishing something extraordinary that one individual could never have achieved alone. Or when they see someone they've mentored surpass their own capabilities. Or when the organization's work brings meaningful impact to a community or industry.

Leaders also describe a deeply personal experience of spiritual transformation. Despite the difficult decisions, navigating conflict and tension, managing complex change, relational-spiritually aware leaders frame the challenges through the lens of service to their team, to their mission, and to stakeholders. They share more significant fulfillment in this focus than personal achievement or advancement and describe a humble realization of the undeniable reality that Bigger-Than-Me opens up an other-focused leadership approach and is also the source of their unique leadership gifts and strengths.

Leader relational-spiritual transformation is connected to significant benefits and rounds out the Leading Becomes You journey in a few important ways:

1. Your leadership relationships and connection become more authentic as you lead from a grounded, truer self-as-leader versus a stagnant or performance-based persona.

2. An expanded relational-spiritual awareness increases empathy for others' journeys, challenges, perspectives, and leadership approaches that differ from your own. This is a domain of emotional intelligence. A bigger-than-me lens reminds me that others' leader terrains are bordering and pollinating mine.

3. You gain capacity to listen and understand how others experience your leadership approach and impact. This is one of the most common take-aways from my leader identity workshops—recognition of how others perceive them.

4. The realization that even the deepest inner investigation, while invaluable and necessary, comes up short. My own growth as a leader has been highly dependent on conversations with others and Other (for me, this is God). In crisis situations, I am not comforted by counsel of one-liners or mantras telling me to exclusively trust my gut or to manifest some-thing from my own will. I'm aware that when big emotions and high-risk, high-stakes situations show up, I can convince myself of some gnarly ideas. For me, finding the answers in myself or relying on others is only one part of the decision pursuit. My internal terrain contributors can get noisy and personally, I need God to help me detangle.

> "I can convince myself of some gnarly ideas.

The spiritual leadership model developed by Louis Fry sees the goal of spiritual leadership as the creation of a workplace characterized by hope, faith, altruistic love, and purpose—not only to enhance productivity but to support the spiritual well-being of both leaders and employees. Fry's model asserts that when individuals feel their work is meaningful and connected to a larger purpose, their motivation, commitment, and performance increase. Spiritual leadership creates environments where people feel seen not just as performers, but as whole human beings.

A related line of work by Dr. Bryan Dik and Dr. Mike Steger (my very first doctoral professor!) highlights the importance of meaning, purpose, and calling in the workplace. Their insights validate the importance of work experienced as calling—a sense of purpose that transcends the self and contributes to the greater good. They have shown how meaningful work is not only psychologically beneficial for the leader but yields *gold* for organizations who prioritize the greater good with outcomes such as higher engagement, resilience, and ethical behavior.[51]

Steger and colleagues developed the Meaning in Work Inventory and Work and Meaning Inventory, which have been used globally to illustrate that meaning at work enhances motivation and reduces burnout. When leaders discover and express their core identity through meaningful work, they flourish—and they help their teams flourish too. I've included the Work and Meaning Inventory in the Resources section (*pg. 343*) for your flourishing self-as-leader toolkit!

Taking this work to real life, many people have natural capacity and skillset to lead. But if they do not feel *called* to pursue leadership, it's probably better that they don't. I can think of several examples where someone's evident talent was tapped for a leadership position. Without consideration and under high pressure to meet the need, they took the job. Sometimes the fallout was costly before they realized formal leadership was not what they wanted and, with relief, returned happily to their individual contributorship role. And of course, sometimes a hesitant new leader surprises themselves with unexpected joy and realization of leading as a great fit.

In the context of leadership, these frameworks all suggest that leaders who cultivate identity clarity and relational-spiritual congruence empower not only their own flourishing but also that of their teams. They help others see their roles as meaningful contributions to something bigger than themselves and model humility, self-awareness, and ethical clarity, creating cultures where dignity, trust, and psychological safety thrive. Spiritual leadership and a purpose of greater good contribute to leadership that is emotionally grounded, ethically anchored, and deeply motivating. Leaders who integrate this focus inspire psychological safety, relational trust, and team resilience—creating cultures where meaning is foundational.

Together, identity clarity and relational-spiritual congruence create fertile conditions for sustainable leadership, innovation, and influence. These leaders are whole—and they help others flourish by leading from that wholeness.

TOP 10 EXTERNAL | ORGANIZATIONAL CONTRIBUTORS

- Mission-values alignment: The organization's core purpose reflects and reinforces leader identity and ethical priorities
- Psychological safety: A culture that supports honest feedback, vulnerability, and relational authenticity at all levels
- Sustainable workload and rhythm: Healthy pace, flexible structures, and built-in recovery practices protect against erosion
- Values-based recognition and rewards: Leaders are affirmed not only for performance outcomes, but for leading with integrity and alignment
- Mutual mentorship and peer learning: Cross-functional support systems encourage growth, wisdom-sharing, and collective development
- Embedded leadership development pathways: Ongoing reflective growth opportunities such as coaching, learning labs, and retreats are normalized
- Integrity-driven decision structures: Transparent policies, ethical frameworks, and consistency across teams protect leader moral grounding
- Co-creation and shared ownership: Leaders are trusted with agency, influence, and meaningful participation in shaping the system
- Whole-person leadership culture: Human identity beyond the role—family, faith, creativity—are welcomed, not compartmentalized

- Purpose-driven rituals and storytelling: Regular reflection on organizational purpose through shared narratives, team rituals, and legacy practices that connect past, present, and future

CORE MOTIVATION

To know and intentionally connect to deepest parts of self via awareness, acceptance, and assimilation—and to translate this to consistent, healthy leadership of self and others.

DEEP BELIEFS OF FLOURISHING MEADOW LEADERS

- "I am enough—and so are the people I lead."
- "I lead best when I am rooted, not rushing."
- "Boundaries are not barriers—they are containers for flourishing."
- "My presence creates more impact than my perfection ever did."

FLOURISHING MEADOW
EMOTIONAL AWARENESS TAKEAWAYS

- Regular self-check-ins to maintain emotional clarity and boundaries
- High emotional literacy: awareness of self and others without over-responsibility
- Comfortable with conflict, feedback, and emotional range
- Willing to rest, recalibrate, and recover without guilt

FLOURISHING MEADOW REFLECTION QUESTIONS

- What practices help me stay anchored to my true self-as-leader when things shift?
- How do I stay connected to the greater good and deeper meaning of leadership?

- Where do I need to re-tend the soil—emotionally, relationally, or soulfully?
- How do I model sustainability, not just talk about it?

Now that we've tackled the terrains, here's a handy quick guide. This can be helpful for your ongoing self-reflection. It's also helpful to consider potential terrain traps for leaders you work with and support.

LEADER TERRAIN QUICK REFERENCE SUMMARY

	Swamp (Lo Identity Clarity × Lo Connection)	**Wasteland** (Lo Identity Clarity × Hi Connection)	**Petrified Forest** (Hi Identity Clarity × Lo Connection)
Identity Clarity & Self-View	• Fragmented or inflated self-concept • Unanchored, reactive identity • Self-worth unclear or inflated • Often self-deceived, not self-aware	• Self-worth tied to output or approval • Other-referenced identity • "I perform; therefore, I matter" • Chameleon self-concept	• Fixed, legacy-based identity • "I am my role" • Resistant to redefinition • Identity fused with past success
Behavior Patterns	• Passive or overly adaptive • Avoids conflict and clarity • Adapts language to survive • Performs for inclusion or hides to avoid scrutiny	• Overcommits and overfunctions • Avoids rest and reflection • High external engagement, low internal alignment • Empathic performance without boundaries	• Controls processes and people • Avoids feedback • Dominates decision-making • Resists innovation or collaboration

Emotional Landscape	• Confused, emotionally fogged • Shame, numbness, moral fatigue • Emotionally reactive or disengaged	• Anxious, depleted, emotionally flat • Shame under productivity • Fear of slowing down or saying no	• Rigid emotional control • Defensiveness, pride, superiority • Feels grief and fear of irrelevance underneath
Relational Dynamics	• Superficial or inconsistent connections • May appear charismatic but lacks depth • Withholds needs and authenticity • Unseen or misunderstood by others	• Highly attuned to others' needs • May become enmeshed or overly responsible • Disconnected from self • Well-liked but personally lonely	• Emotionally distant or intimidating • Rarely shows vulnerability • Creates cultures of compliance • Limited emotional safety or trust
Performance & Influence	• Disengaged or erratic • Output inconsistent • Team may be confused or mistrustful • Role often sustained by reputation, not results	• High activity, low vitality • Effective but unsustainable • Team dependent but uninspired • Output without ownership or innovation	• Predictable execution • Teams stagnate under rigid control • Innovation and dissent suppressed • Long-term legacy at risk of irrelevance
Internal Contributors	• Emotional disorientation • Ego chameleonism	• Self-worth as productivity • Recovery avoidance	• Role-identity fusion • Legacy lock-in
Key Emotional Theme	*"I don't know who I am, and I don't feel like I belong."*	*"I'm doing everything, but I've lost myself in the doing."*	*"If I evolve, I might lose who I've been—and my power."*

Having read through the three languishing terrains and the flourishing terrain, take a moment with your notebook and your chocolate to capture your thoughts regarding how any of these show up in your current self-as-leader terrain. Don't forget the flourishing terrain good stuff that you see and want to nurture too!

_____ BONUS TOOL _____

The following list includes common terrain contributors I've collected from my work with leaders—just to give you more ideas of sneaky contributors that can wreak havoc on your leader terrain. They blend thinking, emotion, and response traps as what's visible above the water line. Since you've looked at both internal and external terrain contributors, you can consider these examples from two perspectives: which ones are internal deep beliefs, tentacled reflex thoughts, emotional habits. And how might these be reinforced or previously unrecognized cultural norms on my team or in my organization.

I've also included the flourishing meadow opportunity which translates perfectly to goals for growth—choosing and test-driving a different response is how you assimilate!

TERRAIN-TRAPPING PATTERN	FLOURISHING MEADOW OPPORTUNITY
Not voicing an opinion or altering how you show up to be more "likeable"	Leading from honest wholeness, trusting that authenticity builds real connection. Speak one small (seemingly risky) opinion this week
Taking responsibility for others' emotional needs	Set one relational or emotional boundary (more on boundaries coming up in chapter X). Review last week specifically gauging your emotion regulation or overfunctioning
Staying in an ill-fitting social circle	Choosing aligned relationships that nourish identity and values. Get honest and intentionally pursue a new relationship or rekindle one that you found fulfilling

TERRAIN-TRAPPING PATTERN	FLOURISHING MEADOW OPPORTUNITY
Overcommitting to avoid disapproval	Ask "is this an overcommitment?" while reviewing your calendar. Offer opportunities that aren't for you to others.
Following a life or leadership timeline others expect	Defining personal and professional success through reconnection to your self-authored purpose and values, not external milestones
Tolerating unclear expectations at work	Courageously requesting clarifying roles, needs, and values, which done effectively co-creates accountability
Being a "team player" at personal cost	Balancing collaboration and support with honesty and clear boundaries
Downplaying personal accomplishments	Receiving recognition with humility and truth, modeling healthy self-worth
Not asking for a raise or promotion	Advocating for fair value of your contribution, aligned with your worth
Staying in a bad situation	Trusting your wisdom to advocate, realign or release what no longer supports your flourishing. Seek outside counsel, starting with your pacer
Choosing safe and stable over passion and purpose	Following what feels deeply alive (or start with the question, "What does deeply alive look like for me?"), even when uncertain or organizationally countercultural; acknowledge fear of failure and fear of success
Suppressing personal values and beliefs to fit in with leadership, a team or the organization	Living value-informed congruently in word, action
Perfectionism procrastination	Choosing "good enough" as a tangible personal reminder (and a reminder to others) that perfection doesn't exist
Staying busy to not feel	Create stillness to reconnect with insight and emotion; rest

TERRAIN-TRAPPING PATTERN	FLOURISHING MEADOW OPPORTUNITY
Not delegating	Trusting others with responsibility and growing leadership in others; choose two things to delegate today
Leading from obligation	Consider a season of stepping away from formal leadership; re-evaluate, take time to discern
Dismissing feedback	Integrate requested feedback with a professional coach. Initiate a 360 assessment
Refusing to acknowledge deeper issues	Naming what matters, even when hard; truth as the path to transformation; *radical* acceptance
Avoiding difficult conversations	Reframing conflict as an opportunity for growth, repair, and clarity; use Brene Brown's word "rumble" for conflict[*]
Resistance to change	Focus on when this happens. Choose an intentional change as a chance to intentionally evolve your identity clarity and impact
Excessive optimism	Remember balance is needed here. Embracing grounded hope; what defines your clear-eyed reality and how do you communicate it
Others: _____	Your flourishing meadow opportunity: _____

Acknowledging those terrain-specific internal contributors is often challenging and relieving at the same time. Putting words to emotions and deep beliefs and the patterns connected to them—that *is* the work!

Don't try to tackle it all at once. Choose one internal contributor or specificpattern at a time. Use focused awareness and test-drive one new responses over a couple of weeks. Then choose another one. It's a journey and avprocess. That neural rewiring and weeding takes some time and repetition.

---

[*] Brené Brown uses the term rumble for those tough-but-worth-it conversations where we stay curious, generous, and open—even when it gets messy. Brown's book is called *Dare to Lead*.

There's plenty of time and chocolate.

_____ EXCAVATING EXTERNAL CONTRIBUTORS_____

The tree depends on sunlight, air, and soil nutrients for soil. The iceberg is at the mercy of water temperature and deep currents. Your inner leader terrain is significantly impacted by external circumstances. You captured earlier environmental influences on your Leader Story Timeline. We're shifting focus to the external factors that may perpetuate or reinforce the inner terrain traps you've identified and how the combination of these contributors impacts your identity clarity and connection.

The Leader Identity Formation Theory (LIFT)[46] emphasizes that a leader's identity is shaped over time by experiences across different life domains (remember the Leader Becoming Compass from chapter 4) over the leader's entire lifespan. Leader identity clarity is greatly influenced by context, reflection, and meaning-making.

Right now, your current context and environment is also impacting your leadership. More specifically, the culture of an organization (influences how a leader expresses their identity. Leaders often suppress, reshape, or emphasize parts of their self-as-leader identity to align with the dominant environment. Like your work in this journey, those influences may need focused attention and acceptance. Ideally your entire team or organization takes the Leading Becomes You journey together!

We are shifting attention to the team, organization, and various influences on your leadership. It seems like the external contributors would be easier to spot but not necessarily. Like a frog in the kettle, leaders often keep leading without stopping to consider what influences are impacting them—for good or bad.

It's important to remember that a languishing leadership terrain like wasteland, swamp, or petrified forest is not *only* caused by internal contributors. In fact, *burnout*, by definition, is a workplace syndrome. Here's the official definition from the International Classification of Diseases (ICD-11):

> Burnout is defined as a syndrome resulting from chronic workplace stress that hasn't been successfully managed, characterized by feelings of energy depletion, increased mental distance from one's job, and reduced professional efficacy.[53]

Burnout is one of many leadership terrain challenges organizationally impacted by many sources, such as:

- Low morale
- Lack of recognition
- Unclear expectations
- Unmanageable workload
- Lack of autonomy
- Dwindling engagement
- Antiquated hiring practices
- Toxic leader residue
- Organizational cultural factors
- Dried up innovation
- Lack of trust and psychological safety

You might use the iceberg or the tree metaphor for the whole team or organization. Deeper level issues beneath the water line or in the deep root system (e.g. culture issues, unaddressed historical ruptures) are influencing what is visible (e.g. morale, cohesion, performance). A leader's internal struggle often reflects the organizational culture. These external contributors may also include bigger, wider, macro-level factors like market shifts, economic downturns, industry disruption, or politics—all of which can be pollutants to a leadership terrain.

Let's look at some common external contributors impacting a leader's inner terrain.

EXTERNAL CONTRIBUTOR #1: MISCONCEPTIONS

Misconceptions are the bridge between the internal and external terrain contributors. Internally, leaders may carry these as mental traps: reflex thoughts or deep beliefs. Externally, a team or organizational culture may perpetuate them. Leader identity myths are a subset of misconceptions subversively hidden in an organization's culture—unspoken but unhelpful all the same. I've seen these misconceptions keep people with incredible leadership potential trapped in a role, team, or organization they've outgrown. These misconceptions also muddy hiring processes.

Leader Myths and Misconceptions

- *The Great Man or Woman Myth*: There is a "best version" of leadership and personality. This was the pervasive theory of leadership one hundred years ago—that leadership is innate and you have it or you don't. Research has disproved this theory, but some people still believe it.[54]
- *The Confident Leader Myth*: Strong and extroverted personalities are the best type of leaders. This myth prioritizes confidence and charisma as the

most important leadership qualities. It overlooks the skillsets of introverts, whose approach is better suited for some situations.

• *The Lone Hero Myth*: A confident leader is not plagued by self-doubt or insecurities. The myth perpetuates leaders trying to solve problems without asking for help.

• *The Martyr Myth*: This myth is often connected to a misunderstanding of servant leadership or relational leadership, that the leader's job is self-sac- rifice—no. We could call this "Fast Track to Burnout."

• *The Control Myth*: This myth mostly lives in the petrified forest wasteland perpetuated by the belief that tight control at all times is the main play in the leadership playbook. An executive leader I coached shared that the CEO texted their leadership team no less than 40 times every weekend; One part insecurity. One part micromanagement.

While the myths and misconceptions can be powerfully believable, the reality is:

• There is not a one-size-fits-all leader identity or personality.

• Leadership capacity, skills, and approach are learnable skills and context dependent.

• Strong personalities are not always the best fit for a leadership situation.

• Leaders who appear to lack confidence may have incredible competence but are often overlooked for promotions. Research also confirms that confidence does not equal competence.

• Leader identity is evolving, just like us. A new role, challenge, or situation shapes the leader's identity and approach.

• Authentic, relational leaders are consistently their own self-as-leader, but know when, why, and how to adapt appropriately.

- Strong leader identity doesn't eliminate self-doubt, but awareness navigates it more effectively.

When considering the potential external and internal wasteland contributors, give some consideration to potential leadership myths and misconceptions from the team or organizational perspective that may be feeding your leadership terrain. Notice how the misconceptions fuel your personal deep beliefs, reflex thoughts, and emotional habits.

EXTERNAL TERRAIN CONTRIBUTOR #2: MEET BANI

The acronym VUCA (volatile, uncertain, complex, ambiguous) was first used by the U.S. Army College to describe leadership challenges post-Cold War. The concept made its way into leadership and marketing literature and education into the 2000s. But as the 21st century has unfolded, with a global pandemic, social upheaval, technological acceleration, and climate challenges, VUCA doesn't capture it all. Author and anthropologist Jamais Cascio proposed an updated acronym, BANI, to better capture characteristics in the present world, leadership and otherwise.[55] Many of the leaders I support resonate with both of these acronyms and position their own challenges in the overlap.

BANI stands for brittle, anxious, nonlinear, and incomprehensible. When applied to leadership, the acronym captures how many leaders might describe not only their challenged inner landscape with its emotionally and psychologically taxing state. BANI gives leaders validation and a means to communicate the realities of major external influences on their leader landscape, and that of their teams. The intersection of VUCA and BANI raises the stakes for identity-rooted leadership prioritizing the psychological resources and resilience of yourself and your team, modeling and developing agency, and the need for collective leadership that hinges on self and other awareness. In the face of nonlinearity and incomprehensibility, leaders must also prioritize connection, intentionally strengthening relational trust and authentic meaning-making—for themselves and for those they lead.

EXTERNAL CONTRIBUTOR #3: MORAL INJURY

I first learned about moral injury from the combat veterans I worked with in the PTSD clinic of a veteran's hospital. Healthcare professionals also resonate with the term which captures their feeling betrayed by administrative and budgetary demands that override their clinical judgment.

Moral injury[56] refers to the psychological, emotional, and spiritual harm that happens when someone behaves or bears witness to behavior that violates their deeply held moral beliefs. The realities of war morally injure soldiers and not having enough ventilators for patients during a pandemic morally injured healthcare professionals. In leadership, a moral injury arises from violated values, system failures, or witnessing unethical behavior. A moral injury occurs when a leader is forced to carry out an action, such as a layoff or harmful policy, that contradicts their moral compass or fails to protect others due to organizational pressure. Leader moral injury occurs when a leader feels betrayed by the company when values are spoken but not lived. Over time, this dissonance and sense of betrayal erodes leadership identity clarity, connection, and spiritual mooring.

In leaders, moral injury is associated with increased rates of burnout, loss of identity and meaning in the role, and decreased ethical decision-making capacity over time. It leads to distressing psychological, behavioral, and social issues and can even lead to mental health issues like depression and anxiety.

In the swamp terrain, moral injury may show up as chronic doubt and disorientation, where a leader no longer trusts their internal compass. In the wasteland terrain, moral injury adds layers to the emotional overresponsibility.

Leadership moral injury is an increasingly pervasive issue challenging the leaders I work with. Prolonged exposure to systems or power structures that reward compliance over conscience, polish over authenticity, and outcomes over ethics lead to a sense of emotional and ethical exile from oneself.

Often, a new coaching client stepping into a higher leadership position realizes that a large contributor to their debris is related to previous unprocessed moral injuries. We work through awareness, acceptance, and assimilation of the hurtful impact of authoritarian, perhaps petrified forest play books that prioritized self-interest, made decisions without concern for long-term implications, scapegoated, and disregarded empathy. A leader's inner landscape can easily turn to languishing terrain if they do not address old moral injuries.

If your Leader Story Timeline and new awareness include realization of a situation or leader impact that caused a moral injury, there is good news. The antidote and healing is the process you have been and will continue working through! Leader moral injury recovery happens through reflection, supportive coaching and creating courageous leader cultures where moral complexity and harmful impact can be verbalized. Healing occurs via the deeper work of re-aligning values, identity work, and prioritizing authentic leadership approaches. It all sounds familiar, doesn't it?

EXTERNAL CONTRIBUTOR #4: THE ORG PARTS

We've looked at your personal mental and emotional landscape, identity clarity factors, and relationships. Every organization has these too, of course with nuanced layers and dimensions for teams, service lines, departments, reporting structures, and org charts. Organizational influence and organizational culture are slippery terms. We know what they mean, but it can be challenging to put words, metrics, and levers to these concepts. To make them more concrete, here are some potential, specific factors within the organizational influence category:

- Shifting organizational and industry expectations
- Balancing stakeholder demands
- Managing remote or hybrid teams
- Communication systems
- Management strategies
- Organizational structure
- Work environment (physical and social)
- Workplace ethics
- Employee demographics
- Resources (financial, tech, human resources)
- Integrating AI
- Attracting and retaining top talent
- Philosophy of work-life integration
- Fostering inclusion

The research supports additional organizational influence challenges for female leaders, such as:

- Gendered leadership expectations
- Lack of mentorship and sponsorship
- Work-life integration
- Underrepresentation in leadership roles, particularly at higher levels in organizations
- Wage gaps

- Increased pressure to prove competence
- Overcoming "the broken rung"[57]

Awareness showed you what's there and not there, with focus on identity clarity and connection. Acceptance lets you stop hiding or fighting what you find.

The acceptance phase is not a blanket approval or co-signing of the external factors that intersect with your inner leader terrain contributors.

Acceptance simply means you can stop pretending that the terrain is something it's not,

that "it's just how my leadership is," or "every organization does this." It *doesn't* mean you have to wrestle every belief, attitude, norm to the ground. But that you've considered the cost and chosen to lead from a fully informed, grounded self-as-leader center rather than a defended partial version.

Your self-as-leader identity marble has been shaped by your rehearsed deep beliefs, choices, habits that you've fed or starved. It has been sculpted by outside forces including organization culture, previous mentors, and system pressures. Acceptance stops hiding or arguing with the contributors and lets them have their dot on the map.

You don't have to like them, but you do need to name them.

_____ FOR REFLECTION_____

With pen and notebook ready, imagine your inner terrain.

Next, draw the outlines—mark areas of your leadership that feel like swamps, wasteland, petrified forest, and flourishing meadow.

Now place the contributors—for each outline area, jot down the internal (e.g. beliefs, emotional habits, behaviors, fears, deep motivations) and external contributors (e.g. culture, past leadership, myths).

Place a star on the map—this indicates the one place where you willingly practice acceptance this week.

CHAPTER RECAP

☐ *Leadership terrain challenges develop over time due to internal and external contributors.* This requires using awareness to identify self-imposed patterns, beliefs, and external dynamics eroding leader effectiveness.

☐ *Internal contributors include perfectionism, fear-based decision-making, burnout, and lack of self-awareness.* These factors create self-as-leader inner terrain business traps that limit growth, authenticity, and effectiveness.

☐ *External contributors stem from workplace culture, organizational demands, and leadership myths.* Industry pressures, toxic environments, and outdated leadership expectations can reinforce wasteland stagnation and depletion.

☐ *Avoidance and denial keep leaders stuck in toxic terrain cycles.* Leaders who resist feedback, overwork to prove worth, or avoid difficult decisions delay needed change, self-renewal, and freedom from authentic leadership.

☐ *Pruning terrain erosion or overgrowth—internal and external—and addressing root causes is essential for Leading Becomes You.* Identifying personal and systemic contributors allows leaders to clear obstacles, realign with purpose, and create personally defined sustainable leadership growth.

LEADING BECOMES YOU BREAKTHROUGHS

In the following space, take a few moments to write notes for what resonated with you from this chapter.

What connections do you see between your internal and external terrain contributors?

Are there aspects of your personal or professional re-flourishing already coming to mind that you would like to focus on? Where do these go on your map?

What rhythm will you create to address these one by one?

Are there other external contributors not listed here?

"You all have a manure pile of memories. Nothing you can do about that. Now you can drown in the stink or turn it into compost and grow a garden."

— Rebecca O'Donnell

"All shall be well, and all shall be well and all manner of things shall be well."

— Julian of Norwich

CHAPTER 10

ASSIMILATION COMPOST

How to Repurpose Your
Dug-Deep Insights

Your gritty self-as-leader has navigated deep excavation, drained bogs, and cleared ground. Those were hard chapters, digging deep in your inner terrain landscape business via awareness and acceptance to clarify the realities of your present situation. You've removed your rootbound self-as-leader from the flimsy plastic and carefully detangled the roots for repotting. You've looked closely at weed patches and zoomed out for a perimeter check. You've taken stock of what your self-as-leader needs to prune and where to replace topsoil. Your last two phases, assimilation and authentic activation will give you opportunity to compost and repurpose what awareness and acceptance unearthed and shoveled aside.

Did she say composting?

Yes, it's the quiet, messy, necessary work of assimilation. It does not smell like chocolate. This is the stage where insight shifts to instinct. Where the parts of you that once felt broken, irrelevant, or burdensome get turned over and repurposed. You only *thought* they were scraps! It's the phase where your values, story, and leadership no longer live in separate compartments. Where your beliefs that once overprotected, habits that hurt more than helped, and the debris you kept tarping becomes fertile ground. When your inner terrain and outer leadership begin to mirror each other—messy, rooted, real.

Assimilation is the process by which your inner work takes root in how your self-as-leader actually shows up in your day to day. It's when your reclaimed story, clarified identity, reconnection to others, purpose, and bigger-than-me begin to show through your choices, tone, timing, and presence.

Your leadership voice no longer competes with the noise of old scripts. It's when you water the wasteland cracks, work the rigid clay of the petrified forest, and spread the swamp muck strategically as nutrients.

It doesn't require you to become someone new. It allows you to fully use and embody the self-as-leader you've reclaimed—undistorted, integrated, alive.

> **Assimilation:** *composting—where everything you've moved through, all that manure, gets broken down, repurposed, and folded into the foundation of who you're becoming.*

The past becomes usable.

Wisdom-rich.

Fuel for aligned, embodied, integrated leadership.

LIFE OR DEATH

I lived in east Tennessee in 2024 when Hurricane Helene devastated our region. Entire neighborhoods vanished beneath muddy waters. Sections of interstate highways were torn apart like paper. Whole communities—homes, families, histories—washed away.[*]

But one story has stayed with me longer than any insight I've taught.

Two neighbors stood outside their homes as water crept higher—ankles, knees, thighs—rushing across their yards and up the porch steps, furiously

---

[*] Hurricane Helene struck the southern Appalachians in September 2024 as one of the most catastrophic storms in the region's history, unleashing up to 30 inches of rain across steep mountain valleys. In western North Carolina and eastern Tennessee, the storm triggered record flooding, landslides, and infrastructure collapse that killed more than 100 people, damaged and destroyed thousands of homes, and washed-out roads, bridges, and utilities. North Carolina alone sustained nearly $60 billion in damages—the costliest disaster in its history—while Tennessee saw more than $1 billion in losses. Entire communities were displaced, businesses shuttered, and rivers and hillsides reshaped, with recovery expected to take years.

overtaking. A rescue boat pulled up, urging both to climb aboard. One man accepted. The other refused. "I can't leave my house. I've gotta stay here with it," he insisted, even as the walls groaned behind him. The boat pushed away. When they looked back, the man—and the house—were gone.

Leaders do this too. They anchor themselves to outdated versions of who they were, identities built for survival in a previous storm. They cling to roles, personas, or beliefs that once offered protection or significance—but no longer serve their truth. From the outside, it may not look catastrophic. But the inner erosion is real. Clinging to what no longer fits leads to misalignment, stagnation, and in time, burnout or disintegration.

It doesn't feel like life or death in the moment, but I've watched leaders lose everything because they didn't do the inner work. Awareness-knowing and acceptance-welcoming are not enough.

Leaders are often rewarded for constant evolution—for iterating, performing, and problem-solving. But sustainable leadership doesn't come from reflex reinvention and performance alone. It comes from identity clarity—the alignment between who you are, how you lead, and what you stand for. From this foundation, effective, fulfilling sustainable performance follows.

Assimilation moves you from the factors to flow. It's where you stop bracing—and start becoming. The opposite of assimilation is what you've already worked through—avoidance, division, denial, separation, detachment.

HOW ASSIMILATION TRANSFORMS LEADERSHIP

High-performing leaders are conditioned to believe that relentless progress and constant problem-solving equal success. While agility and execution matter, what sustains leadership over time is the ongoing synthesis (aka composting) of inner clarity, emotional truth, values, and behavior. Research on identity development, psychological flexibility, and authentic leadership supports this shift:

Leader identity clarity is strengthened through reflective assimilation, leading to greater self-efficacy, resilience, and direction.[58]

Assimilation renews *Psychological flexibility*—the ability to adapt to changing demands without abandoning core values—reduces burnout and increases well-being.[59]

Authentic leadership theory shows that leaders who internalize their values and *assimilate* them into action build trust, cohesion, and higher team engagement.

Assimilation is also emotional. It clears the static of disconnection and frees up the mental and emotional bandwidth you recognized via awareness for creativity, presence, and strategic clarity. You're no longer split between past identity versions and your emerging voice, your "then you" and your "right now you"—

you're rooted cohesively in what is and who you are and right now leadership.

FROM THE CADRE: A COMPOSTING STORY

Mel was a high-achieving leader in the recruiting industry when we began our four-day personal coaching intensive. Her resume gleamed—building and scaling a high-performance team, guiding executive hiring, and helping countless professionals and companies with win-win hires. From the outside, she was a model of executive success. But inwardly, Mel didn't know who she was.

"I feel unreal, unseen, unlovable," she told me in our first session. Her words were compelling and metered. Practiced. And as she dug deeper, she disclosed that she wasn't just tired—she was disoriented. Lost.

Mel quickly identified in her awareness and acceptance phases that she had been living for years in the wasteland terrain—not recognizing her low identity clarity and disconnection from her inner compass. On paper, she was thriving. But she wasn't living from her own leadership agenda. She was entangled in the agendas of others—anticipating needs, accommodating demands, overfunctioning to prove her worth, and constantly shape-shifting to fit the moment.

She also attributed this to an identity fragmentation problem. And hard to recognize because her success, by all stakeholders' terms, was significant. She had built her professional standing and reputation on hard-earned excellence, but parts of her were missing—parts she hadn't even noticed were gone.

She described it like this:

"At work, I'm competent and clear. I lead teams, make tough calls, trust my instincts. But at home, it's like I lose all that. I second-guess myself constantly. I can't make a simple decision without overthinking how everyone else will feel. I apologize for things that aren't mine. I wait too long to speak up—then I overreact. I'm either silent or overwhelmed. I've lost track of who I really am anymore."

When we started working together, Mel described her behavior as reactive instead of rooted. She deferred small decisions until resentment built. She avoided conflict to keep the peace but stewed internally. She lost time scrolling, zoning out, or replaying conversations. She questioned whether her feelings were valid and described feeling like a background character in her own life. Her boundaries weren't just porous—they were nonexistent.

She had no map, no coordinates, no perimeter.

This wasn't about a lack of ability. It was about low identity clarity and connection to self. Her leadership clarity didn't translate to her personal world because she didn't feel entitled to that same authority in relationships that weren't defined by her role. She was leading from confidence in one space and from fear in the other.

TRUE-TO-YOU TOOLS

Mel's self-as-leader *a-ha* didn't begin with a major insight. It began with a sticky note.

After a conversation about self-abandonment, Mel committed to tracking each time she dropped one of her priorities to respond to someone else's need. By the end of the week, the page was full—dozens of sticky notes. These weren't just moments of overfunctioning—they were a leak map. Evidence of where her leadership identity was slipping through the cracks.

That led to a deeper practice: a two-column tracking tool. In the first column, "I Feel," Mel rated her emotional state and authenticity on a 0 to 10 scale. In the second column, "Connected to Self," she noted how aligned she felt with her true leader identity in each interaction. What emerged was a stunning correlation. Every time she deferred, overaccommodated, or prioritized someone else's vision over her own, her scores plummeted.

It wasn't just the actions—it was the invisible cost. Her clarity dropped. Her vitality dropped. And her connection to her leadership purpose dimmed. Her intentional awareness and acceptance led to core insights explaining why she felt so disconnected and fragmented.

MEL'S COMPOST

Mel didn't need to burn it all down. She needed to compost it. The wasteland wasn't devoid of growth—it was full of material waiting to be broken down and repurposed. Her overfunctioning, her self-silencing, her people-pleasing—they weren't character flaws. They were survival strategies. Once, they'd kept her safe. Now, they were keeping her stuck.

But naming them changed everything. The sticky notes became an act of rebellion. A daily declaration: "I see where I'm leaking. And I choose to lead differently."

Mel wasn't creating a new identity—she was reclaiming the one buried beneath years of distortion.

Her assimilation shift arrived one morning in her car.

She was halfway to the office when she realized her hands weren't clamped to the steering wheel. For the first time in decades, her body was at ease. Since her teenage years, driving had symbolized freedom—but also fear. It was her escape from the chaos in her home. Her initiation into control. And ever since, she'd gripped that wheel like her life depended on it.

That morning, something was different. Her body had received what her mind had been working toward for weeks and it all came together in a simple but profound experience: She no longer needed to white-knuckle her way through life—or leadership.

The shift was physical.

Emotional.

Spiritual.

All ways of knowing converged.

Mel had spent months building awareness and accepting what she found. She had traced the roots of her overfunctioning, plotted where her beliefs about worth and safety had shaped her leadership posture. That morning, the work lined up. Her nervous system got the memo.

She didn't have to perform. She didn't have to grip. She didn't have to lead from fear.

POST-COMPOST LEADING

From that point on, Mel's leadership changed. Not overnight. Not dramatically. But deeply.

She no longer contorted herself to match others' needs. She paused before saying yes and stopped editing her tone to soften her strength.

Her voice became steadier and her decisions became clearer. For the first time in years, it felt like her leadership was hers. She could clearly define her very own leadership approval rooted in her full self-as-leader identity.

Her shift didn't stop at the office door.

At home, she began applying the same inner authority she once reserved for work. She named what she needed without guilt. She started making small decisions—where to eat, when to rest, what to say yes to—without spiraling into overthinking. She held boundaries without apology. She stopped managing others' emotions as her full-time job.

Her relationships and rhythms transformed her relationships at work and at home. She didn't swing between extremes anymore—confident in one space, invisible in another. She was becoming one whole person.

One whole leader.

For Mel, assimilation meant she no longer led from a divided self. She had integrated the parts. Her story, her strengths, her needs, her voice—they showed up everywhere.

She had emerged from the wasteland—not by escaping it, but by composting its debris into something nourishing, rooted, and real.

TIMELINE COMPOSTING

Look back at your Leader Story Timeline. We've used this to help you bring things into focus—moments, conversations, dynamics, or decisions that have continued to echo internally, even if they seemed small at the time. Awareness pointed you to areas where acceptance could say, "ah, yes!"

I can remember how a single sentence from a teacher, a subtle dismissal from a colleague, an idea that went bust, or a moment I silenced myself in a meeting— those seemingly small experiences shaped how I learned to hold back, perform, or prove. Even though my responses were misaligned with my values, preferences, or needs. Awareness turns the lights on so we can accept and then compost-assimilate for forward.

Consider your Leader Story Timeline as the whole truth for deeper assimilation insights. When you look at your timeline from a compost-assimilation lens, do you see new connections and opportunities for integration?

YOUR TURN

Here are some specific questions to guide this focus, pulling together all three phases of awareness, acceptance, and assimilation together:

• Are there moments, decisions, or conversations that still carry emotional "charge?" (awareness)

• What did you notice about your emotional responses and choices? Where were they effective? Or not? (acceptance)

• Where have you historically made yourself small, silent, or secondary? (disconnection from self)

• Where have you made yourself big, loud, and primary? (overconnection to self)

• How have your responses impacted relationships? (connection to others)

• What tarp-covering habits or behaviors have been quietly pulling you away from active assimilation and integration?

• What truths about yourself are coming into view now—truths that may have been buried, edited, or forgotten? (assimilation)

• What old debris and lessons learned from it can you repurpose right now? (assimilation)

- How do you want to lead?

Here's a specific example of someone moving through the process or reviewing their Leader Story Timeline through awareness, acceptance and assimilation:

Identified moment of emotional charge (**awareness**): Remembered when a direct report said, "It's hard to step up when it seems like you've already decided everything." That hit hard—it wasn't the leader I wanted to be.

Pattern (**acceptance**) *of internal contributors*: My leadership timeline showed a trend: In times of pressure, I overfunction *(behavior awareness)*. I take on too much. I don't delegate, not because I don't trust others, but because of constant internal pressure to prove my value. So I fear *(emotional awareness)* slowing down or disappointing.

Acceptance *of connection impact:* In my pursuit of excellence, I actually disempowered others. I led from control instead of collaboration. My team met deadlines—but didn't grow.

Awareness *and* **acceptance** *of tarp-covering behaviors:* Micromanaging. Rewriting others' work. Saying yes to too many projects.

Awareness*-recovered buried truth:* I feared being perceived as lazy or replaceable. I conflated being needed with being valuable.

*Composted shift to **assimilation**:* Now that I see the pattern, I lead more slowly. I intentionally share decisions earlier. I coach instead of correct (*intentional connection*). My leadership strengths are still functioning—but they are distributed, more human, and leadership has become much more fulfilling.

REFRAMING

If you prefer examples to help you recognize composting opportunities in your own experience, here are ten composts from awareness to active assimilation. Assimilation is retelling the story—moving from the challenges, painful parts, and recognized growth edges to how new awareness and acceptance becomes part of identity clarity—not just an isolated insight. The behaviors on the left represent hard truths, each with their own mental and emotional habits and the right side illustrates usable truths. The process supports absorbing and integrating internal influences plus external contributors. Use these to springboard your own ongoing deep dives:

1. From saying yes by default → Practicing the strategic "no"

2. From emotionally reactive mode → Creating margin for reflection and emotional awareness

3. From image at all costs → Sharing and inviting from the middle, "we" language

4. From micromanagement → Empowering others, delegating

5. From avoiding conflict → Naming the truth in real time

6. From self-forgetting tone → Speaking with integrity

7. From overfunctioning for the team → Letting others rise

8. From dismissing the body → Honoring physical and gut-informed cues

9. From role-driven identity → Values-driven presence

10. From isolation → Reaching for connection

Depending on your levels of swamp, wasteland, or petrified forest, your assimilation shifts will correlate directly to those map areas you outlined. This is behavior meeting up with awareness and acceptance.

What will you *do* differently? Your answer is evidence of your integration and your becoming!

BEWARE RESISTORS

Composting can get hijacked in a few different ways. It may not work due to too little moisture, poor aeration, an imbalance of materials (too many browns or too few greens). The size of the compost pile may even be too small—in that case you could see what else awareness and acceptance can unearth!

In J.R.R Tolkien's famous Lord of the Rings story, Frodo is a courageous hobbit charged with carrying a golden ring—the One Ring—to its necessary destruction in order to save Middle Earth. The ring is inscribed with "One Ring to rule them all," symbolizing the lure of power and tension between the dark character traits of those tempted by its control and the struggle to maintain one's moral integrity.

Without delving too deeply into existential waters, this internal resistance is wired into our humanity. Deep tension is part of human nature, the spiritual part of our person and what we've connected to the soul of leadership. Look no further than box-office-busting movies like Star Wars, Harry Potter, *The Dark Knight,* and literature classics like *Dr. Jekyll and Mr. Hyde* and *Paradise Lost,* all illustrating the tension between good and evil, the pursuit of control, and the deep bigger-than-me capacity to prioritize others over self (and the problem when this is backwards). It's why relational leadership works. It's also why I remain firm in my position that self-help doesn't work—and why your Leading Becomes You packing list implored you to journey with your pacer.

Resistance is a tension. In fact, resistance can be good and is essential for resilience. Resistance prompted you to undertake the Leading Becomes You journey. Resistance helped you discover thinking traps, emotional habits, and other internal terrain contributors.

But too much resistance holds us back. And certain resistance threatens your ability to lead effectively by keeping you from assimilation-composting. In the spirit of Gandalf the Grey—the wise leader and counselor to Frodo—I urge you to say to each resistor I introduce below: "Thou shalt not pass" or "Stay out of my leadership flourishing terrain!"

These assimilation resistors are not terrain specific. But they can keep a leader trapped in the piles of cleared manure and wasteland brush versus composting them. Now that your awareness eyes are sharp, I want you to see these deeper level threats before they interfere any further with your journey to leadership flourishing.

Resistor 1: Blame

"It's my fault." | *"I should have done better."* | *"If they had supported me, I would not be here."*

Blame is a sneaky assimilator resistor because it can feel productive—like accountability or honesty. But it's actually a trap. It keeps you circling the ouch or the duct-taped box without moving toward acceptance. Blame shows up in two distinct but equally limiting forms:

1. *Blame of self*: attributing negative outcomes to your own shortcomings, even the ones you had nothing to do with

2. *Blame of others*: attributing fault to external factors or other people, even the ones you're directly responsible for

The first version, blame of self, says: "Everything that went wrong is because of *me*."

Self-blame often has deep roots in a leader's personal history—early environments where they were criticized or made to feel responsible for others' emotions and outcomes out of their control. Over time, that conditioning forms an unconscious deep belief and tentacle reflex thoughts like, "If something goes wrong, it must be my fault."

In leadership, this blame resistor manifests as overfunctioning, perfectionism, or self-silencing. Even though blame is not terrain specific, self-blame is a common resistor for wasteland-trapped leaders. Leaders stuck in self-blame often:

- Apologize for things that aren't theirs to own
- Absorb the emotional fallout of team dynamics
- Struggle to set boundaries or delegate
- Question their right to lead when something goes wrong
- Dismiss their needs, preferences, and limits

The emotional awareness element is shame, and some tentacle reflex thoughts are:

- "I am the problem, and I don't deserve to lead well—or to flourish."
- "I cannot change."
- "I can't make up for what I did."

Self-blame beliefs may show up in awareness but they're often very deep. The leader who hasn't worked through self-blame plays small, avoids risk, and eventually disconnects from their own power.

Other blame is a very different version of blame. Blame of others, says: "I'm stuck because of what *they* did."

Blame of others says: "I'm stuck because of what *they* did."

Blame of others often stems from betrayal, injustice or repeated experiences of disempowerment. This assimilation resistor can cause a leader to feel righteous and justified—because sometimes they are. But when blame of others becomes the default lens, it keeps the leader tethered to either power identity like the petrified forest or powerlessness like the wasteland.

Common unhelpful beliefs and attitudes related to blame of others sound like:

- "If leadership had listened, I wouldn't have burned out." (powerlessness belief trap)
- "If my team were stronger, I wouldn't be so stressed." (powerlessness belief trap)
- "If my colleague, partner, boss would have supported me, I'd be further along." (powerlessness belief trap)

- "We wouldn't be in this situation if people followed the process." (power identity trap)
- "I've tried giving them more ownership, but they're not ready." (power identity trap)
- "I'm the only one who sees the big picture." (power identity trap)

This form of blame outsources your agency. It keeps you from fully accepting and assimilating the reality of what's yours to recover and change. The cost? You stay stuck in resentment while your forward motion stalls. And your leadership is stifled by wasted resentment energy.

Please do not misinterpret naming this resistor as ignoring the very real and challenging experiences and impact of your personal and professional story. It's a tenuous line between awareness or acceptance and blame. But blame ultimately evades personal responsibility for your leadership growth and solution-oriented mindset. Blaming others hands over self-as-leader agency and keeps leaders trapped in stagnant wasteland water, fixated on the past and stewing in fixed mindset resentment, cut off from their vision and tools.

You cannot re-root and flourish if you are fixated on blame.

We will look at the antidotes to the resistors in the next chapter. For now, consider a potential mindset shift, such as "While the actions of others impacted me, I hold the power to choose my intentional response."

Resistor 2: Regret

"I should have taken that opportunity." | "I missed my chance."

The regret resistor shows up creatively in unfulfilled goals, missed relation-ship or career opportunities, lifestyle choices. The thinking traps of "could have" or "should have" or "what if" are clues to the regret resistor. It also shows up in wasteland overgrowth as comparison, with emotions of illegitimate guilt, sadness, and fear. Regret blocks acceptance by holding tightly to unaccepted, unacknowledged paper-stuffed boxes.

Potential core and tentacle beliefs might be "I should have known better," "I missed my only chance," "I ruined everything," "My past defines me," or "I could be so much farther ahead right now." Throw in some big emotions of inadequacy, guilt, and shame, and that stagnant pool of blame will soon be filled with regret debris.

Regret erodes a leader's identity and terrain by:

- Decimating confidence
- Washing away opportunities for joy and connection
- Allowing the mistake to become the overriding definition of a leader's identity
- Anchoring identity to past decisions versus future possibilities
- Creating a narrative of "diminished potential"
- Fragmented identity between past and present versions of self-as-leader

Common unhelpful deep beliefs and identity thinking traps related to regret sound like:

- "I should've known better than to take this role."
- "If I had spoken up earlier, none of this would've happened."
- "I missed my chance to lead the way I wanted to."

- "I wasted years in the wrong environment."
- "I should've seen the signs—I failed my team."
- "If I had handled that one conversation differently, I wouldn't have lost their trust."
- "Other people don't seem to carry the same regret—I must not be cut out for this."

Mindset shifts that loosen the hold of the regret acceptance resistor. These perspectives compost the regret resistor as clarity and fuel for good, value realignment, and template for future choices:*

- "I've realized what I don't want; I'm pursuing what I do want."
- "While others' actions impacted me, I have the power to choose my response."
- "I can grow from this experience, even if it was painful."
- "I can create solutions, regardless of the challenges I've faced."

Resistor 3: Avoidance

"I don't really have to look in that box." | "What I've worked through is enough."

This is a hefty assimilation resistor that I see showing up across all three unhealthy types.

---

*Daniel Pink's *The Power of Regret* reframes regret as a healthy, universal emotion—evidence that we care about doing better—showing that when we confront and reinterpret our regrets (whether about missed chances, broken connections, moral missteps, or shaky foundations) with self-compassion and perspective, they become powerful teachers, sharpening our values, guiding wiser decisions, and fueling bolder, more meaningful action going forward. It's a great read.

Avoidance is extra sneaky because it fuels all of the other unhelpful elements you've worked on: mental habits, emotional habits, internal contributors. It can also disguise itself as seemingly good—like overwork.[60] Avoidance of deep work and flourishing terrain-building is arguably the most dangerous resistor—not because it's the loudest or most obvious, but because it silently fuels the others. Avoidance shrouds awareness and denies acceptance.

This avoidance resistor sets up a cycle—-starting with the brief relief from not noticing or tackling the discomfort of an unhelpful element. This leads to disregarding the need to step into a challenge or opportunity, do business with a deep belief, or chart the pattern of emotionally-charged responses. The brief relief leads to more inaction, more tarping over potential pockets of swamp, wasteland, or petrified forest. In turn, this inaction triggers increased disconnection, lower identity clarity, and the leader is right back in a languishing inner terrain. Inaction also leads to the feared thing getting bigger and bigger, taking back over the flourishing meadow. As more and more feared things increase, leadership life and impact gets smaller and smaller.

Avoidance can disguise itself as other forms and tactics:

- "I don't have time to tackle that challenging goal" (avoid failure)
- "That position or opportunity is not suited to me" (avoid risk)
- "I'll get to that later" (avoid the unpleasant)
- "I don't have the necessary information to make that call" (avoid decision or failure)
- "Everything is fine" (avoid discomfort)

I've had personal experience with the harmful effect of avoidance-tarping on my own career development. Let me share how I did business with this one.

DON'T WAIT FOR THE FACEPLANT

I shared the season in my life that led to a wasteland. Some of my early tarp-avoidance strategies were mental avoidance traps: "I'm doing good work here in Africa" and "Other people have challenges too" and "Who am I to complain when these people are working so hard for one meal for their children?" I also fell into some specialized avoidance beliefs called spiritual bypassing*. These sounded like: "Everything happens for a reason" and "It's not about me; this is God's work" and "I must not be grateful enough."*

My ultimate supersized tarp for when the wasteland really started leaking was a doozy: I thought I would fix everything by going to graduate school.

Getting a PhD was a perfect avoidance strategy—it justified not returning to Africa and the fear of telling anyone "I don't want to."

What I needed in that season was to *stop* and assess the terrain. I needed to climb higher for a perimeter check, to see where my terrain was being overtaken.

I needed a break—time to grieve my mother's death. I needed to talk honestly with someone, take permission to re-evaluate what I wanted and didn't. Eventually, the overload of graduate school blew the tarp right off. No more denial.No more avoidance. I was not functioning. With the help of a great therapist and friend support network, I slowly reclaimed my land one square foot at a time.

---

*Spiritual bypassing—coined by psychologist John Welwood—describes using spiritual beliefs or practices to sidestep uncomfortable emotions, wounds, or growth work. While not something all people of faith or all traditions engage in, any belief system can be misused this way; when faith language (prayer, gratitude, surrender, "light and love") is used to avoid pain or complexity, it shifts from being a source of grounding to an escape hatch, leaving hard truths unspoken and growth work unfinished. You could think of it as a form of what is referred to as toxic positivity, the pressure to maintain a positive front that's actually unhelpful avoidance of negative emotions and experiences

Avoidance keeps you stranded and rootbound. It can go undetected for a long time, passively overtaking terrain through various creative leadership strategies—mental and emotional traps and behaviors like:

- *Avoiding criticism:* In leadership, this looks like brushing off feedback or turning it into a joke—protecting ego at the expense of growth.
- *Avoiding hard conversations:* Leaders may sugarcoat messages, delay performance discussions, or allow tension to fester rather than address it.
- *Avoiding responsibility by blaming others:* In the workplace, this surfaces as finger-pointing when things go wrong, weakening accountability and trust.
- *Avoiding with procrastinating:* Leaders may delay strategic decisions or action steps, citing "needing more data," when fear or uncertainty is the real issue. It can also be due to inner critic and imposter chatter.
- *Avoiding people and connection such as withdrawing from the team:* A leader might physically isolate, emotionally check out, stop communicating clearly, or delegate without direction—leaving others to guess at expectations.
- *Avoiding the inner work by seeking validation versus self-reflecting:* When a leader over-relies on external praise to feel effective as a leader—while ignoring the deeper internal misalignment.

Avoidance adds waste to all of the languishing leadership terrain types andkeeps your self-as-leader roots trapped tighter. It shows up physically as muscle tension, poor sleep, and GI issues. Avoidance impacts relationships when withdrawal leads to disconnection and distrust. Ultimately, like my example, it can lead to lost seasons. The refusal to admit to myself and others that I couldn't finish my lifelong self-contract in Africa, or in another season admit that I couldn't fill the pipeline for my business, was costly.

RESISTOR AWARENESS

Let's pause here so you can collect your thoughts about how the three assimilation resistors may have or are showing up in your life and leadership.

Can you think of any other resistors that may keep you from assimilation?

Write them here.

HOW DO I KNOW I'VE COMPOSTED?

I left home at age 17 carrying a small duffel bag and combat boots. I had only flown twice before. I hugged my family goodbye in the Toledo, Ohio airport and traveled to Colorado Springs with 1,000 other high school graduates to attend the U.S. Air Force Academy (USAFA). Day 1 of Basic Cadet Training begins with stepping over a literal line painted on the ground. On one side of the line you are free to do, say, eat, walk however you want. The moment you step over that line, you are wrong. And the "do as I say" begins—from your haircut to your uniform to how many times you chew your food before swallowing. Life is prescribed.

That first night in Vandenberg Hall surrounded by army green bags filled with my new standard-issued life's possessions, I remember asking my 17-year-old self what I was thinking to choose hell in exchange for a prestigious education. At one of the in-processing stations, a gracious civilian woman who was not yelling looked at me and said, "Honey, they can't ever take away who you are." It was an important moment.

The service academies develop some incredible officers. For me in that life season, the system authority was a lot to navigate. For several reasons, I transferred to another college after completing the rigorous first year but unwittingly continued subscribing to the "no questions asked" mantra, in other systems too. I believed that system's authority was to be followed at all costs. I trusted that my loyalty and dependability would be affirmed and rewarded. It's taken my own commitment to the leader re-becoming process to step back over the line, reclaim my inner authority, and do business with careless words by low-insight leaders and the toxins of good ole boy clubs over the course of my career. Because of the intentional trek, my self-as-leader agency is stronger than it would have been.

In your Leading Becomes You journey of *re*-rooting and *re*-flourishing, stepping over the metaphorical acceptance line and doing business with your assimilation resistors might be the most significant moment of your process.

DECLARATIONS

Sometimes assimilation is simply a moment-in-time decision, a volitional stepping over the line in your mind. Maybe that moment is now. Or schedule it within the next week or two, once you've had more time to push back the resistors. It can be as simple as saying to yourself and sticky-noting your bathroom mirror with one or more of the following assimilation declaration statements:

- I've got this.
- I've done the work.
- Let's compost that manure pile.
- My leadership approach is valid.
- I know who I am.
- The old stuff doesn't define my self-as-leader.
- I see a new aspect of myself that I have faithfully repurposed.
- I'm leading from what's real, not rehearsed.
- I've reclaimed what matters—and I'm ready to lead from it.
- The part of me that used to feel like a liability is a strength.
- I don't need to overexplain who I am.
- I've integrated the lessons. They live in my self-as-leader approach now.
- I no longer need to earn my place—I already belong.
- I can be both unfinished _and_ fully capable.
- I trust my inner compass more than the old maps other people gave me.
- I'm not who I was—but he/she is still in there and that's a good thing.
- It's safe to lead as myself now.
- The friction is gone; I'm leading and living in alignment with what's true.
- I carry my past wisely, not as weight but as wisdom.
- Others:

Assimilation is stepping over the line and looking back at the cleared, excavated space, and the big pile of sorted empty boxes ready for recycling. Maybe it's a manure pile you've spread across a new bed of leadership growth seeds in the flourishing meadow.

Assimilation is relief meets satisfaction meets repurposing of the hard stuff.

_____ YOUR COMPOSTING TOOLS _____

I remember when my uncle used the manure spreader on the fields by our house. It's amazing how something that smells so bad can be transformed for good growth and nourishment. Our family also gardened so we collected food scraps, coffee grounds, and banana peels for our garden compost. Rotting scraps become nutrition for new garden growth.

You have confronted the internal and external leader terrain contributors and timelined the challenges and places where you picked up hurtful deep beliefs, identity thinking traps, and emotion habits that never suited you. You've reclaimed your potential and your new pot for a flourishing leader identity.

Now let's spread some manure so you can grow your flourishing leadership landscape.

Remember: This is not erasing what awareness and acceptance excavated, cleared, and sorted from the past. Rather, it's reconciling the leader you have been at every chapter and season with the leader you are becoming. Reconciling means "to bring one thing into correspondence with another."

> "Now let's spread some manure so you can grow your flourishing leadership landscape.

THE BIG FOUR COMPOSTING TOOLS

Like tools, there are countless practices that could help you keep turning the manure of old habits, hurts, and beliefs into rich soil. But you don't need them all to get started. I'm sharing the core tools you do need—the ones that offer the heaviest lifting. They're simple enough to use right away and are meant to be returned to again and again. Like all the tools I've shared, your pacer or a professional coach can help you personalize these. You can also design a custom tool for your unique self-as-leader terrain and climate.

Composting Tool #1: Boundaries

Boundaries are the fences that protect your leadership vision and your self-as-leader. Good boundaries are not concrete barricades, but fences that someone can see through and talk over. They are sturdy but pleasant, like a lattice or picket fence. Boundaries also protect those you lead. Without clear boundaries, your leadership is at risk of being diluted and tainted by external contributors of unrealistic expectations, overcommitments, and unhealthy team or cultural dynamics. Boundaries define what your re-rooted self-as-leader will and will not accept—both for yourself and the teams, systems, and processes you lead.

Boundaries are important for relationships and for all parts of your healthy leadership: physical, emotional, psychological, and spiritual. They impact your personal and professional time, your work, your stuff, and your conversations. Healthy boundaries yield healthy respect for others and self. In fact, they are the most other-respecting and self-respecting way to live and lead. Boundaries protect your well-being, your values, and your sense of self-as-leader. They clarify where your self-as-leader ends and where someone else begins. Healthy boundaries preserve appropriate autonomy and respect—yours and theirs.

We often think of external boundaries, like those specifically in relationships. But internal boundaries with self are important too. These are the internal limits you can set to support your assimilation and alignment with your values, energy, and priorities—even when no one else is watching. Unlike external boundaries, which involve navigating others' behavior and choices, internal boundaries are a self-honoring discipline: the choices you make to stay congruent with your recovered and authentic self-as-leader, not reactive habits, people-pleasing, or old survival patterns.

For leaders, this kind of boundary is vital. It creates inner structure, protects against overextension, and keeps your leadership rooted rather than scattered.

Here are some specific, practical boundary-setting examples:

Time: "I don't check email before 9 a.m. so I can lead from reflection, not reactivity."

Emotion: "I pause before responding to differing opinions or feedback so I can respond from clarity, not defensiveness."

Protecting energy: "I limit back-to-back meetings because I know I lead best when I have margin."

Staying aligned to values: "I don't agree to strategy shifts that violate my core values, even if they're popular."

Limit overfunctioning: "I let my team own their work—I don't rescue or rewrite unless it's truly needed."

Sabbath-like practices: "I block one afternoon a week for creative thinking and long-view reflection."

Mindset: "I stop myself from spiraling into self-criticism and re-center with my assimilation declaration statement."

Boundaries are guardrails that establish an agreement about what communication, behaviors, and interactions are acceptable in your personal and professional interactions with others. They clarify roles, expectations, and limits.

Did you ever have a boss, employee, or even a college roommate with no boundaries?

Sometimes external factors erode boundaries, like unpredictability. When others' responses are all over the place and day-to-day operations are vulnerable to the whims of others' inconsistent leadership, your boundaries will let you know when and how to intervene.

Another external factor is power imbalance. Sometimes the power differential feels like a David versus Goliath situation, and you feel vulnerable, pressured to do extra, take on more, or do things that compromise your values. Goliaths have lots of tactics, like threats ("If you don't *xyz*, you'll never get a raise or promotion") or empty promises ("I'll never ask you to *xyz*" or "I'll never *xyz* to you again"). Overwhelm, exhaustion, and resentment live here and are clues that power imbalance is overriding necessary boundaries.

BOUNDARIES HOW-TO

Let's look back at your Leader Story Timeline. Do you see a connection to boundaries? Sometimes there are belief traps directly related to boundaries, like "I don't deserve to have boundaries" or "No one respects my boundaries."

Rebuilding Boundary Fences

1. Find the broken boundary.

Here are ten key questions to assess your self-as-leader boundaries:
- What are the non-negotiables for my leadership approach?
- How do I ensure that my values remain intact amid organizational pressures and changes?
- Where do I need to set clearer boundaries with my team or colleagues? With myself?

- How do I communicate these boundaries without falling into guilt traps or over-explanation?
- Are there patterns of recurring unpredictability or power imbalance that especially threaten my leadership boundaries?
- Have I been mis-prioritizing someone else's needs over my own (or vice versa)?
- Why is this boundary important to me?
- What does this boundary protect for me?
- How does this boundary contribute to my well-being? Someone else's well-being?

2. Rebuild the boundary—take action.

Direct communication is key here. I like Kim Scott's book *Radical Candor* for striking a good balance. It's important not to dilute the message in "niceness." I'm not from the South but lived "southern" for many years, where my clients' situations illuminated that etiquette sometimes creates boundary challenges. Brené Brown says, "Clarity is kindness and nice is not kind." Nice untruth is still dishonesty. And "no" is still a complete sentence.

Other boundary strategies include:
- Reject passive-aggressive responding. It's easy to confuse a passive-aggressive response for boundary-setting. Not saying what you mean, rehashing, not offering opinions, or agreeing but not really meaning it translates to nothing getting accomplished.
- "Is that how you really feel?"
- "Does that really work for you?"
- "You said you were okay with this, but is there more to it?"

A well-defined boundary might sound like:

- "I am available for my team during work hours, and I protect my evenings for personal renewal."
- "I welcome constructive feedback, and I do not tolerate disrespectful communication."
- "I believe in collaboration, and I expect team members to take personal accountability."
- "I'm willing to share half my chocolate."

3. Follow through.

Consistency is key, especially for leaders. You are teaching others how to be in a professional relationship with you. If you speak a boundary and let the override happen—or you do the thing you didn't want to do—what are you communicating? If you don't hold the boundary, it feels confusing for them and for you. That hard-earned boundary will erode right off your reclaimed flourishing leaderscape.

4. Adjust if needed.

Your leadership context and approach will continue evolving—as will team and organizational dynamics. Boundary needs and focus will change over time and can be tightened or loosened. Intentionality is the key.

5. Grace is good.

Like the many new skills and leader tools you've developed, new habits do not roll out perfectly on the first take. Boundaries are challenging for many people (myself included). Bigger-than-me is a key factor here. Which leads to your next powerful composting tool.

Composting Tool #2: Forgiveness

Mistakes, miscommunication, and interpersonal offenses are inevitable in life and leadership so forgiveness is a critical leadership capacity. Forgiveness does *not* mean forgetting, excusing, or condoning. Rather, forgiveness is the emotional composting process and how leaders transform the ouch—the regret, the resentment, the hurt—into nutrient-rich insight. It is the intentional release of the need to punish—yourself or someone else—for harm that has already happened.

It's the antidote to those resistors of self-blame, other blame, avoidance, and regret.[61]

Outcomes of forgiving leadership include the good stuff we've seen before:

- Increased team trust and cohesion
- Reduced interpersonal stress and workplace tension
- Improved conflict resolution and communication
- Lower leader and team burnout
- Higher psychological safety
- Innovation

Forgiveness is a personal act of emotional freedom and not necessarily a relational repair or reconciliation—though maybe. Forgiveness says, "What happened mattered. And I'm not going to let it poison my leadership or my choices." Like composting, forgiveness

> "Forgiveness is a specific moment when waste becomes wisdom.

Forgiveness allows you, my leader friend, to re-enter your role, season, or new opportunity not hardened, but whole.

Forgiveness does not mean:
- Condoning the hurtful action
- Removing any consequences
- Forgetting
- Automatically reconciling the relationship

It may include:
- Second chances
- Clearing up how holding onto anger is serving you
- Compassion for the person you're angry with

And forgiveness definitely does not happen:
- Via revenge

Forgiveness composting may take some additional time revisiting awareness and acceptance to move toward self-as-leader reconciliation. No problem. We talked about that. The process is on your timetable.

Don't forget self-forgiveness. Leader self-forgiveness is essential because no one leads perfectly—and without it, we stay stuck in self-condemnation instead of growth. When leaders learn to forgive themselves—not to excuse poor choices or responses, but to integrate and learn from them—they create the inner freedom to lead with humility, resilience, and renewed clarity. Self-forgiveness is what transforms regret into wisdom and allows your self-as-leader to move forward without dragging shame behind you.

Composting Tool #3: Leader Andlightenment

It is not a typo. It's the Leading Becomes You *special!* I've been excited to share this tool with you since your journey started! It's the Swiss army knife in your self-as-leader trek pack. This tool can not only help with composting but is useful for doing inner business with your internal wasteland contributors' acceptance resistors, deep beliefs, and emotion traps. As the trainer at the gym says about the exercise called the plank: It's simple, but not easy.

Your self-as-leader *and*lightenment obviously focuses on *and*. The *and* offers a practical way to think *and* choose, live *and* lead, and enjoys time with our good friend, acceptance. I have ampersand symbols all over my office because this tool helps me out of a lot of my own mental, emotional, deep belief, and Edna-fueled traps!

Binary thinking—seeing the world in two categories—is inherent and important to leading. It's vital for clarity in a crisis, establishing what's safe or not, a new launch requiring a yes/no decision framework, and decision-making to narrow choices. Holding multiple agendas, overseeing varied projects, and tackling problems on a daily basis reinforces the brain's penchant to think in black and white—right or wrong, success or failure, strong or weak, good or bad.

Flourishing and relational leadership also requires the ability to hold two truths at the same time. *And*lightenment is the secret sauce for leading with realism *and* optimism, compassion *and* accountability, fast *and* slow, efficient *and* comprehensive.

This includes holding two truths about your self-as-leader too. Using *and*-lightenment acknowledges the real-life tension and discomfort that comes with effective leadership. You likely discovered some of these tensions in your reflections: "How can I believe this and that?" or "Can this value and that value both be important to me?" or "How do I follow this rule and that non-negotiable?"

Many of our mental and emotional habits happen because our brains love and need efficiency and self-protection. We categorize and order the steady mass of incoming data into our life and leadership daily examples.

Here are some more examples of binary, either/or thinking:

- True or false
- Possible or impossible
- Helpful or not helpful
- Safe or dangerous
- Successful or failure
- Strong or weak
- Perfect or mediocre
- Approval or rejection
- Right or wrong
- Good or bad

See what happens when you replace the "or" with "and"? Real life and leadership are usually both, at the same time—more messy than clean.

We can even add the assimilation resistors to this list too:
- Regret or no regret
- Overcontrol or no control
- Blame or responsibility
- Avoidance or everything at once

Let's try out the *and*lightenment tool on the hurtful deep belief we looked at earlier, lurking in many leaders' identity frameworks:

"I'm not enough."

If this belief is 100% true versus false, there are lots of associated belief tentacles, like:

- I depend on others to validate my worth.
- I don't deserve happiness.
- I am not wanted on the team.

When you use *and*lightenment, watch what happens:

- I'm not enough AND I led that project successfully.
- I'm not enough AND I got the promotion.
- I'm not enough AND that conversation went really well.

Just adding "and" forces you to consider the data that does not confirm the statement as 100% truth. It forces a reconsideration and a rewrite of the starting belief.

Since "I'm not enough" cannot co-exist with the addition of truth statements, we can shift to some healthier mindful reframing alternatives such as:

- I've made some mistakes.
- I may feel "not enough" but I have what I need for a next step.
- I'm working on myself.
- Learning something new is enough for today.

Let's try *and*lightenment on the tentacle beliefs:

- I depend on others to validate my worth *and* I'm taking time myself to notice the good work I did today.
- I don't deserve happiness *and* I enjoyed that sandwich.
- I am not wanted on the team *and* I was invited to lead another project.

Even if the starting beliefs are not helpful and untrue, *and*lightenment loosens them up. Then you can reframe the unhealthy deep beliefs or reflex thoughts to healthier versions. Using *and*lightenment shakes things up, especially when the belief or attitude is well-practiced and seems locked in.

As you move to the end of your Leading Becomes You process, take *and*lightenment with you as a prevention tool—like a fire rake that stops the spread of wildfires. It would be easy after looking at the deep beliefs and emotion traps of languishing terrains to fall into a new mental trap like, "I am either a wasteland-trapped leader or a flourishing meadow leader." This is not helpful.

Your self-as-leader can be languishing and flourishing at the same time. No one is 100% flourishing all the time.

Here are some *and*lightenment statements for each of the languishing terrain types:

- Wasteland: I can care deeply for others and care for my own needs and limits.
- Swamp: I can feel uncertain of success and take the next step.
- Petrified Forest: I can hold to my standards and invite others into the process.

Composting Tool #4: Burn and Chuck

Your final composting tool is like shampoo and conditioner in the same bottle—a two-in-one! And it happens to include two things I love: rocks and the smell of campfire. This should not be a surprise since chocolate is often present at campfires. After an evening by the fire, rather than tossing my clothes into the washing machine, I sleep in them because I love the smell.

This composting tool is based on ritual. You already have lots of ordinary rituals in your daily routine—morning coffee, a favorite cake for your birthday, how you answer the phone, when you eat lunch, a nightly bathroom routine. Rituals exist in many arenas of our lives, such as religion, athletics, business,and the military. Ordinary words or actions become meaningful and symbolic expressions of someone's commitment to God (prayers), coming of age initiations (Latin American cultures' quinceaneras), cultural greetings (handshakes, bowing, cheek kisses), a marriage ceremony (vows, releasing doves), military (etiquette, salutes).

Rituals are psychologically helpful. A ritual can help to regulate emotions or supercharge a "just do this" mindset. Did you have a pre-game playlist? Have you ever stopped by the bathroom to take some breaths before the big meeting?

But back to fire and rocks. Fire is fascinating—it's self-sustaining, can double in seconds, changes color based on the oxygen level, and only burns on Earth. It also destroys evidence—like newly realized mental or emotional traps, outdated rules, pesky emotional hooks, old stuff that has been messing with your leader identity and holding you back from leading as yourself.

Writing these on paper and then dropping that paper into flame is powerful and cathartic. Watching the paper burn to ash while the smoke drifts into the sky brings an intentional closure, freedom, and clearing to move on...

...and lead like you.

You can do the same thing with rocks, but chuck them instead of burning them. I keep a basket of rocks in my office for my coaching clients for this very purpose. The beauty of a rock is that you can hold it in your hand, feel the coolness, and rub off the dirt. You can write on rocks with Sharpie pens.

Things like:
- Illegitimate guilt
- Unforgiveness
- Self-condemnation
- Worthlessness
- Control
- Fear
- Not my script
- Not my rules
- Leading like him or her
- Comparison
- Imposter
- Regret
- No boundaries
- Not-enoughness
- Fear of vulnerability
- Distrust
- Isolation
- Avoidance
- Denial
- Others:

Once you've written what you want to let go of on your rock(s), the next step is taking it to a big body of water—a lake, river, reservoir. If you're in the city, you may need to take a drive because the mission is rock-chucking. You may have lots of rocks. I have walked with people to a literal mountainside with a bucket of rocks. I've had clients who kept their rocks in a cup in their truck or in their aquarium.

I've been honored to bear witness to and participate in many rock-chuckings. There's something about writing whatever you're letting go of in black Sharpie on a rock, winding up, and hurling it across the water, or down the mountain, never to be seen again. It's up to you if your pacer's presence would be meaningful or if you take this one solo.

If you don't like fire or rocks, use something else! You could also let a balloon go, tear up the paper and put it in the lake, write in sand near a shore and let the waves wash it away. It could even be the soap suds going down the drain of a sink or shower.

The goal is to identify a ritual you will use as you revisit this process. Rituals put an experience with the letting go. It takes your stepping over the acceptance and assimilation line to a new level with a fresh data point to remember when the unhelpful traps or contributors try to sneak back in. You remember your fire or rock-chucking ritual moment and say, "Nah, I let that go."

I'd love to hear yours.

_____ FOR REFLECTION _____

In the space below, write down the things you want to let go. There is no wrong answer.

What ritual will you use to honor the letting go of what's been holding you back?

CHAPTER RECAP

☐ *Composting transforms the past into fuel for future leadership growth*: Rather than simply discarding past experiences, leaders can repurpose lessons, setbacks, and awareness to build a flourishing leadership ecosystem.

☐ *Boundaries protect leadership vision and integrity*: Establishing clear personal and professional boundaries ensures leaders stay aligned with their values, avoid burnout, and maintain respect in relationships.

☐ *Forgiveness frees leaders from resentment and regret*: Letting go of past hurts, mistakes, and unhelpful beliefs enables leaders to move forward with clarity and emotional resilience.

☐ *Andlightenment helps leaders navigate nature-of-the-job complexity*: Embracing both/and thinking (versus all-or-nothing thinking) allows leaders to balance confidence with humility, progress with setbacks, and structure with flexibility.

☐ *Rituals reinforce transformation and closure*: Whether through fire-burning, rock-throwing, or your own symbolic gesture, your self-as-leader can solidify your commitment to growth by physically or mentally letting go of what no longer serves you.

LEADING BECOMES YOU BREAKTHROUGHS

In the following space, take a few moments to write notes for what resonated with you from this chapter.

Don't miss the many places in your leadership where you have alignment and can keep growing in those places.

Is there a particular composting tool you plan to try out?

"And the day came when the risk to remain tight in a bud was more painful than the risk it took to blossom."

— Anaïs Nin

"We can't go over it. We can't go under it. Oh, no! We've got to go through it!"

— Michael Rosen

CHAPTER 11

AUTHENTIC ACTIVATION REPOTTING

Your Leadership Becomes
You—How Will You Prune It?

The oak tree doesn't rush.

In its early years, it doesn't shoot skyward or demand attention—it roots. Deep and wide, beneath the surface, it invests in the unseen. Its strength doesn't come from speed, but from patience, consistency, and grounded development. What looks slow above ground is, in truth, the essential work of becoming unshakable.

This is the ultimate metaphor for your Leading Becomes You journey. As leaders, we often expect transformation to look like acceleration. But the most enduring growth happens like the oak's—deep first, then tall. And only after you've freed yourself from flimsy plastic rootbound to repotting in recovered terrain. Your self-as-leader story may have included seasons that felt stalled, overgrown, barren, or invisible. Yet every one of those chapters was composting the old and rooting the new. You've been preparing, becoming, stretching downward so you could rise upward—not fast, but faithfully.

Now, you're not just emerging—you're activated.

Rooted.

Ready to lead from the deep work you've done.

We've arrived at the summit of your Leading Becomes You trek—using everything you've dug deep to discover and mapping those insights to build a leader landscape and terrain that supports and sustains your revived self-as-leader! This is the activate phase of your trek.

True flourishing begins when you reach the sweet spot and repot:

With plenty of space for roots to keep growing identity clarity.

Balanced and authentic connection—not just to others, but to your values, your body, your voice, your vision.

There is no room in the pot or the meadow for trying to earn, perform, or preserve your leadership.

You're living it.

Growing it!

The ingredients for human flourishing have been considered throughout human history. Aristotle's ancient concept of eudaimonia described flourishing not as fleeting pleasure, but rather a virtuous, meaningful life. Flourishing leaders don't merely succeed; they thrive by becoming more of who they already are meant to be.

I referenced *The Global Flourishing Study* in our first chapter and the data that flourishing includes happiness, health, character, social relationships, and purpose. Significantly, the study shows that people—like leaders—who report a strong sense of meaning and purpose live longer, perform better, and experience higher well-being overall.

In leadership, this is transformative.

Flourishing leaders:
- Make confident, values-aligned decisions
- Communicate with clarity and resonance
- Build resilient, psychologically safe teams
- Recover from failure without identity collapse

Flourishing is not fluff. It's the highest form of leadership capacity.

BEYOND BECOMING

You've done the excavation. You've unearthed truth, composted the past, and reclaimed the leader you were always meant to be. But now comes the part that determines whether this growth takes hold or withers: How you sustain.

Leadership doesn't stop at self-as-leader recovery. Ongoing flourishing continues to rebecome as you build a team, culture, and impact that multiplies—fueled by the daily practices, relationships, environments, and rhythms that spread your hard-earned inner leader clarity to your corner of the world.

Authenticity + Sustainability = Authentic Activation and Leadership that lasts.

This chapter is your invitation to intentionally plan the consistent work of tending your inner terrain now that you've repotted and rerooted in the flourishing meadow.

SUSTAINABILITY

What comes to mind as essential for your ongoing self-as-leader flourishing?

What internal or external contributors do you need to stay particularly mindful of?

How will you nourish your ecosystem day by day? Season by season?

Take a moment to write your clarified self-as-leader mission.

YOUR FLOURISHING MEADOW

Authentic activation is the translation of your hard-earned and well-won insights to a long-term inner terrain formula that continues to foster and nurture your fulfillment and your influence on others. This will be your quick reference when you find old mindset traps and deep-seated internal or external terrain contributors trying to sneak in.

When you began your leader re-becoming, your flourishing vision may have felt foggy. And your leadership "why" may have been outdated—written a position or more ago. Perhaps it belonged to another leader. Now that you have journeyed through the phases of leader identity clarity—awareness, acceptance, assimilation, and authentic activation—I encourage you to revisit your leader "why" and purpose.

YOUR TURN

Complete the following statements. Share them with your pacer.

Consider the perspective of flourishing, the themes from your LeaderStory Timeline, insights from your mindset and emotional awareness, what youhave acknowledged and assimilated from the previous chapters—what you've chucked and what you've recovered.

Your Flourishing Self-as-Leader Mission Statement Template

Step 1: Who I Am
What core values and identity truths have emerged for you?

"I am a leader who values _____, is grounded in

_____,

and brings _____ to the people and systems I serve."

Step 2: Why I Lead
What meaningful purpose fuels your leadership?

"I lead to _____ because I believe _____. My work is
an expression of _____."

Step 3: How I Lead
What guiding principles or relational commitments define your
leadership behavior?

"I lead with _____ and strive to create spaces that are
_____, _____, and _____."

Step 4: The Impact I Intend to Have
What outcomes do you want to shape for others and your landscape?

"Through my leadership, I intend to _____ and cultivate a
culture of _____."

As Anne Lamott eloquently writes in *Grace (Eventually): Thoughts on Faith*, "What if you wake up some day, and you're 65, or 75, and you never got your memoir or novel written, or you didn't go swimming in those warm pools and oceans all those years because your thighs were jiggly and you had a nice big comfortable tummy; or you were just so strung out on perfectionism and people-pleasing that you forgot to have a big juicy creative life, of imagination and radical silliness and staring off into space like when you were a kid? It's going to break your heart. Don't let this happen."[62]

Anne's reminder that embracing imperfection and uncertainty allows us to keep stepping forward in life and leadership—even when it's messy and painful. She does not shy away from loss and grief but beautifully illustrates how meaning can emerge if we allow it to.

TERRAIN PATHS TO THE MEADOW

The inner leader terrains of swamp, wasteland, and petrified forest we have explored in this book have their own challenges on their paths to flourishing. Now that you've moved through awareness, acceptance, assimilation, and are authentically activating, you're equipped to action step new habits and leadership behaviors that transform how you show up—and how your self-as-leader terrain thrives.

As always, I'm offering ideas to get you started. These are based on my experience working with leaders trapped in each terrain type. I'm also including a bigger-than-me transformation statement for each terrain type. Pick and choose the practical strategies and focus areas that make sense for your self-as-leader re-becoming right now.

When you revisit this process again next year (because you will be a different self-as-leader as your becoming unfolds), you will be pleasantly surprised to see how your activation has become second nature.

The Wasteland Terrain
- Core shift: From rigid standards, imposter and inner critic chatter, and self-judgment to compassion and flexibility
- Activation practices: Reframe failure, prioritize progress over perfection, build emotional self-trust, rewire mental chatter for positive truth
- Flourishing competency focus:
  - Decision-making: Allow intuition and flexibility to balance structure

- Emotional intelligence: Cultivate self-compassion and internal permission
- Mindset: Shift from "never enough" to "good enough to grow"
- Team motivation: Create and model safety for risk-taking and mistakes
- Communication: Speak from grace, not perfectionism
- Conflict resolution: Move from hyper-correction to relational repair

- Bigger-Than-Me idea: Transformation emerges as the leader lifts their eyes from the never-ending needs of now to a much greater horizon that stretches beyond the present and even beyond their leadership. The leader is relieved from the burden of holding it all together.

The Swamp Terrain

Core shift: From stuck and inauthentic shapeshifting to grounded, authentic, and purposeful

- Activation practices: Redefine success, commit to values-driven consistency, admit where hiding happens
- Flourishing competency focus:
  - Decision-making: Move from reactive, what do they want indecision to values-aligned intention, hold the decision when made
  - Emotional intelligence: Name emotions and direct them, let emotional data contribute
  - Mindset: Embrace sufficiency and progress over success at all costs
  - Team motivation: Model vision and consistency

- Communication: Shift from venting to vision-casting
- Conflict resolution: Step into necessary tension
- Bigger -Than-Me idea: The swamp terrain binds the leader to others' in-the-moment expectations and emotional currents, but beneath the murk lies the truth: You are not here just to win. Transformation emerges when the leader disentangles and listens for a call that flows beyond perception and performance—toward unnoticed contribution, vision, and legacy

The Petrified Forest Leader
- Core shift: From overcontrol and fear to trust and creativity
- Activation practices: Delegate, invite feedback, foster collaborative innovation
- Flourishing competency focus:
    - Decision-making: Share authority, integrate diverse input
    - Emotional intelligence: Regulate dominance impulses, build empathy
    - Mindset: Shift from scarcity of control to abundance of trust
    - Team motivation: Foster shared ownership
    - Communication: Speak less to control, more to empower
    - Conflict resolution: Practice vulnerability and truth-telling
- Bigger-Than-Me idea: The soul of your leadership were made to evolve. Your control and status can co-exist with vulnerability. Transformation begins in the courageous loosening of the grip: You are not just what you've built, you are who you become when you release it. Transformation becomes possible when image gives way to impact.

The Flourishing Meadow Leader
- Core strength: Aligned, fulfilled, generative
- Sustaining practices: Reflect, recalibrate, deepen presence and purpose
- Flourishing competency focus:
  - Decision-making: Trust and refine intuitive, values-based direction
  - Emotional intelligence: Maintain compassionate presence with self and others
  - Mindset: Lead from sufficiency, not urgency
  - Team motivation: Inspire through clarity, authenticity, and shared vision
  - Communication: Communicate with resonance and relational depth
  - Conflict resolution: Model direct, respectful, and generative tension navigation
- Bigger-Than-Me idea: In the meadow, the leader has tasted flourishing—but transformation lifts the horizon higher. It is no longer just about living and leading well but about leading beyond oneself. The call to legacy rings clear with calling: Use your life and self-as-leader impact to water others' roots and pollinate others' terrains.

WHAT DO YOU CALL IT?

Now that you've built it, what do you want to call your flourishing leadership terrain?

Like a boat or a beach cabin whose name reflects the owner's personality and the sanctuary of that space.

For me, there's an old, forgotten picnic table deep in the forest where I trail run. Weathered, moss-laced, and softened by time, it's where I stop—to breathe. Sometimes I sit. Sometimes I lay flat on my back gazing up through the treescape to the clouds. My little dog rests his head on my stomach. And there I'm thinking. Praying. Becoming.

I call it *The Wayfaring Place*.

The name fits because that's what I think this journey is, Wayfaring.

Traveling the leader's development path.

Intentionally slowing to recover the sacred.

Returning to what's true.

The table itself certainly isn't special. But it holds space for my integration of that week—for laying down the days, sorting the moments, listening inward, and remembering who I am when no one's watching.

Where's your place? What do you call it? Maybe it's the room or the porch or the desk where you've done your Leading Becomes You work.

Through this journey, you've re-entered your leadership **from the inside out**.

Wherever and whatever your leader terrain represents for you, name it—and return to it often.

Write it here:

RE-FLOURISHING

From here, everything becomes an expression of your integrated self. Challenges still come. Conflicts still arise. But now, you face them from integrated wholeness, not fragmentation.

Your team can feel it. Your impact multiplies. And best of all—you're leading in a way that doesn't cost your soul.

This is what it means when **leading becomes you**.

CHAPTER RECAP

☐ *Flourishing leadership* requires deep-rooted preparation: Like the oak tree, true transformation takes time and unseen ground-work.

☐ A clear leadership vision hinges on a *clear leader identity*: Your leadership "why" is only as good as your leadership "who am I?"

☐ Flourishing self-as-leaders integrate *emotional intelligence, strengths, and values to build resilience*: Good stuff like autonomy, mastery, meaningful relationships, and personal well-being are key ingredients for the thriving landscape.

☐ *Intentional transformation* fosters lasting leadership fulfillment: Connecting leadership to something bigger-than-self—through mentorship, service, or mission-driven work—deepens purpose and impact.

☐ A *sustainable leadership landscape* requires a continuous rhythm of reflection and renewal: Leaders must check internal and external contributors, revisit values, strengths, and growth areas to hold steady on alignment and prevent losing land.

"Nothing in life is more exciting and reward-ing than the sudden flash of insight that leaves you a changed person."

— Arthur Gordon Webster

"The soul should always stand ajar, ready to welcome the ecstatic experience."

— Emily Dickinson

"Life is a journey not a destination."

— St. Therese of Liseaux

"Tell me, what is it you plan to do with your one wild and precious life?"

— Mary Oliver, "The Summer Day"

CHAPTER 12

LEADING RE-BECOMES YOU

Commit to a Re-Becoming
Rhythm and Pay It Forward

I have a shelf on the bottom of my bookcase stacked with dusty folders of handouts and notes from conferences. I have digital stacks too. Don't let this happen to your Leading Becomes You work. Re-rooting your self-as-leader is an ongoing process of tending. Maintaining your flourishing terrain for sustainable leadership is an ongoing process of nurture.

At the very least, revisit this full process once a year. I encourage my coaching clients to schedule quarterly retreats. Sometimes I'm a part of those. Other times they take a clean copy of what is now this book and their notes from last year's personal strategic planning retreat. I instruct them to start with reviewing last year's responses and noting how they've grown.

Another option is to dedicate each quarter to one of the four As in the process: Q1 revisits awareness, Q2 focuses on acceptance, Q3 is dedicated to assimilation, and Q4 recalibrates authentic activation.

I also encourage you to use this book with your team. It is perfect for a team development offsite.

_____ CLOSING REFLECTION_____

To close this Leading Becomes You trek, know that I hold your self-as-leader in the highest regard for taking your own growth journey. Now savor the journey with this closing reflection of your **leading becomes you**.

_____ **[Your Name]'s Commitment to Lifelong Leading From the Inside Out, and to Re-Becoming and Re-Flourishing**

A Personal and Professional Contract with Your Re-Becoming Self-As-Leader

Date: [_____]

I have walked through my Leader Identity Story and seen how it impacts the terrain of my leadership. I used my gritty honesty to see my self-as-leader defenses: my own version of defended armor, whether performance, approval, or pressure. I've gotten clear about where I'm building connection and identity clarity or the places these may be lacking. I've gained understanding of my inner leader terrain, whether it's the wasteland of burnout or overextension, the eroded swamp of inauthentic and shapeshifting, areas petrified by control, perfectionism, or overconfidence, or the inevitable debris from hard situations. I have looked squarely at my growth edges and courageously undertaken the Leading Becomes You process of awareness, acceptance, assimilation, and authentic activation.

Now, from this new vantage point of freshly flourishing terrain, I declare a deeper promise to myself and those I lead—not to perfection, but to presence. Not to performance, but to purpose. Not to external validation, but to internal congruence.

1. I commit to pursuit of identity clarity and authentic, relational leadership.

I will lead as myself—not as a mask, a role, or an expectation. I will free myself from outdated scripts and ego-driven strategies that shrink my leadership. I will embody clarity, speak truth, and act in alignment with my deepest values.

2. I commit to maintaining connection to self and others and the soul of leadership.

Leadership is relational, not solitary. I will seek feedback, invite constructive dialogue, and be open to learning from trusted individuals. I commit to the ongoing courageous work of self-examination and the sometimes-uncomfortable work of growth—knowing that it strengthens my ability to serve and lead effectively while growing resilience for me, for my team, and my organization.

3. I commit to reflection and emotional awareness.

I will practice ongoing self-awareness—of mindset and emotions—using tools like reflection, journaling, time with my pacer, and intentional time to check in with myself. A great leader knows their self-as-leader deeply—strengths, weaknesses, motivations. The iceberg and the tree require attention to see how the weather and other elements are affecting them. I will set aside time to continue refining my leadership skills via emotional intelligence, ensuring that I lead from a place of intention, not reaction. This keeps me connected and my self-as-leader identity clarified.

4. I commit to accepting my full and ongoing Leader Story Timeline.

I honor the terrain I have walked. I embrace my strengths and struggles, past experiences and aspirations—knowing that my authentic wholeness, hard-earned experience, and unique combination of self, identity, and personality—not my perfection—is what makes me trustworthy, wise, and relatable. I will embrace my full professional and leader story. I will leverage all parts of my story to lead with compassion and acceptance—for self and others. My leadership approach rests on my contentment with self AND my striving to transform each day. I acknowledge and want to honor others' stories too.

5. I commit to releasing what no longer serves me or my leadership.

I will continually audit my leadership for ego, fear, and mindset or emotion patterns that constrict my growth and best influence. I will let go of the behaviors, systems, or relationships that have kept me in the wasteland, swamp, or petrified forest. I will courageously make room for what aligns with my self-as-leader flourishing. This does not mean avoiding discomfort or hard decisions—it means refining and appropriately protecting my leadership so that it remains effective, meaningful, and values-driven.

6. I commit to valuing the process, not just the outcomes.

I will not measure success only by metrics and results, but by the congruence, meaning, and presence I bring and that others share with me. I will embrace the unfolding, the imperfect steps, and the joy of growing into the leader I already am and the leader I will continue to become. I will honor leadership as a journey, not just the milestones. I acknowledge that growth is continuous and that leadership is about adapting, evolving, and embracing each phase—from seasons of clarity to times of challenge. I will celebrate progress, no matter how small, and remain committed to learning along the way.

7. I commit to cultivating a flourishing terrain.

I will use my new awareness and clarity not only for my own thriving, but to build team and organizational cultures of trust, dignity, safety, growth, and shared purpose. I will lead in ways that generate life, not depletion. Leadership is about empowering others. I will strive to create environments where people feel seen, valued, and encouraged to grow. I will use my influence to uplift, mentor, and invest in those around me, recognizing that great leadership is measured by the growth of others, not just personal achievement.

8. I commit to recommitting, re-becoming, and re-flourishing.

I understand that distractions, challenges, and resistance will arise. I will revisit this commitment, sharpen my tools, and renew my promise to lead with intention, purpose, and heart. Growth is a lifelong pursuit, and I embrace the responsibility of staying engaged in my own evolution. I know there will be resistance, forgetfulness, and detours. I will return to myself often. I will revisit this contract when needed. I will keep my chocolate supply intact and share with others. I will forgive myself freely and begin re-becoming again,

and again,

and again.

Signature: _____ **Date:** _____

True leadership starts with self-leadership.

You've done that.

The world needs leaders like you who are willing to re-root, re-become, build awareness, and commit to ongoing growth and re-flourishing.

You are that leader.

And will keep becoming that leader.

For having walked the Leading Becomes You journey, I would follow your self-as-leader anywhere.

SELF-AS-LEADER VALUES INVENTORY

**Leading Becomes You: Leadership Values Inventory
(100 Values)**

This Self-As-Leader Values Inventory is designed to help you reflect on the values that define your authentic leadership identity.

Instructions:

1. Read through the full list of 100 leadership values.

2. Highlight or mark the 12 to 15 values that feel most essential to your leadership right now.

3. Narrow those to your top five self-as-leader values.

4. Reflect on where and how these values show up (or don't) in your daily leadership.

Groundedness	Transparency	Legacy
Voice	Accountability	Flexibility
Presence	Self-trust	Forgiveness
Discernment	Drive	Depth
Resonance	Curiosity	Excellence
Bravery	Confidence	Decisiveness
Compassion	Creativity	Relationship
Wholeness	Boldness	Ethics
Generosity	Resourcefulness	Respect
Alignment	Autonomy	Wisdom
Clarity	Stewardship	Patience
Integrity	Communication	Restraint
Resilience	Vision	Hope
Purpose	Meaning	Strength
Humanity	Emotional depth	Vulnerability
Identity	Trust	Culture
Reflection	Risk	Diligence
Calm	Belonging	Influence
Ownership	Community	Tenacity

Mastery	Responsibility	Order
Humility	Presence	Generosity
Service	Stability	Courage
Hospitality	Strategy	Loyalty
Initiative	Fairness	Maturity
Responsiveness	Growth	
Disruption	Compassion	
Authority	Learning	
Emotional honesty	Forgiveness	
Awareness	Balance	
Persistence	Self-respect	
Focus	Clarity of intent	
Dignity	Willingness	
Boundaries	Reflection	
Perspective	Connection	
Listening	Encouragement	
Renewal	Safety	
Alignment	Empathy	
Collaboration	Grit	

THE WORK AND MEANING
INVENTORY (WAMI)

———————

Work can mean a lot of different things to different people. The following items ask about how you see the role of work in your own life. Please honestly indicate how true each statement is for you and your work.

1=Absolutely Untrue

2=Mostly Untrue

3=Neither True nor Untrue

4=Mostly True

5=Absolutely True

1. I have found a meaningful career..1 2 3 4 5

2. I view my work as contributing to my personal growth.................1 2 3 4 5

3. My work really makes no difference to the world 1 2 3 4 5

4. I understand how my work contributes to my life's meaning..........1 2 3 4 5

5. I have a good sense of what makes my job meaningful...................1 2 3 4 5

6. I know my work makes a positive difference in the world..............1 2 3 4 5

7. My work helps me better understand myself 1 2 3 4 5

8. I have discovered work that has a satisfying purpose 1 2 3 4 5

9. My work helps me make sense of the world around me 1 2 3 4 5

10. The work I do serves a greater purpose 1 2 3 4 5

Scoring instructions.

Add the ratings for items 1, 4, 5, and 8 to get the "Positive Meaning" score. The Positive Meaning scale reflects the degree to which people find their work to hold personal meaning, significance, or purpose. Add the ratings for items 2, 7, and 9 to get the "Meaning-Making through Work" score. The Meaning-Making through Work score reflects the fact that work is often a source of broader meaning in life for people, helping them to make sense of their lived experience. Subtract the rating for item 3 from 6 (e.g., if a client gave item 3 a rating of 2, then their converted rating would be 4 [6-2=4]); add this number to the ratings for items 6 and 10 to get the "Greater Good Motivations" score.

The Greater Good Motivations score reflects the degree to which people see that their effort at work makes a positive contribution and benefits others or society. The Positive Meaning, Meaning-Making through Work, and Greater Good Motivations scores can all be added together to get the test-taker's overall Meaningful Work score. The Meaningful Work score reflects the depth to which people experience their work as meaningful, as something they are personally invested in, and which is a source of flourishing in their lives.

Low scores on any of these scales reflect an absence of work meaning, and may be predictive of poor work engagement, low commitment to one's organization and intentions to leave, low motivation, a perceived lack of support and adequate guidance from leadership or management. People who score low on these scales are also more likely to be absent from work and experience both low levels of well-being and higher levels of psychological distress.

For more information on the development of the WAMI, please consult: Steger, M. F., Dik, B. J., Duffy, R. D. (2012). Measuring Meaningful Work: The Work and Meaning Inventory (WAMI). Journal of Career Assessment

NOTES

INTRODUCTION

1 **pg. 14 the key findings of the Global Flourishing Study.** The Global Flourishing Study (2023), a five-year longitudinal collaboration between Harvard University's Human Flourishing Program, Baylor University, and Gallup, examines how people around the world experience and sustain flourishing across diverse life domains. With over 200,000 participants in 22 countries, the study defines flourishing as a multidimensional construct encompassing six domains: happiness and life satisfaction, mental and physical health, meaning and purpose, character and virtue, close social relationships, and financial/material stability. For leaders, the study underscores that flourishing is not only an individual state, but an ecosystemic condition—leaders who flourish create the cultural conditions for others to thrive. It provides empirical support for leadership models rooted in authenticity, identity clarity, and human-centered design over traditional performance-first paradigms.

See: VanderWeele, Tyler J., et al. The Global Flourishing Study Baseline Report. Harvard University and Baylor University, in partnership with Gallup, 2023. https://hfh.fas.harvard.edu/global-flourishing-study

CHAPTER 1

2 **pg. 27 more effective, resilient, and influential than those who do not.** Leaders who carve out time for personal growth, reflection, and imaginative thought are more effective in navigating complexity and sustaining impact. Reflection enhance emotional intelligence, improves decision-making, and builds resilience—key traits of transformational leadership. Conversely, overemphasis on productivity without space for reflective practice can lead to rigidity, short-term thinking, and eventual burnout.

See: Ashkanasy, NealM., and Catherine S. Daus. "Rumors of the Death of Emotional Intelligence in Organization-al Behavior Are Vastly Exaggerated." Journal of Organizational Behavior, vol. 26, no. 4, 2005, pp. 441-452.; Avolio, Bruce J., and William L. Gardner. "Authentic Leadership Development: Getting to the Root of Positive Forms of Leadership. "The Leadership Quarterly, vol. 16, no. 3,2005, pp. 315-338.; Goleman, Daniel. Leadership: The Power of Emotional Intelligence. More Than Sound, 2011.; McAlpine, Lynn, and Cheryl Amundsen. "Identity Formation and University Academics: Outside Their Institutional Context." Teaching in Higher Education, vol.17, no. 2, 2012, pp. 183-194.; Roberts, Laura Morgan, et al. "How to Become a Better Leader. "Harvard Business Review,2018. https://hbr.org/2018/01/how-to-become-a-better-leader

3 **pg. 28 because they gain experience over time.** Research shows that managers don't automatically get better just by being in the role longer. Without deliberate reflection, feedback, and opportunities to grow, added years of experience alone do not translate into effectiveness or stronger leadership.

See: McCall, Morgan W., Michael M. Lombardo, and Ann M. Morrison. The Lessons of Experience: How Successful Executives Develop on the Job. Lexington Books, 1988.

See also: Day, David V. "Leadership Development: A Review in Context." The Leadership Quarterly, vol. 11, no. 4, 2000, pp. 581–613.

4 pg. 30   Default Mode Network (DMN) builds and locks in your sense of self.

See: Raichle, M. E., MacLeod, A. M., Snyder, A. Z., Powers, W.J., Gusnard, D. A., & Shulman, G.L. (2001). A default mode of brain function. Proceedings of the National Academy of Sciences, 98 (2), 676-682.https://doi.org/10.1073/pnas.98.2.676

CHAPTER 2

5 pg. 39 internalized the role as part of your identity?

See: Day, D. V., Harrison, M. M., & Halpin, S. M. (2009). An Integrative Approach to Leader Development: Connecting Adult Development, Identity, and Expertise. Routledge.

6 pg. 41 lack of fulfillment and satisfaction for the leader. Struggling to internalize a leader identity is not merely a personal challenge—it carries organizational consequences. Research confirms that when leaders lack a strong internalized leader identity, they are more likely to demonstrate inconsistent behaviors, which can result in follower uncertainty and decreased morale. This misalignment not only impacts team performance but also contributes to lower leader satisfaction and greater risk of burnout due to identity conflict and role strain. Leadership fulfillment is strongly tied to identity integration; without it, both personal and collective outcomes suffer.

See: Ely, Robin J., Herminia Ibarra, and Deborah M. Kolb. "Taking Gender Into Account: Theory and Design for Women's Leadership Development Programs. "Academy of Management Learning & Education, vol.10, no.3, 2011, pp.474-493.; Ibarra, Herminia. Working Identity: Unconventional Strategies for Reinventing Your Career. Harvard Business Press, 2003.; Lord, Robert G., and Rosalie J. Hall. "Identity, Deep Structure and the Development of Leadership Skill." The Leadership Quarterly, vol. 16, no. 4, 2005, pp. 591-615.

7 pg. 43 Widely credited to Michelangelo; original source unknown.

8 pg. 43 MBTI, Hogan, NEO-PI, DISC, Enneagram.

See: Myers, Isabel Briggs, Mary H. McCaulley, Naomi L. Quenk, and Allen L. Hammer. MBTI Manual: A Guide to the Development and Use of the Myers-Briggs Type Indicator.3rd ed., Consulting Psychologists Press,1998.; Goldberg, Lewis R. "The Development of Markers for the Big-Five Factor Structure." Psychological Assessment, vol.4, no.1,1992, pp. 26-42.; Hogan, Robert, and Joyce Hogan. Hogan Personality Inventory Manual. 2nd ed., Hogan Assessment Systems, 1992.; Costa, Paul T., Jr., and Robert R. McCrae. Revised NEO Personality Inventory (NEO-PI-R) and NEO Five-Factor Inventory (NEO-FFI) Professional Manual. Psychological Assessment Resources, 1992.; Lapid-Bogda, Ginger. What Type of Leader Are You? Using the Enneagram System to Identify and Grow Your Leadership Strengths and Achieve Maximum Success. McGraw-Hill, 2007.

9 pg. 49 leader selection and development assessment I use, the Hogan.

See: Hogan, Robert, and Joyce Hogan. Hogan Personality Inventory Manual. 2nd ed., Hogan Assessment Systems, 1992.

10 pg. 53 "Being a leader is important to me." These self-statement items originate from the Leader Self-Identity Scale developed by Hiller (2005), which has been widely utilized in leadership research. This scale measures the extent to which individuals internalize the leader role as part of their self-concept. It has been employed in various studies to examine leader identity development over time.

See: Day, David V., and Hock-Peng Sin. "Longitudinal Tests of an Integrative Model of Leader Development: Charting and Understanding Developmental Trajectories." The Leadership Quarterly, vol. 22, no.3, 2011, pp.545;560. Elsevier, https://doi.org/10.1016/j.leaqua.2011.04.011; Hiller, N.(2005). An examination of leadership beliefs and leadership self-identity: Constructs, correlates and outcomes. (Doctoral dissertation, The Pennsylvania State University).

Also See: Day &Sin (2011),who found that leader identity grew over time in response to increasing leadership challenges, and Miscenko, Guenter & Day (2017), who showed that identity development tracked with leadership skill growth in MBA students.

11 pg. 53 valuing diversity, and creating commitment.

See: Kragt, Darja, and David V. Day. "Predicting Leadership Competency Development and Promotion Among High-Potential Executives: The Role of Leader Identity." Frontiers in Psychology, vol. 11, 2020, article 1816. https://doi.org/10.3389/fpsyg.2020.01816

12 pg. 56 mutual goodness-of-fit for their values. In fact, there is a leadership approach called values-based leadership, which prioritizes humility and self-reflection and is connected to trust-building and high-performance cultures.

See: Cable, Daniel M., and Timothy A. Judge. "Person-Organization Fit, Job Choice Decisions, and Organizational Entry." Organizational Behavior and Human Decision Processes, vol. 67, no. 3, 1996, pp.294-311. https://doi.org/10.1006/obhd.1996.0081; Deci, Edward L., and Richard M. Ryan. "The 'What' and 'Why' of Goal Pursuits: Human Needs and the Self-Determination of Behavior." Psychological Inquiry, vol. 11, no. 4, 2000, pp. 227-268. https://doi.org/10.1207/S15327965PLI1104_01; Bass, B. M. and Steidlmeier, P. "Ethics, Character, and Authentic Transformational Leadership Behavior." The Leadership Quarterly, vol. 10, no. 2, 1999, pp. 181-217.https://doi.org/10.1016/S1048-9843(99)00016-8

CHAPTER 3

13 pg. 67 same neural pathways as physical pain. Social exclusion and interpersonal rejection are not just emotionally distressing—they are neurologically painful. Functional MRI studies demonstrate that experiences of social pain, such as being excluded, overlooked, or betrayed, activate the same neural regions associated with physical pain, particularly the dorsal anterior cingulate cortex (dACC) and anterior insula. Eisenberger and Lieberman's foundational 2004 study introduced the concept that "social pain shares a common neuroanatomical basis with physical pain," suggesting that our brains evolved to treat social connection as a survival imperative. This insight has profound implications for leadership: team dynamics, psychological safety, and inclusion are not just "nice to have"—they'rebiologicallynecessaryforwell-beingandengagement.Subsequentresearch has validated and extended these findings, confirming that social rejection—whether subtle (e.g., being left off an email) or overt (e.g., being scapegoated)—can trigger threat responses that impair cognitive functioning, decision-making, and emotional regulation in professional settings.

See: Eisenberger, Naomi I., and Matthew D. Lieberman. "Why It Hurts to Be Left Out: The Neurocognitive Overlap Between Physical and Social Pain." Trends in Cognitive Sciences, vol. 8, no. 7, 2004, pp. 294-300.; MacDonald, Geoff, and Mark R. Leary. "Why Does Social Exclusion Hurt? The Relationship Between Social and Physical Pain." Psychological Bulletin, vol. 131, no. 2, 2005, pp. 202-223.; Kross, Ethan, et al. "Social Rejection Shares Somatosensory Representations with Physical Pain." Proceedings of the National Academy of Sciences, vol. 108, no. 15, 2011, pp. 6270-6275.; Lieberman, Matthew D. Social: Why Our Brains Are Wired to Connect. Crown Publishers, 2013.

14 pg. 68 on par with smoking or obesity A robust body of research confirms that strong relational connection enhances mental, emotional, and even physical health. Meaningful social ties not only increase well-being and life satisfaction, but also serve as a protective factor against anxiety, depression, and early mortality. In a pivotal meta-analysis, individuals with strong social relationships had a 50% increased likelihood of survival, comparable to eliminating major risk factors like smoking and obesity. Similarly, the Harvard Study of Adult Development, one of the longest-running longitudinal studies on human flourishing, concluded that close, high-quality relationships are the most consistent predictors of long-term happiness and health—not career achievement, wealth, or fame. On the flip side, loneliness and chronic social disconnection are increasingly recognized as public health threats, even associated with elevated risks of heart disease, cognitive decline, and mental health disorders. In professional and leadership life, this underscores the vital role of connection—not just as a "soft skill," but as a foundational dimension of leader sustainability and team resilience.

See: Holt-Lunstad, Julianne, Timothy B. Smith, and J. Bradley Layton. "Social Relationships and Mortality Risk: A Meta-Analytic Review." PLOS Medicine, vol. 7, no. 7, 2010, e1000316.; Waldinger, Robert J., and Marc Schulz. The Good Life: Lessons from the World's Longest Scientific Study of Happiness. Simon & Schuster, 2023. Cacioppo, John T., and William Patrick. Loneliness: Human Nature and the Need for Social Connection. W.W. Norton, 2008.

15 pg. 70 are more likely to be resilient, satisfied, and effective.

See: Edmondson, Amy C. "Psychological Safety and Learning Behavior in Work Teams." Administrative Science Quarterly, vol. 44, no. 2, 1999, pp. 350-383. Kahn, William A. "Psychological Conditions of Personal Engagement and Disengagement at Work." Academy of Management Journal, vol. 33, no. 4, 1990, pp. 692-724. Grant, Adam M., and Sharon K. Parker. "Redesigning Work Design Theories: The Rise of Relational and Proactive Perspectives." Academy of Management Annals, vol. 3, no. 1, 2009, pp. 317-375. Reitz, Margaret, et al. "Connections at Work: How Friendship, Kindness, and Social Support Matter for Leadership." Leadership Quarterly, vol. 32, no. 5, 2021, Article 101393.

16 pg. 70 it's the medium of leadership itself. Research shows that task-oriented leadership styles—such as transactional or directive approaches—are useful in high-stakes, high-urgency, or highly structured environments, where clarity, speed, and output are essential, like the military. However, they tend to fall short in fostering long-term engagement, creativity, and adaptability. In contrast, relational leadership—rooted in emotional intelligence, trust-building, and psychological safety—correlates more strongly with team performance, organizational commitment, and individual flourishing. The most effective leaders know how to adaptively blend both styles: setting direction while investing in relationships and recognizing that leadership is not a solo act but a co-created process within dynamic social systems.

See: Avolio, Bruce J., and William L. Gardner. "Authentic Leadership Development: Getting to the Root of Positive Forms of Leadership." The Leadership Quarterly, vol. 16, no. 3, 2005, pp. 315-338. Bass, Bernard M., and Bruce J. Avolio. Improving Organizational Effectiveness Through Transformational Leadership. Sage, 1994. Dinh, Jessica E., et al. "Leadership Theory and Research in the New Millennium: Current Theoretical Trends and Changing Perspectives." The Leadership Quarterly, vol. 25, no. 1, 2014, pp. 36-62. Goleman, Daniel. "Leadership That Gets Results." Harvard Business Review, vol. 78, no. 2,2000, pp. 78-90. Judge, Timothy A., et al. "Personality and Leadership: A Qualitative and Quantitative Review." Journal of Applied Psychology, vol.87, no. 4, 2002, pp. 765-780.Uhl-Bien, Mary. "Relational Leadership Theory: Exploring the Social Processes of Leadership and Organizing." The Leadership Quarterly, vol.17, no.6,2006, pp. 654-676.Caza, Brianna Barker, and Stephanie J. Creary. "The Construction of Professional Identity." Oxford Handbook of Positive Organizational Scholarship, edited by Kim S. Cameron and Gretchen M. Spreitzer, Oxford UP, 2012, pp. 493-503.; DeRue, D. Scott, and Susan J. Ashford. "Who Will Lead and Who Will Follow? A Social Process of Leadership Identity Construction in Organizations." Academy of Management Review, vol. 35, no. 4, 2010, pp.627-647.

17 pg. 71 increased resilience adaptability and performance Empirical studies across leadership and organizational psychology demonstrate that a clearer, well-integrated leader identity—combined with relational connection—enhances resilience, adaptability, and performance. For instance, resilience has been consistently linked to higher leadership effectiveness, job satisfaction, and organizational commitment. Moreover, research in identity leadership shows that leaders who infuse group-based pride and a shared social identity among team members significantly improve team performance. These findings align with broader frameworks of leader development that place self-awareness and adaptive identity integration at the heart of leadership effectiveness.

See: Goh, Jonathan, et al. "Resilience and Leadership: Performance, Job Satisfaction, and Organizational Commitment." Building Leadership Resilience: The CORE Framework, CCL Innovation, 2023.;Joyce, Sadhbh, et al. "Road to Resilience: A Systematic Review and Meta-analysis of Resilience Training Programmes." BMJ Open, vol. 8, no. 6, 2018.; Hou, Liang, et al. "Linking Identity Leadership and Team Performance: The Role of Group-Based Pride and Leader Political Skill." Frontiers in Psychology, vol. 12, 2021.; Day, David V., and Lisa Dragoni. "Leader Development: A Review in Context." The Leadership Quarterly, 2015. Ryan, N.F., and Michelle Hammond. "A Qualitative Study Unpacking the Leader Identity Development Process." Leadership & Organization Development Journal, vol. 45, no. 4, 2024.

18 pg. 74 buried their essence of self-as-leader identity Research across healthcare, education, nonprofit, social services, and other mission-driven sectors consistently shows elevated rates of compassion fatigue, burnout, and identity strain among leaders and staff. These environments often attract high-empathy, high-capacity individuals who feel personally responsible for others' well-being, a dynamic linked to people-pleasing, emotional over functioning, and role overload. The emotional labor required—particularly in female-dominated or caregiving-oriented cultures—blurs boundaries and can erode resilience over time. Faith-based organizations, HR, and mental health roles share this vulnerability, as cultural and organizational norms often reward constant relational availability. Without deliberate boundary-setting and strong identity clarity, connection—a leadership strength—can tip into exhaustion, self-neglect, and diminished leadership effectiveness.

See: Brotheridge, Céleste M., and Alicia A. Grandey. "Emotional Labor and Burnout: Comparing Two Perspectives of 'People Work.'" Journal of Vocational Behavior, vol. 60, no. 1, 2002, pp. 17–39.; Figley, Charles R. Compassion Fatigue: Coping with Secondary Traumatic Stress Disorder in Those Who Treat the Traumatized. Brunner/Mazel, 1995.; Gilligan, Carol. In a Different Voice: Psychological Theory and Women's Development. Harvard University Press, 1982.; Grant, Louise, and Gail Kinman. "Enhancing Wellbeing in Social Work Students: Building Resilience in the Next Generation." Social Work Education, vol. 31, no. 5, 2012, pp. 605–21.; Hochschild, Arlie Russell. The Managed Heart: Commercialization of Human Feeling. University of California Press, 1983.; Joinson, Carla. "Coping with Compassion Fatigue." Nursing, vol. 22, no. 4, 1992, pp. 116–21.; Maslach, Christina, and Michael P. Leiter. Burnout: The Cost of Caring. Malor Books, 2016.; Skovholt, Thomas M., and Michelle Trotter-Mathison. The Resilient Practitioner: Burnout Prevention and Self-Care Strategies for Counselors, Therapists, Teachers, and Health Professionals. 3rd ed., Routledge, 2016.; Stamm, Beth Hudnall. The Concise ProQOL Manual. 2nd ed., ProQOL. org, 2010.

CHAPTER 4

19 **pg. 89 despite challenges and setbacks.** Leadership grit refers to the perseverance and sustained passion leaders exhibit toward long-term goals, especially in the face of obstacles, uncertainty, or failure. Rooted in Angela Duckworth's foundational work on grit, recent research has examined how leaders with high grit are more likely to persist through adversity, model resilience, and create cultures of perseverance within their teams. Leadership grit has been positively correlated with transformational leadership behaviors, goal commitment, and organizational performance, especially in volatile or high-pressure contexts.

See: Duckworth, Angela L., et al. "Grit: Perseverance and passion for long-term goals." Journal of Personality and Social Psychology, vol. 92, no. 6, 2007, pp. 1087-1101. For a leader-ship-specific application: Kelly, David R., Matthews, Michael D., and Paul T. Bartone. "Grit and hardiness as predictors of performance among West Point cadets." Military Psychology, vol. 26, no. 4, 2014, pp. 327-342.

20 **pg. 92 such as the authentic leadership approach.** Bill George, former Medtronic CEO and Harvard Business School professor, introduced the concept of authentic leadership in his 2003 book, Authentic Leadership: Rediscovering the Secrets to Creating Lasting Value. He later expanded the concept in True North (2007) and subsequent works. George argues that authentic leaders are grounded in their values, lead with purpose, and build trust through honesty and consistency. Rather than conforming to external models of leadership or charisma, authentic leaders develop a deep sense of self-awareness, emotional intelligence, and internal moral compass—all elements of the process in Leading Becomes You. These authentic leaders demonstrate transparency, practice balanced processing (seeking out diverse perspectives), and are guided by a commitment to service rather than ego or image. Research based on George's framework suggests that authentic leadership correlates with increased employee engagement, psychological safety, and performance. It's especially relevant in these VUCA meets BANI times as followers seek trustworthy and stable guidance.

See: George, Bill, et al. True North: Discover Your Authentic Leadership. Jossey-Bass, 2007.

Bokhorst (2020), explores authentic leadership from acritical and developmental perspective, emphasizing that authenticity is not just about individual self-expression, but also about relational and contextual alignment(connection!). The article critiques overly simplistic or individualistic models of authentic leadership and calls for acknowledgement of the social construction of identity and the ethical responsibilities of leaders to others. Bokhorst integrates insights from existential and dialogical philosophy, proposing that authentic leadership requires ongoing reflexivity, openness to being shaped by others, and a continuous engagement with one's values and environment. This view pushes authentic leadership beyond trait-based models into a relational and moral practice.

See: Bokhorst, Joost A. C. "Authentic Leadership: A Phenomenon, Not a Formula." Leadership, vol. 16, no. 1, 2020, pp. 91-107. SAGE Journals, https://doi.org/10.1177/1742715019885762

21 **pg. 97**

See: Lazar, Mona. "Are You an Introvert? Here's 5 Ways You Intimidate People without Doing a Thing." Medium, 31 Aug. 2022, https://medium.com/illumination/are-you-an-intro-vert-heres-5-ways-you-intimidate-peopl e-without-doing-a-thing-93ba2936d577

22 pg. 98 naturally foster deep-thinking environments A substantial body of research challenges the traditional assumption that extroversion is the default or ideal leadership trait. While extroverted leaders often excel in high-visibility, socially intensive contexts, studies show that introverted leaders can match or even surpass their extroverted peers—especially when leading proactive, self-starting teams. Introverted leaders tend to engage in active listening, carefully consider diverse perspectives, and encourage autonomy, which can unlock greater team engagement and innovation. They often create reflective, deep-thinking environments where individuals feel heard and valued, a dynamic linked to higher satisfaction and problem-solving capacity. This perspective aligns with broader leadership literature emphasizing that effectiveness is highly contingent on the match between leader traits, team needs, and situational demands, rather than on a single "ideal" personality profile. Susan Cain's influential work Quiet brought this research to public awareness, reframing introversion as a leadership asset rather than a liability.

See: Cain, Susan. Quiet: The Power of Introverts in a World That Can't Stop Talking. Crown Publishing Group, 2012.; Grant, Adam M., Francesca Gino, and David A. Hofmann. "Reversing the Extraverted Leadership Advantage: The Role of Employee Proactivity." Academy of Management Journal, vol. 54, no. 3, 2011, pp. 528–550.; Judge, Timothy A., et al. "Personality and Leadership: A Qualitative and Quantitative Review." Journal of Applied Psychology, vol. 87, no. 4, 2002, pp. 765–780.; Kahnweiler, Jennifer B. The Introverted Leader: Building on Your Quiet Strength. 2nd ed., Berrett-Koehler, 2013.; Zaccaro, Stephen J. "Trait-Based Perspectives of Leadership." American Psychologist, vol. 62, no. 1, 2007, pp. 6–16.

23 pg. 98 make better decisions and pivot more effectively. Research shows that leaders who actively participate in peer learning communities and mentoring networks benefit from improved decision-making, adaptability, and leadership development. Peer engagement enhances cognitive diversity, provides real-time feedback, and fosters reflective practice—factors that help leaders navigate complexity and pivot more effectively.

See: Bruce, Chrystal D., et al. "The Value of Peer Mentoring Networks for Developing Leaders and Inspiring Change." Journal of Chemical Information and Modeling, vol. 62, no.12, 2022, pp. 6292-6296.; Young, Dallin George, et al. "The Quality and Quantity of Participation in Peer Leader Experiences and Student Outcomes: A Cross-National Validation of Constructs and Predictive Model." Research in Higher Education, vol. 65,2024, pp. 893-13.; Murray, Denise E., and Mary Ann Christison. "Peer Mentoring and Coaching as Tools for Leadership Development and Learning." Language Teacher Leadership, Springer, 2023, pp.153-179.

CHAPTER 5

24 pg. 107 Awareness is the foundation of change. Awareness, in psychological terms, refers to the state of being conscious of what's happening to us, on the inside and outside. It encompasses the ability to perceive, feel, and be cognizant of events, objects, thoughts, emotions, and our sensations. It's a main player in how psychologists understand human cognition and behavior. Sudden awareness, often described as an "Aha!" moment or insight, is characterized by an abrupt realization or comprehension that was previously elusive. Cognitive neuroscience research indicates that these "a-ha!" moments result from unconscious processing and culminate in a sudden reorganization of information in the brain. This reorganization leads to a lightning-fast shift in understanding. You might think of awareness on a spectrum that ranges from unconsciousness to "super" consciousness. This range includes unconsciousness: we are not aware of the environment or what's happening internally; subconscious: thinking process occurs below the level of conscious awareness but still influences our thoughts and behaviors; consciousness: we are actively aware of our environment and what's happening internally; self-awareness: recognizing our own self or self-as-leader individually and separate from the environment, others' influences on our internal process; and supraconsciousness: a hyperawareness that goes beyond personal identity, often associated with spiritual experiences. It's helpful to consider that we can have these different "levels" of awareness in different situations, contexts, or chapters of our lives. Our goal is to build more capacity in the self-awareness zone.

See: American Psychological Association. "Awareness." APA Dictionary of Psychology. https://dictionary.apa.org/awareness; Kounios, John and Mark Beeman. "The Cognitive Neuroscience of Insight." Annual Review of Psychology, vol. 65,2014, pp. 71-93.; Reid, Sophie. "Eureka! The Science Behind Moments of Sudden Insight. "WHYY, 1 Sept. 2015.https://whyy.org/segments/eureka-moments-q/; "Understanding the 5 Levels of Awareness in Psychology." Listen Hard.https://listen-hard.com/cognitive-and-ex-perimental-psychology/5-levels-awareness-psychology/listen-hard.com

25 pg. 107 but only 10 to 15% do.

See: Eurich, Tasha. Insight: The Surprising Truth About How Others See Us, How We See Ourselves, and Why the Answers Matter More Than We Think. Crown Publishing Group, 2017.

26 pg. 109 foundational for authentic leadership Leadership researchers have long documented that self-reflection on one's life story is foundational to authentic leadership development. Psychologist Dan P. McAdams describes this as creating a narrative identity—an internalized life story that integrates past, present, and future into a coherent sense of self. Research shows that leaders who explore their personal story "come to know, claim, and enact their leader identity," linking formative experiences to their current purpose. Authentic leadership emerges from an ongoing cycle of self-awareness and relational transparency, both rooted in reflection on the events and relationships that shaped a leader's values. Research differentiates between "horizontal" leader development (focused on skills) and "vertical" development (expanding self-concept, purpose, and relational capacity), emphasizing that without reflective integration, leadership remains shallow and scripted. These findings align directly with the Leading Becomes You model, where Connection to Purpose is strengthened when leaders locate meaning in their own timeline, and Connection to Others grows when they share those stories, empathize with others' journeys, and lead with vulnerability.

See: Avolio, Bruce J., and William L. Gardner. "Authentic Leadership Development: Getting to the Root of Positive Forms of Leadership." The Leadership Quarterly, vol. 16, no. 3, 2005, pp. 315–338.; Day, David V., Michelle M. Harrison, and Stanley M. Halpin. An Integrative Approach to Leader Development: Connecting Adult Development, Identity, and Expertise. Psychology Press, 2009.; McAdams, Dan P. The Redemptive Self: Stories Americans Live By. Revised and expanded ed., Oxford University Press, 2013.; Shamir, Boas, and Galit Eilam. "What's Your Story? A Life-Stories Approach to Authentic Leadership Development." The Leadership Quarterly, vol. 16, no. 3, 2005, pp. 395–417.

CHAPTER 6

27 pg. 135 approximately 6,200 thoughts per day Neuroscientific research suggests that the average adult brain generates approximately 6,200 thoughts per day, based on findings using "thought worms"—patterns of neural activity detected through fMRI. This sheer volume of mental activity means the brain favors efficiency, often using heuristics and automatic processing to keep up with the demands of daily life and leadership. While efficiency is helpful for speed, it increases vulnerability to overgeneralization, assumptions, and implicit bias—our thinking traps. However, research in mindfulness and metacognition (our ability to think about our thinking) shows that reflective awareness practices can help interrupt these automatic thought patterns, allowing more deliberate and intentional thinking, which is especially relevant for leaders seeking greater mental clarity and behavioral agility.

See: Kiken, Laura G., et al. "From a state to a trait: Trajectories of state mindfulness in meditation during intervention predict changes in trait mindfulness." Personality and Individual Differences, vol. 81, 2015, pp. 41-46. https://doi.org/10.1016/j.paid.2014.12.044; Tseng, Jennifer, et al. "Thoughts as dynamic entities: Identifying transitions in thought using brain network activity patterns." Nature Communications, vol. 11, no. 1, 2020, article no. 1796. https://doi.org/10.1038/s41467-020-15532-4; Zeidan, Fadel, et al. "Mindfulness meditation improves cognition: Evidence of brief mental training." Consciousness and Cognition, vol. 19, no. 2,2010, pp. 597-605.https://doi.org/10.1016/j.concog.2010.03.014;

28 pg. 136 identity thinking traps. The "reflex thoughts" are taken from "cognitive biases" in psychology and some have a long history. Each of them have their own line of research and I'll list some of those here. Nickerson, Raymond S. "Confirmation bias: A ubiquitous phenomenon in many guises." Review of General Psychology 2, no. 2 (1998): 175–220.; Tversky, Amos, and Daniel Kahneman. "Judgment under uncertainty: Heuristics and biases." Science 185, no. 4157 (1974): 1124–1131.; Baumeister, Roy F., et al. "Bad is stronger than good." Review of General Psychology 5, no. 4 (2001): 323–370.; Ross, Lee, David Greene, and Pamela House. "The 'false consensus effect': An egocentric bias in social perception and attribution processes." Journal of Experimental Social Psychology 13, no. 3 (1977): 279–301.; Thorndike, Edward L. "A constant error in psychological ratings." Journal of Applied Psychology 4, no. 1 (1920): 25–29.

What I refer to as "thinking traps" and have written to match our ecosystem and repotting metaphor draw from the clinical concept of cognitive distortions, first introduced by psychiatrist Aaron T. Beck in his influential 1963 paper, "Thinking and Depression: Idiosyncratic Content and Cognitive Distortions." Beck identified what we call in psychology" maladaptive thought patterns"—such as catastrophizing, personalization, and all-or-nothing thinking—that were prevalent in his patients with depression. These distorted patterns laid the foundation for what would become a widely used and researched approach to psychotherapy called cognitive therapy and eventually cognitive behavioral therapy (CBT). Psychologist David D. Burns later brought these concepts into public awareness and accessibility in his bestselling book, Feeling Good: The New Mood Therapy (1980), in which he outlined and labeled specific distortions in a highly relatable way. However you want to refer to them, it's a great tool for leaders to recognize habitual thought patterns that may undermine self-awareness, decision-making, and leadership presence.

See: Beck, Aaron T. "Thinking and Depression: I. Idiosyncratic Content and Cognitive Distortions." Archives of General Psychiatry, vol. 9, no.4, 1963, pp. 324-333. https://doi.org/10.1001/archpsyc.1963.01720160014002; Burns, David. Feeling Good: The New Mood Therapy. William Morrow, 1980.

29 pg. 136 essential for leader identity clarity Psychological research consistently demonstrates that we all carry deep beliefs—sometimes called schemas or core beliefs—that function as mental blueprints for how we view ourselves, others, and the world. Schema therapy and related research in cognitive, developmental, and personality psychology support the idea that these deeply held beliefs are enduring mental frameworks that shape how we perceive ourselves, others, and the world. Jeffrey Young's schema therapy model identifies early unhelpful schemas as pervasive patterns formed in childhood or adolescence developed through the interaction of temperament and unmet core emotional needs. These beliefs can be helpful—providing stability and guiding values—or harmful, contributing to low self-worth, mistrust, overcompensation, and rigid role adherence. Beck's cognitive theory similarly emphasizes that core beliefs, once formed, filter all new experiences, often outside of conscious awareness. In leadership contexts, unexamined deep beliefs can unconsciously influence decision-making, interpersonal dynamics, and self-concept clarity, either reinforcing healthy leadership identity or perpetuating distorted, limiting patterns. Recognizing and addressing these beliefs is therefore essential for leader identity clarity and sustainable leadership effectiveness.

See: Beck, Aaron T. Cognitive Therapy and the Emotional Disorders. Penguin, 1976.; Harms, P. D., Seth M. Spain, and Sean T. Hannah. "Leader Development and the Dark Side of Personality." The Leadership Quarterly, vol. 22, no. 3, 2011, pp. 495–509.; Young, Jeffrey E., Janet S. Klosko, and Marjorie E. Weishaar. Schema Therapy: A Practitioner's Guide. Guilford Press, 2003.;

30 pg. 137 an hour and a day. In cognitive psychology, automatic thoughts are fast, habitual interpretations that occur almost instantly in response to situations. Aaron Beck's foundational work on cognitive therapy identified these thoughts as the immediate expressions of underlying core beliefs—what we're calling deep beliefs—, shaping emotional and behavioral responses often without conscious awareness. While automatic thoughts are essential for efficiency and quick decision-making, their content and patterns are directly influenced by deep beliefs formed earlier in life. Daniel Kahneman's dual-process theory describes these as "System 1" processes—fast, intuitive, and often emotionally charged—contrasting with the slower, more deliberate "System 2" thinking used for complex problem-solving. In leadership contexts, positive and accurate automatic thoughts can enhance responsiveness, decisiveness, and relational connection. However, when these mental shortcuts are negative, biased, or outdated, they can narrow perspective, undermine mental agility, and perpetuate unexamined patterns of reaction, ultimately impacting leader effectiveness and identity clarity. Recognizing and reframing unhelpful automatic thoughts is a critical component of developing adaptive leadership habits.

See: Beck, Aaron T. Cognitive Therapy and the Emotional Disorders. Penguin, 1976.; Kahneman, Daniel. Thinking, Fast and Slow. Farrar, Straus and Giroux, 2011.

31 pg. 142 the constant calculation of how to be Cognitive load theory explains that the human brain has a limited capacity for processing information at any given time. When demands exceed this capacity—known as cognitive overload—it negatively affects concentration, memory, and decision-making, leading to stress, fatigue, and decreased productivity. For leaders, this may look like decision fatigue, avoidance of challenges, and higher error rates—likely more noticeable during periods of sustained complexity or crisis. Research demonstrates that women leaders face a double bind contributing to their cognitive load: If they are assertive, they may be perceived as too harsh; if they are nurturing, they risk being seen as weak. This constant identity management imposes a cognitive "tax" that can further contribute to less fulfillment, burnout and disengagement over time. These intersecting pressures highlight the need to recognize and address not only the visible workload but the invisible mental and emotional labor that shapes the leadership experience for women. Doing so is critical for fostering sustainable leadership and equity.

See: Paas, Fred, Alexander Renkl, and John Sweller. "Cognitive Load Theory: Instructional Implications of the Interaction between Information Structures and Cognitive Architecture." Instructional Science, vol.32, no. 1/2, 2004, pp. 1-8. Springer, https://doi.org/10.1023/B:TRUC.0000021806.17516.d0; Sweller, John. "Cognitive Load Theory, Learning Difficulty, and Instructional Design." Learning and Instruction, vol. 4, no.4, 1994, pp. 295-312. Elsevier, https://doi.org/10.1016/0959-4752(94)90003-5; Brescoll, Victoria L. "Leading with Their Hearts? How Gender Stereotypes of Emotion Affect Women's Evaluation as Leaders." The Leadership Quarterly, vol. 27, no.3, 2016, pp.415-428. https://doi.org/10.1016/j.leaqua.2016.02.005; Williams, Joan C., and Rachel Dempsey. What Works for Women at Work: Four Patterns Working Women Need to Know. NYU Press, 2014. Ely, Robin J., Herminia Ibarra, and Deborah M. Kolb. "Taking Gender into Account: Theory and Design for Women's Leadership Development Programs." Academy of Management Learning & Education, vol.10, no.3, 2011, pp.474-493. https://doi.org/10.5465/amle.2010.0046

32 **pg. 144 rather than impossible obstacles**. Research on optimism in leadership underscores the benefits of grounded hope while warning against blind positivity. The psychological definition of optimism is a generalized expectation that good things will happen and that challenges are temporary and manageable. Psychologist Martin Seligman distinguishes between flexible, realistic optimism and blind positivity—emphasizing that sustainable well-being and effective leadership stem from optimism grounded in truth and personal agency. Optimistic leaders are shown to be more resilient, solution-focused, and better at motivating teams during uncertainty. Studies also suggest that leader optimism contributes to higher employee engagement, psychological safety, and innovation, especially when leaders model hopeful thinking while acknowledging real constraints. However, an overreliance on positivity that bypasses pain or minimizes barriers can lead to disconnection, mistrust, and emotional suppression— undermining the very growth optimism intends to fuel. A balanced mindset that acknowledges difficulty while remaining hopeful is key to both personal leadership development and healthy workplace cultures.

See: Seligman, Martin E.P. Learned Optimism: How to Change Your Mind and Your Life. Vintage, 2006.; Forgeard, Marie J. C., and Martin E. P. Seligman. "Seeing the Glass Half Full: A Review of the Causes and Consequences of Optimism." Pratiques Psychologiques, vol. 18,no.2, 2012, pp.107-120. https://doi.org/10.1016/j.prps.2012.02.002; Avolio, Bruce J., and Fred Luthans. "The High Impact Leader: Moments Matter in Accelerating Authentic Leadership Development." McGraw-Hill, 2006.; Rego, Arménio, et al. "Leader Self-Confidence and Positive Psychological Capital: The Mediating Role of Leader Psychological Empowerment." Journal of Leadership & Organizational Studies, vol. 19, no. 1, 2012, pp. 29-41.https://doi.org/10.1177/1548051811404895

33 **pg. 152 the brain grows, learns, and changes** Neuroplasticity refers to the brain's remarkable ability to reorganize itself by forming new neural connections across the lifespan. Once thought to be fixed after childhood, neuroscience now confirms that the adult brain can adapt in response to learning, environment, habits, and even intentional reflection. For leaders, this matters deeply: How you think, behave, react to stress, and relate to others is not hardwired—it can be reshaped through awareness, practice, and feedback. In workplace contexts, neuroplasticity underpins emotional intelligence, leadership development, resilience, and unlearning outdated or limiting beliefs. It means that change is biologically possible, not just motivationally encouraged—offering real hope for transformation at both the individual and organizational level.

See: Doidge, Norman. The Brain That Changes Itself: Stories of Personal Triumph from the Frontiers of Brain Science. Penguin Books, 2007.; Draganski, Bogdan, et al. "Changes in Grey Matter Induced by Train-ing." Nature, vol. 427, no. 6972, 2004, p. 311.https://doi.org/10.1038/427311a; Davidson, Richard J., and Sharon Begley. The Emotional Life of Your Brain. Hudson Street Press, 2012.

CHAPTER 7

34 **pg. 161 self-management, and other management.** Emotional awareness refers to the capacity to notice, identify, and name one's emotions accurately in real-time. It is foundational to emotional intelligence and linked to self-awareness, stress regulation, and interpersonal effectiveness. Emotional agility, a concept developed by psychologist Dr. Susan David, builds upon awareness and emphasizes the ability to move through emotions with openness, curiosity, and choice. Rather than being driven by difficult thoughts or feelings, emotionally agile individuals observe their inner experience without fusion, allowing them to align their actions with core values rather than with reactive emotion. In leadership and workplace contexts, emotional awareness helps leaders understand their internal state, while emotional agility enables them to respond rather than react—a distinction critical to adaptive leadership,

resilience, and psychological safety.

See: Goleman, Daniel. Emotional Intelligence: Why It Can Matter More Than IQ. Bantam Books, 1995.; David, Susan. Emotional Agility: Get Unstuck, Embrace Change, and Thrive in Work and Life. Avery,2016.

35 **pg. 164 critical role in rational thought** Neuroscientist Antonio R. Damasio demonstrated that emotion is not the enemy of reason but its indispensable partner. Working with patients who had damage to the parts of the brain that inhibit emotional signaling, Damasio showed these individuals could still think logically about choices, yet they struggled to decide. Without the "somatic markers" provided by emotion, their rational calculations stalled in endless cost-benefit thinking loops. The finding upended the old "reason versus feeling" split, proving that healthy judgment relies on emotional signals to tag options as good, bad, or uncertain and to motivate timely action—insight with profound implications for leadership and ethical decision-making.

See: Damasio, Antonio R. Descartes' Error: Emotion, Reason, and the Human Brain. G. P. Putnam's Sons, 1994.

36 **pg. 170 Inside Out and Inside Out 2.**

Docter, Pete, and Ronnie del Carmen, directors. InsideOut. Walt Disney Studios Motion Pictures, 2015.; Mann, Kelsey, director. Inside Out 2. Walt Disney Studios Motion Pictures, 2024.

37 **pg. 174 more effective in some leadership situations** Research consistently shows that women, on average, tend to demonstrate higher empathic accuracy, interpersonal sensitivity, and relational attunement than men. These relational strengths—often cultivated through both socialization and life experience—contribute to greater effectiveness in leader situations requiring emotionally intelligent leadership, team cohesion, and trust-building. Women leaders are also more likely to adopt transformational leadership styles, which emphasize collaboration, support, and development of others—qualities strongly linked to higher engagement and team performance. This relational edge does not suggest that all women lead alike, nor that men cannot develop these skills, but it does highlight the value of relational intelligence in leadership and the need to recognize and sup-port it as a critical strength and essential skill.

See: Christov-Moore, Leonardo, et al. "Empathy: Gender Effects in Brain and Behavior." Neuroscience & Biobehavioral Reviews, vol.46,2014, pp.604-627. https://doi.org/10.1016/j.neubiorev.2014.09.001; Eagly, Alice H., and Mary C. Johannesen-Schmidt. "The Leadership Styles of Women and Men." Journal of Social Issues, vol.57, no.4, 2001, pp.781-797.https://doi.org/10.1111/0022-4537.00241;Bartol,Kathryn M., and David M. Butterfield. "Sex Effects in Evaluating Leaders: A Role Congruity Perspective." Journal of Applied Psychology, vol. 84, no. 5, 1999, pp. 765-776. https://doi.org/10.1037/0021-9010.84.5.765 (18); Anjali Singh, Seema Das, Sumi Jha. Women leadership and emotions: Knowledge structure and future research opportunities, European Management Journal, Volume 41, Issue 6, 2023, 864-882,https://doi.org/10.1016/j.emj.2023.05.004

38 **pg. 176 and even perception of risk** Recent studies have highlighted the intricate relationship between the gut and the brain, emphasizing how gut-derived signals can influence emotional states and decision-making processes. For instance, research has shown that the gut microbiome can affect the syn-thesis of neurotransmitters like serotonin, which plays a crucial role in mood regulation. Additionally, the gut-brain axis has been implicated in modulating responses to stress and risk, suggesting that our "gut feelings" are grounded in physiological processes. In leadership scenarios, this underscores the importance of integrating intuitive insights with conscious self-re-flection to make balanced and effective decisions.

See: Holzer, P. (2022). Gut Signals and Gut Feelings: Science at the Interface of Data and Beliefs. Frontiers in Behavioral Neuroscience,16, 929332.https://doi.org/10.3389/fnbeh.2022.929332; Neuroba. (2025). The Role of Gut-Brain Connection in Emotional Awareness. Retrieved from https://www.neuroba.com/post/the-role-of-gut-brain-connection-in-emotional-awareness-neuroba;Angela,V.(2025).The Art Of Leading With Intuition: Why Gut Feeling Is Your Best Ally. Forbes Coaches Council. Retrieved from https://www.forbes.com/councils/forbescoachescouncil /2025/02/18/the-art-of-leading- with-intuition-why-gut-feeling-is-your-best-ally/; Lacasse, K. (2015). Going with your gut: How William James 'theory of emotions brings insights to risk perception and decision-making research. New Ideas in Psychology, 39, 1-6. https://doi.org/10.1016/j.newideapsych.2015.04.001; Pearson., Donkin, C.,& Lufityanto, G. (2016). Intuition: It's More Than a Feeling. Association for Psychological Science. Retrievedfromhttps://www.psychologicalscience.org/news/minds-business/intuition-its-more-than-a-feeling.htmlMayer EA; Gut feelings: the emerging biology of gut-brain communication. Nat Rev Neurosci. 2011 Jul

13;12(8):453-66. doi: 10.1038/nrn3071, PMID: 21750565; PMCID: PMC3845678.

39 **pg. 176**

See: Paul, Annie Murphy. The extended mind: the power of thinking outside the brain. Boston: Houghton Mifflin Harcourt, 2021.

CHAPTER 8

40 **pg. 187 hard things without complaining. Now hardiness** Psychological hardiness, first conceptualized by Suzanne Kobasa in the late 1970s, is a personality style characterized by three interrelated attitudes: commitment (remaining engaged and finding purpose in work and relationships), control (believing one can influence outcomes rather than being powerless), and challenge (viewing change and stress as opportunities for learning and growth). Her studies found that individuals high in hardiness were less likely to develop stress-related illness despite experiencing high levels of workplace stress. Later research extended these findings, demonstrating that hardiness not only buffers against burnout and health decline but also predicts adaptive coping, improved performance under pressure, and persistence in the face of adversity. In leadership contexts, hardiness fosters resilience during organizational change, supports ethical decision-making under stress, and enables leaders to model psychological safety—creating healthier, more stable, and higher-performing teams. These benefits align with contemporary leadership frameworks that emphasize adaptability, resourcefulness, and sustained well-being as cornerstones of effective leadership.

See: Bartone, Paul T. "Resilience Under Military Operational Stress: Can Leaders Influence Hardiness?" Military Psychology, vol. 18, no. S1, 2006, pp. S131–S148.; Kobasa, Suzanne C. "Stressful Life Events, Personality, and Health: An Inquiry into Hardiness." Journal of Personality and Social Psychology, vol. 37, no. 1, 1979, pp. 1–11.; Maddi, Salvatore R., et al. "Hardiness Training Facilitates Performance in College." The Journal of Positive Psychology, vol. 4, no. 6, 2009, pp. 566–577.; Maddi, Salvatore R., Suzanne C. Kobasa, and Stephen C. Hoover. "An Existential-Humanistic Theory of Hardiness." In Existential-Humanistic Therapy, edited by Kirk J. Schneider and Orah T. Krug, American Psychological Association, 2010, pp. 73–82. Maddi, Salvatore R. "The Story of Hardiness: Twenty Years of Theorizing, Research, and Practice." Consulting Psychology Journal: Practice and Research, vol. 54, no. 3, 2002, pp. 173-185.https://doi.org/10.1037/1061-4087.54.3.173;Bartone, Paul T. "Resilience Under Military Operational Stress: Can Leaders Influence Hardiness?" Military Psychology, vol. 18, suppl.1, 2006, pp. S131-S148. https://doi.org/10.1207/s15327876mp1803s_10

CHAPTER 9

41 **pg. 223 into a stable self-concept** Research on self-concept clarity—how clearly and confidently people define and maintain their sense of self—underscores why acceptance is essential for leader identity clarity. People with high self-concept clarity report greater psychological well-being, self-esteem, and resilience, whereas low clarity is linked to rumination, indecision, and emotional instability. Identity researchers further show that clarity develops not just through self-awareness, but through integration—accepting and making sense of the different parts of one's identity across time and context. In leadership, this integration process means moving from simply noticing strengths, weaknesses, and patterns (awareness) to embracing them as part of a coherent, evolving identity (acceptance). Without acceptance, awareness can lead to self-critique or performative change; with acceptance, it becomes the foundation for authentic, stable, and adaptive leadership.

See: Campbell, J. D., Trapnell, P. D., Heine, S. J., Katz, I. M., Lavallee, L. F., &Lehman, D.(1996). Self-concept clarity: Measurement, personality correlates, and cultural boundaries. Journal of Personality and Social Psychology, 70(1), 141-156.https://doi.org/10.1037/0022-3514.70.1.141; Luyckx, K., Schwartz, S. J., Goossens, L., &Pollock, S. (2011). The relationship between identity development and adjustment in emerging adults: The moderating role of identity style. Identity: An International Journal of Theory and Research, 11(3), 228-247.https://doi.org/10.1080/1 5283488.2011.585164

42 **pg. 223 more trustworthy in relationship, personally and professionally** In the Leading Becomes You model, acceptance is not a passive stance but an active capacity that deepens both self-connection and connection to others. Research on self-compassion provides a strong empirical foundation for this link. A randomized controlled trial of the Mindful Self-Compassion program demonstrated that cultivating self-acceptance through mindfulness and kindness toward oneself reduced self-criticism, increased emotional resilience, and strengthened interpersonal connection. Other research found that self-compassion predicted more adaptive interpersonal behaviors, such as

greater responsiveness, empathy, and reduced defensiveness during social interactions. For leaders, this means that acceptance of one's own imperfections and contradictions creates the psychological safety to extend that same acceptance to others. In turn, this fosters trust, belonging, and open communication—key elements of the connection dimension. Without this self-grounded acceptance, leaders risk building relationships on performance or compliance rather than on genuine, human-to-human connection.

See: Neff, K.D., & Germer, C.K. (2009). A pilot study and randomized controlled trial of the mindful self-compassion program. Journal of Clinical Psychology,65(6),613-626. https://doi.org/10.1002/jclp.20543; Reis, D. L., Grenier, J., & Manczak, E. (2016). Self-compassion and adaptive interpersonal behavior. Personality and Individual Differences,90, 1-6.https://doi.org/10.1016/j.paid.2015.10.043

43 pg. 228 disengagement, or internalized shame This disorientation erodes the leader's capacity to access stable internal cues—such as personal values or intrinsic motivation—leaving them vulnerable to over-reliance on external feedback or shifting expectations. Without a clear internal compass, emotional decision-making becomes reactive or avoidant, which accelerates feelings of depletion and can contribute to depressive symptoms or shame-based self-perception.

See: Brown, Kirk Warren, and Richard M. Ryan. "The Benefits of Being Present: Mindfulness and Its Role in Psychological Well-Being." Journal of Personality and Social Psychology, vol. 84, no. 4, 2003, pp. 822-848; Campbell, Jennifer D., et al. "Self-Concept Clarity: Measurement, Personality Correlates, and Cultural Boundaries." Journal of Personality and Social Psychology, vol. 70, no. 1, 1996, pp. 141-156; Diehl, Manfred, CarrieT. Hastings, and Annette L. Stanton. "Self-Concept Differentiation across the Adult Life Span: Longitudinal Findings from a Cohort of Married Couples." Psychology and Aging, vol.21, no. 3, 2006, pp. 63-645; Luyckx, Koen, et al. "Unpacking Commitment and Exploration: Prevalence and Correlates of Identity Statuses in Late Adolescence." Journal of Adolescence, vol. 29, no. 3, 2006, pp. 361-378.; Rogers, Carl R. On Becoming a Person: A Therapist's View of Psychotherapy. Houghton Mifflin, 1961.

44 pg. 228 within their professional relationships. This dynamic aligns with Deci and Ryan's Self-Determination Theory, which asserts that psychological well-being depends on the fulfillment of three basic needs: autonomy, relatedness, and especially competence—the belief that one can effectively manage life's challenges. When leaders tether their worth to flawless performance, the innate need for competence becomes distorted into chronic self-monitoring and over-functioning. Neff (2011) argues that lacking self-compassion in such environments leads to harsh self-judgment and isolation, which only deepen performance-fueled burnout. Petriglieri (2020) describes how these conditions hollow out the leader, as individuals feel forced to wear a mask of capability while privately unraveling, disconnected from any authentic sense of identity or vitality.

See: Deci, Edward L., and Richard M .Ryan. "The 'What' and 'Why' of Goal Pursuits: Human Needs and the Self-Determination of Behavior." Psychological Inquiry, vol. 11, no. 4, 2000, pp. 227-268.; Neff, Kristin D. Self-Compassion: The Proven Power of Being Kind to Yourself. William Morrow, 2011; Petriglieri, Gianpiero. "The Psychology Behind Burnout." Harvard Business Review, 4 Feb. 2020, https://hbr.org/2020/02/the-psy-chology-behind-burnout; Padesky, Christine A., and Kathleen A. Mooney. "Strengths-Based Cognitive-Behavioural Therapy: A Four-Step Model to Build Resilience." Clinical Psychology & Psychotherapy, vol. 19, no. 4, 2012, pp. 283-290. https://doi.org/10.1002/cpp.1795; Verg-es, Alexandria S., et al. "The Impostor Phenomenon Among Leaders: Understanding Experiences and Organizational Impacts." The Leadership Quarterly, vol. 34, no. 1, 2023, Article 101679.https://doi.org/10.1016/j.leaqua.2022.101679

45 pg. 229 and trust erodes quietly Many leaders in the wasteland suffer from impostor phenomenon—a persistent internal experience of feeling like a fraud despite significant external success. This self-doubt often triggers a harsh inner critic, a recurring internal voice that magnifies flaws, invalidates accomplishments, and anticipates failure. The inner critic not only sustains impostor feelings but also heightens perfectionism, shame, and hypervigilance in professional settings. Studies have found this internal dynamic to be associated with emotional exhaustion, decreased self-efficacy, anxiety, and a chronic fear of being "found out". Leaders may appear competent and engaged, but internally they are waging a relentless battle with a voice that insists they don't belong. The result is a reactive, over functioning leadership style rooted in self-protection rather than grounded self-worth. Psychologically, this pattern aligns with research on contingent self-worth, which links self-esteem to external validation and performance-based outcomes. Neurologically, leaders operating from this mindset often override internal cues for rest or reflection due to chronic activation of the stress response. Emotionally, the leader may feel increasingly numb or resentful but continue working harder, believing that exhaustion is the price of being enough.

See: Bravata, Dena M., et al. "Prevalence, Predictors, and Treatment of Impostor Syndrome: A Systematic Review."

Journal of General Internal Medicine, vol. 35, no. 4, 2020, pp. 1252-1275. https://doi.org/10.1007/s11606-019-05364-1; Clance, Pauline Rose, and Suzanne A. Imes. "The Impostor Phenomenon in High Achieving Women: Dynamics and Therapeutic Intervention." Psychotherapy: Theory, Research & Practice, vol. 15, no. 3, 1978, pp. 241-247; Gilbert, Paul, et al. "Fears of Compassion and Happiness in Relation to Alexithymia, Mindfulness, and Self-Criticism." Psychology and Psychotherapy: Theory, Research and Practice, vol. 85, no. 4, 2012, pp. 374-390. https://doi.org/10.1111/j.2044-8341.2011.02046.x; Neureiter, Magdalena, and Eva Traut-Mattausch. "An Inner Barrier to Career Development: Preconditions of the Impostor Phenomenon and Consequences for Career Development." Frontiers in Psychology, vol. 7, 2016, Article 48. https://doi.org/10.3389/fpsyg.2016.00048

46 **pg. 234 beneath the armor of competence** The pattern described here aligns with research on contingent self-worth—a self-esteem structure in which personal value depends on meeting certain standards, gaining approval, or achieving specific outcomes. Leaders with contingent self-worth often tie identity to performance metrics, status, or others' evaluations, making their self-esteem vulnerable to fluctuations in external feedback. This dynamic can lead to over functioning, perfectionism, and emotional suppression as leaders work to maintain the appearance of competence while neglecting authentic self-expression. Research linked these patterns to workaholism and burnout, showing that excessive work investment, particularly when tied to identity, undermines health and sustainable performance. Low identity clarity exacerbates this risk, as leaders lack an internal anchor for self-definition and rely heavily on perceived external agendas. Petriglieri describes the outcome as the "hollowing out of self beneath the armor of competence"—a gradual erosion of authenticity and vitality masked by professional success. In leadership contexts, this trap undermines both personal fulfillment and the depth of connection with others, as relationships become mediated by role performance rather than genuine engagement.

See: Crocker, Jennifer, and Connie T. Wolfe. "Contingencies of Self-Worth." Psychological Review, vol. 108, no. 3, 2001, pp. 593–623. https://doi.org/10.1037/0033-295X.108.3.593.; Petriglieri, Gianpiero. "Don't Let the Pandemic Sink Your Company Culture." Harvard Business Review, 15 May 2020, https://hbr.org/2020/05/dont-let-the-pandemic-sink-your-company-culture.; Schaufeli, Wilmar B., Toon W. Taris, and Arnold B. Bakker. "It Takes Two to Tango: Workaholism Is Working Excessively and Working Compulsively." The Long Work Hours Culture: Causes, Consequences and Choices, edited by Ronald J. Burke and Cary L. Cooper, Emerald Group Publishing Limited, 2008, pp. 203–226.

47 **pg. 234 fraud despite significant external success** The impostor phenomenon—first described by Clance and Imes—refers to the persistent internal experience of feeling like a fraud despite objective evidence of competence and success. Leaders experiencing this phenomenon often attribute achievements to luck, timing, or others' overestimations, and fear eventual "exposure." This dynamic is frequently accompanied by inner critic dominance—a harsh, self-critical internal voice that magnifies perceived shortcomings—and by perfectionism-as-protection, in which excessively high standards are maintained to prevent failure or criticism. Research links impostor feelings in leaders to increased emotional exhaustion, reduced job satisfaction, and diminished self-efficacy. Perfectionism, while sometimes rewarded in high-achievement environments, has been associated with elevated stress, anxiety, and burnout. For leaders in the wasteland terrain, these patterns are compounded by low identity clarity and high dependence on external validation, making authentic connection and sustainable performance more difficult to maintain.

See: Clance, Pauline Rose, and Suzanne Ament Imes. "The Impostor Phenomenon in High Achieving Women: Dynamics and Therapeutic Intervention." Psychotherapy: Theory, Research & Practice, vol. 15, no. 3, 1978, pp. 241–247. https://doi.org/10.1037/h0086006.; Flett, Gordon L., and Paul L. Hewitt. Perfectionism: Theory, Research, and Treatment. American Psychological Association, 2002.; Vergauwe, Jasmine, et al. "Fear of Being Exposed: The Trait-Relatedness of the Impostor Phenomenon and Its Relevance in the Work Context." Journal of Business and Psychology, vol. 30, no. 3, 2015, pp. 565–581. https://doi.org/10.1007/s10869-014-9382-5.

48 **pg. 235 avoid vulnerability and judgment**

See: Brown, Breneé. The Gifts of Imperfection: Let Go of Who You Think You're Supposed to Be and Embrace Who You Are. Hazelden Publishing, 2010.

49 **pg. 240 dominance rather than development** Role-identity fusion occurs when a leader's identity becomes inseparable from their professional role, which has the negative result of interpreting feedback or even change into perceived existential threats. Psychologically, this mirrors identity foreclosure, a concept introduced by James Marcia as the unexamined adoption of an identity informed by external expectations. An example would be the eldest son in a third-generation family business who stepped into the CEO role straight out of business school, fulfilling

a lifelong expectation set by his parents and community; without ever exploring alternative paths or questioning whether the role aligned with his personal values, he now leads from a place of inherited duty, equating challenges to the company's traditions with personal failure. A related theory to identity foreclosure is identity fusion theory, its revised form—Comprehensive Identity Fusion Theory (CIFT)—offers a refined lens: that fusion involves a blurred integration between personal and role identities, forging a strong and synergistic defense that drives individuals to defend their role even against disruptive or even adaptive forces. In leadership contexts, such blurry and enmeshed fusion can lock in a rigid identity to the point that adaptability feels like self-erasure, necessitating defensiveness and explaining a leader's preference for dominance over development.

See: Gómez, Ángel, et al. "Comprehensive Identity Fusion Theory (CIFT): New Insights and a Revised Theory." Advances in Experimental Social Psychology, edited by Mark P. Zanna, vol. 70, Elsevier, 2024, pp. 275–332, doi:10.1016/BS.AESP.2024.03.003.; Marcia, James E. "Development and Validation of Ego Identity Status." Journal of Personality and Social Psychology, vol. 3, 1966, pp. 551–558.

50 pg. 240 petrifies the leader's identity and impact. In the context of narrative control, self-enhancement bias describes a leader's tendency to inflate their contributions and filter out feedback that threatens their preferred self-story. This bias maintains self-esteem, but in high-status roles, it can harden into a selective, self-protective narrative. This vulnerability is amplified by identity foreclosure—a premature commitment to a fixed self-concept without adequate exploration. When leaders merge these two tendencies, they risk locking their leadership identity into a rigid storyline that resists growth, adaptation, and honest feedback. Over time, the combination can "petrify" their identity, narrowing impact, alienating others, and reducing the flexibility needed to navigate complex leadership challenges. Breaking this cycle requires deliberate feedback-seeking, openness to disconfirming evidence, and the willingness to revise one's narrative in light of new perspectives.

See: Keltner, Dacher, Deborah H. Gruenfeld, and Cameron Anderson. "Power, Approach, and Inhibition." Psychological Review, vol. 110, no. 2, 2003, pp. 265–284. https://doi.org/10.1037/0033-295X.110.2.265.; Marcia, James E. "Development and Validation of Ego-Identity Status." Journal of Personality and Social Psychology, vol. 3, no. 5, 1966, pp. 551–558. https://doi.org/10.1037/h0023281.; Sedikides, Constantine, and Aiden P. Gregg. "Self-Enhancement: Food for Thought." Perspectives on Psychological Science, vol. 3, no. 2, 2008, pp. 102–116. https://doi.org/10.1111/j.1745-6916.2008.00068.x.

51 pg. 247 resilience, and ethical behavior Scholars Fry, Dik, and Steger have each advanced foundational frameworks explaining how spiritual meaning, purpose, and identity influence leadership and workplace flourishing. Together, Fry, Dik, and Steger argue that purpose-driven, identity-integrated leadership is not a soft ideal—it's a measurable driver of human and organizational flourishing. Leaders who connect to purpose, model authenticity, an Louis W. Fry's theory of spiritual leadership integrates intrinsic motivation, vision, and altruistic love to promote higher levels of organizational commitment and productivity. He defines spiritual leadership as the process of creating a vision where team members experience a sense of calling and membership, enabling them to find meaning in their work while feeling understood and valued. His model includes hope/faith, altruistic love, and meaning/ calling as central dimensions that not only elevate well-being but also improve individual and organizational outcomes.

See: Fry, Louis W. "Toward a Theory of Spiritual Leadership." The Leadership Quarterly, vol. 14, no. 6, 2003, pp. 693-727. Elsevier, https://doi.org/10.1016/j.leaqua.2003.09.001;

Bryan J. Dik, a leading researcher in vocational psychology, focuses on the concept of calling—a deeply personal sense of purpose aligned with one's work. He emphasizes that perceiving work as a calling is associated with increased job satisfaction, engagement, and psychological resilience. Dik argues that helping individuals discern their unique sources of meaning is a moral imperative in modern leadership and organizational development. His work often uses the Discern-Integrate-Know (DIK) model to foster purposeful engagement with one's career path.

See: Dik, Bryan J., and Ryan D. Duffy, editors. Make Your Job a Calling: How the Psychology of Vocation Can Change Your Life at Work. Templeton Press, 2012.

I had the privilege of collaborating with Michael F. Steger early in my career on research exploring whether experiencing work as a "calling" is rooted in something sacred or whether it can also be understood in a broader, secular sense. We found that the real power of calling comes from the meaning people experience in their work—whether or not it's tied to religion, which in turn supports well-being and positive work attitudes. This theme continues through Steger's body of work, where he shows that meaningful work predicts engagement, lowers burnout, and helps people thrive. His Meaning in Life Questionnaire (MLQ) remains a go-to tool for measuring these important connections.

See: Steger, Michael F., et al. "Work as Meaning: Individual and Organizational Benefits of Engaging in Meaningful Work." Purpose and Meaning in the Workplace, edited by Bryan J. Dik, Zinta S. Byrne, and Michael F. Steger, American Psychological Association, 2013, pp. 131–142.

See also: Steger, Michael F., Pickering, N. K., Shin, J. Y., & Dik, B. J. (2010). Calling in work: Secular or sacred? Journal of Career Assessment, 18(1), 82–96.

52 pg. 255 Leader Identity Formation Theory (LIFT) describes leader identity as a dynamic, evolving construct shaped by experiences across multiple life domains—professional, personal, relational, and community—over the course of one's lifespan. This process is influenced by context (the environments and cultures in which a leader operates), reflection (the intentional examination of experiences), and meaning-making (integrating those experiences into a coherent self-concept). LIFT research emphasizes that leader identity clarity is not static but continually refined as leaders encounter new challenges, roles, and perspectives. This aligns with the Leader Becoming Compass on pg 93. in Leading Becomes You, which maps how diverse life experiences collectively inform leadership approach, purpose, and values. By actively engaging with context, reflection, and meaning-making, leaders can strengthen their identity clarity and, in turn, their authenticity, adaptability, and impact.

See: Skinner, L. J. (2020). Leader Identity Formation Theory: Exploring the development of leader identity across the lifespan. Philosophy of Coaching: An International Journal, 5(2), 37-58. https://philosophyofcoaching.org/v5i2/03.pdf

53 pg. 256 ICD-11 reduced professional efficacy

See: World Health Organization. International Classification of Diseases, 11th Revision (ICD11): Mortality and Morbidity Statistics. World Health Organization, 2019. ICD-11 for Mortality and Morbidity Statistics, https://icd.who.int/browse11/l-m/en#/http://id.who.int/icd/entity/129180281. Accessed 12 Aug. 2025.

54 pg. 257 some people still believe it The Great Man (or Woman) Myth—the notion that leadership is an innate trait one either possesses or lacks—dominated early leadership theories in the 19th century. It was rooted in Thomas Carlyle's view that history is shaped by extraordinary individuals. However, empirical research over the mid-20th century, notably by Ralph Stogdill, demonstrated that leadership effectiveness depends on a dynamic interplay between personal traits and situational context, debunking the idea of a fixed, innate "leadership gene." This shift laid the foundation for updated behavioral and contingency-based leadership models that emphasize adaptable, learned leadership capacities (e.g. Leadership is teachable and learnable.) rather than "you have it or you don't" leadership attributes.

See: Bourque, Donald D. Understanding Leadership: From Great Man to Emotional Intelligence. In Herausvorderungen an das Management, vol. 10. Springer, 2003, pp. 3–12.; Stogdill, Ralph M. Handbook of Leadership: A Survey of Theory and Research. 2nd ed., Free Press, 1974. "The Evolution of Leadership Thinking: From Great Man Theory to Authentic Leadership." iManage Performance, 2023, imanageperformance.com/blog/the-evolution-of-leadership-thinking-from-great-man-theory-to-authentic-leadership/. iManage Performance. The Evolution of Leadership Theory." BMJ Leader, vol. 5, no. 1, 2018, p. 3, leader.bmj.com/content/5/1/3.full.pdf.

55 pg. 259 world, leadership and otherwise

See: Saleh, A., & Watson, R. (2017). Business excellence in a volatile, uncertain, complex and ambiguous environment (BEVUCA). TQM Journal, 29(4), 705-724; Tshetshe, Zoliswa. (2025). Recognising 'Being' in the BANI world. International Journal for Multidisciplinary Research. 7. 1-9.

56 pg. 260 moral injury

See: Dean, William, Zoe Talbot, and Suzanne Dean. "Moral Injury and Burnout in Healthcare Workers during COVID-19: A Review of the Current Literature." Psychiatry Research, vol. 302, 2019, 114024.https://doi.org/10.1016/j.psychres.2021.114024; Harris, Joshua I., et al. "Moral Injury, Burnout, and the Ethical Demands of Leadership." Journal of Health Care Chaplaincy, vol. 28, no. 1, 2022, pp. 45-63.https://doi.org/10.1080/0885472 6.2021.1942956 ; Koenig, Harold G., et al. Moral Injury and Moral Repair in Clinical Practice. Springer, 2022.;Litz, Brett T., et al. "Moral Injury and Moral Repair in War Veterans: A Preliminary Model and Intervention Strategy."

Clinical Psychology Review, vol. 29, no. 8, 2009, pp. 695-706.https://doi.org/10.1016/j.cpr.2009.07.003; Papazoglou, Konstantinos, and Brian Chopko. "The Role of Moral Injury in PTSD among Law Enforcement Officers: A Brief Report." Frontiers in Psychology, vol.8, 2017, 798. https://doi.org/10.3389/fpsyg.2017.00798; Shay, Jonathan. Moral Injury. Lecture, U.S. Department of Veterans Affairs, 2014.

57 pg. 63 Overcoming "the broken rung" Recent research underscores the complex interplay of gender stereotypes, structural barriers, and work-life integration in shaping women's leadership experiences. Female leaders are still evaluated through a lens of gendered expectations, with stereotypical views favoring male-associated leadership traits (e.g., assertiveness) while undervaluing relational or communal qualities more often attributed to women. This contributes to biased perceptions that can undermine women's credibility or advancement. Research also shows that women leaders frequently encounter career obstacles, including limited access to influential networks, lack of mentorship, and organizational cultures resistant to change—while also naming systemic and policy-level interventions that could facilitate progress. Additionally remains the often-overlooked impact of work-life balance on women's leadership sustainability, with supportive environments that honor personal and professional integration contributing significantly to women's well-being and long-term leadership success. Together, these findings point to the necessity of addressing gender-based assumptions and creating workplace structures that enable leadership equity, sustainability, and authentic expression across gender lines.

See: Tremmel M, Wahl I. Gender stereotypes in leadership: Analyzing the content and evaluation of stereotypes about typical, male, and female leaders. Front Psychol. 2023 Jan 27;14:1034258. doi: 10.3389/fpsyg.2023.1034258. PMID: 36777214; PMCID: PMC9912935; Coleman, Marianne. (2019). Women leaders in the workplace: perceptions of career barriers, facilitators and change. Irish Educational Studies. 39. 1-21. 10.1080/03323315.2019.1697952; Brue, Krystal. (2018). Harmony and Help: Recognizing the Impact of Work-Life Balance for Women Leaders. Journal of Leadership Education. 17. 219-243.10.12806/V17/I4/C2

CHAPTER 10

58 pg. 274 self-efficacy, resilience, and direction Research suggests that leader identity clarity, deepened through a process of reflective assimilation—where leaders meaningfully integrate feedback and experiences into their self-concept—builds stronger self-efficacy, fosters resilience, and provides clearer direction in leadership. For example, new leaders who continuously reflect on their leadership identity develop greater self-awareness and alignment with their roles. Reflective practices, like journaling or structured self-assessment, have been empirically shown to enhance resilience and well-being by helping leaders process challenges and recommendations more effectively. Additionally, leaders who cultivate self-leadership—aligning actions with personal values—report increased emotional resilience and self-efficacy, underscoring the practical power of identity clarity.

See: Alessandri, Guido, et al. "Self-Efficacy in Managing Negative Emotions at Work: A Resource for Managing Job-Related Stress." Frontiers in Psychology, vol. 8, 2018.; Crane, Monica, et al. "Reflective Practice Can Improve Resilience: A Self-Reflective Framework to Navigate Stressful Moments." HALO Psychology, 10 Mar. 2025, halo-psychology.com/2025/03/10/why-leaders-should-engage-in-reflective-practice/.; "Leadership and Followership Identity Processes: A Multilevel Review." The Leadership Quarterly, vol. 28, 2017 Self-Leadership: Strengthening Leadership Effectiveness from the Inside Out. Bakken Center for Spirituality & Healing, University of Minnesota, 2024, csh.umn.edu/for-community/wellbeing-workshops/self-leadership-strengthening-leadership-effectiveness-inside-out.

59 pg. 274 reduces burnout and increases well-being The integration of one's experiences and insights and aligning these with their core values—can renew psychological flexibility: the capacity to adapt effectively to changing demands without compromising identity or priorities. Enhanced psychological flexibility has been shown to reduce burnout and elevate overall psychological well-being, often acting as a conduit for interventions inspired by Acceptance and Commitment Therapy (ACT) and mindfulness-based approaches. (Acceptance and mindfulness are in your wheelhouse now too!)

See: Puolakanaho, Anne, et al. A Psychological Flexibility-Based Intervention for Burnout: A Randomized Controlled Trial. 2020, DOI:10.1016/S2212-1447(19)30100-0. ; Russo, A., Mansouri, M., Santisi, G., and Zammitti, A. "Psychological Flexibility as a Resource for Preventing Compulsive Work and Promoting Well-Being: A JD-R Framework Study." International Journal of Organizational Analysis, vol. 33, no. 12, 2025, pp. 18–34. ; Kashdan, T. B., & Rottenberg, J. (2010). Psychological flexibility as a fundamental aspect of health. Clinical Psychology Review, 30(7), 865-878.https://doi.org/10.1016/j.cpr.2010.03.001

60 pg. 290 seemingly good —like overwork. Avoidance is one of the most insidious barriers to authentic leadership because it often masquerades as productivity—particularly in high-performing leaders. Rather than facing discomfort, feedback, or emotional friction, leaders may overwork, micromanage, or over-rely on external validation, reinforcing patterns that prevent identity development. You've taken a good look at these for yourself, already! This subtle form of resistance undermines self-awareness, acceptance, and assimilation—key processes in building clear leader identity. As researchers note, avoidance coping erodes psychological flexibility and blocks reflective growth, making it difficult for leaders to evolve their self-as-leader identity clarity or re-connect with purpose. Over time, this avoidance disrupts leader resilience and integrity, separating who they are from who they feel they must appear to be.

See: Hofmann, Stefan G., and Ann F. Hay-Schmidt. "Avoidance in Leadership: The Hidden Driver of Resistance and Rigidity." Journal of Leadership and Organizational Psychology, vol. 28, no. 1, 2025, pp. 44–58.; Kashdan, Todd B., and Julianne A. Rottenberg. "Psychological Flexibility as a Fundamental Aspect of Health." Clinical Psychology Review, vol. 30, no. 7, 2010, pp. 865–78, https://doi.org/10.1016/j.cpr.2010.03.001.; Grant, Anthony M., and Margie Warrell. "Authenticity and Avoidance: How Leaders Lose Themselves While Trying to 'Do It All'." Harvard Business Review Online, 17 Aug. 2023, https://hbr.org/2023/08/how-leaders-lose-authenticity.

61 **pg. 302 other blame, avoidance, and regret** In organizational settings, mistakes, miscommunication, and interpersonal harm are inevitable. Leaders who cling to grudges or adopt punitive postures often erode trust, increase psychological distress among team members, and fuel toxic cultures. In contrast, forgiveness promotes psychological safety, strengthens team cohesion, and fosters a growth mindset. Mc-Cullough's evolutionary psychology research positions forgiveness as a prosocial behavior that enables long-term cooperation. Forgiveness allows individuals and groups to move beyond retaliation and retribution, repairing relationships after violations of trust. His studies show that people who forgive are less prone to rumination, anxiety, and stress—and leaders who embody this stance create environments where people feel emotionally safe to admit missteps and innovate. Worthington's REACH model (Recall, Empathize, Altruistic gift, Commit, and Hold onto forgiveness) offers a structured framework for teaching forgiveness in clinical and organizational contexts. His research demonstrates that forgiveness interventions can improve emotional regulation, reduce burnout, and restore working relationships after conflict. Both scholars emphasize that forgiveness is not passive or permissive. Instead, it is an active leader-ship behavior that requires strength, emotional maturity, and clarity of boundaries. Forgiving leaders do not excuse poor behavior—they choose not to be controlled by resentment. They can hold others accountable while also creating space for repair, learning, and reintegration. Forgiveness is especially important in high-change, high-pressure environments, where unresolved conflict and perfectionism can hinder collaboration and learning. Leaders who embody forgiveness create cultures where people feel seen, humanized, and resilient.

See: McCullough, Michael E. Beyond Revenge: The Evolution of the Forgiveness Instinct. Jossey-Bass, 2008; McCullough, Michael E., Kenneth I. Pargament, and Carl E. Thoresen, editors. Forgiveness: Theory, Research, and Practice. Guilford Press, 2000; Worthington, Everett L. Jr. Forgiving and Reconciling: Bridges to Wholeness and Hope. InterVarsity Press, 2003; Worthington, Everett L. Jr. Moving Forward: Six Steps to Forgiving Yourself and Breaking Free from the Past. Waterbrook Press, 2013.

CHAPTER 11

62 **pg. 289**

See: Lamott, Anne. Grace (Eventually): Thoughts on Faith. Riverhead Books, 2007.

ABOUT
THE AUTHOR

———————————

Natalie Pickering, PhD, is an author, TEDx speaker, organizational psychologist, and executive coach who helps leaders trade performance pressure for authentic influence. For more than two decades, she has partnered with executives, founders, and teams across healthcare, education, startups, and global organizations to navigate change, strengthen culture, and lead with courage. Natalie is known for making leadership both practical and profound. Her identity-first approach blends research-based psychology with real-world strategies to prevent burnout, deepen emotional intelligence, and create sustainable impact. With equal parts candor, warmth, and humor, she equips leaders to gain clarity on who they are, confidence in how they lead, and connection that inspires others to follow. She is the founder of Becoming Works, a leadership development firm dedicated to helping leaders, teams, and organizations scale without losing soul. She lives in Tennessee, where she writes, coaches, hikes wooded trails, eats chocolate, and—when she remembers—waters her houseplants.

Connect with Natalie at www.drnataliepickering.com